The Treasury of London's Past

Francis Sheppard

AN HISTORICAL ACCOUNT OF
THE MUSEUM OF LONDON
AND ITS PREDECESSORS,
THE GUILDHALL MUSEUM
AND THE LONDON MUSEUM

LONDON: HMSO

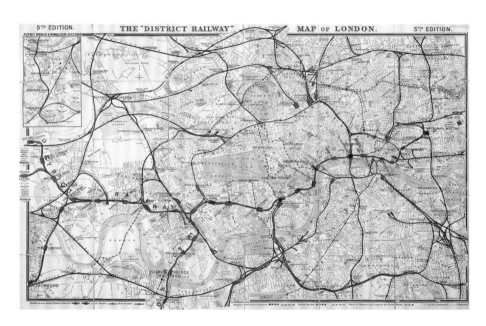

Dedicated to
Michael Robbins

EDITOR
Valerie Cumming

PHOTOGRAPHIC PRODUCTION
Barrington Gray
and museum staff photographers

DESIGN AND PRODUCTION
David Milbank Challis

Set in Lasercomp Bell

Typesetting by
Jolly & Barber Limited, Rugby

Origination and printing by
Balding + Mansell plc, Wisbech

Bound in England

ISBN 0 11 290492 0

*British Library Cataloguing in Publication Data
A CIP catalogue record for this book is available
from the British Library*

HMSO Publications are available from:

HMSO PUBLICATIONS CENTRE
(*Mail and telephone orders only*)
PO Box 276, London SW8 5DT
Telephone orders 071 873 9090
General enquiries 071 873 0011
(*queuing system in operation for both numbers*)

HMSO BOOKSHOPS
49 High Holborn, London WC1V 6HB
  071 873 0011 (*Counter service only*)
258 Broad Street, Birmingham B1 2HE
  021 643 3740
Southey House, 33 Wine Street, Bristol BS1 2BQ
  0272 264306
9–21 Princess Street, Manchester M60 8AS
  061 834 7201
80 Chichester Street, Belfast BT1 4JY
  0232 238451
71 Lothian Road, Edinburgh EH3 9AZ
  031 228 4181

HMSO'S ACCREDITED AGENTS
(*see Yellow Pages*)

and through good booksellers

1 *'Britannia visits the London Museum':
gouache drawing for a poster design by Rex
Whistler, 1928.
Probably commissioned by Ernest Makower
and deposited by the executors of J M
Makower at the Museum of London,
September 1990*
(*page 1*)

FRONTISPIECE
2 *The Lord Mayor's Coach and the
figurehead from HMS London as displayed
at the Museum of London.
The gilded wood and enamelled coach with
panel paintings attributed to G B Cipriani
was built in 1757 and marks the end of the
permanent galleries. HMS London greets
visitors as they enter the galleries*

3 *The 'District Railway' Map of London,
fifth edition (first state), c.1892*
(*above*)

ENDPAPERS
*Details taken from the two sheets of the
engraved copperplate map of London, c.1558,
now in the possession of the museum.
These two plates are the only ones known to
have survived and cover the Moorfields area
and the heart of the City*

CONTENTS

4 Poster for the Underground advertising the London Museum, designed by E McKnight Kauffer, 1922

ACKNOWLEDGEMENTS

I acknowledge the gracious permission of Her Majesty the Queen to make use of material in the Royal Archives at Windsor relating to the early history of the London Museum. I am grateful to the Hon. Mrs Crispin Gascoigne for permission to use the correspondence (now at the Bodleian Library) of her grandfather, Lewis, first Viscount Harcourt. My warm thanks are also due to Viscount Esher, who kindly read much of my typescript and allowed me to publish many of the papers (now at Churchill College, Cambridge) of his grandfather, Reginald, second Viscount Esher. I acknowledge, too, with pleasure, the help given to me by Ms Priscilla Greville, who talked so freely about her grandfather, Sir Harry Waechter, and great grandfather, Sir Max Waechter.

Much of the research for this book was done at the Museum of London, where many members of the staff helped me in innumerable ways and showed me great kindness over a long period of time. I am deeply grateful to all of them. It has been a privilege to work amongst them. I have also had the pleasure of talking to many former members of the staffs of the Guildhall Museum, London Museum and Museum of London. To Norman Cook, Beatrice de Cardi, Philippa Glanville, the late W F Grimes, Donald Harden, John Hayes, the late Walter Henderson, Martin Holmes, Tom Hume, Jean Macdonald, Ralph Merrifield, Mary Speaight, Brian Spencer and Arthur Trotman I tender my warm and respectful thanks.

I am much indebted to Mr Oliver Everett and the staff of the Royal Library, Windsor; to the Master, Fellows and Scholars of Churchill College in the University of Cambridge, for allowing me to study the Esher Papers there, and to Miss Marion M Stewart, archivist at the Churchill Archives Centre, for much assistance; to the President and Fellows of the Society of Antiquaries of London and their sometime librarian, Mr John Hopkins; to Mr J R Wynter Bee of Walker Martineau, and Mr G W Rowley, town clerk of the City of London, for reading parts of the text; to Susan Hibbert for making the index; and to the staffs of the Bodleian Library, the British Museum, the Guildhall Library, the London Library, the Corporation of London Records Office and the Public Record Office.

The illustrations have been drawn mainly from the Museum of London's archives and collections, augmented by those of Guildhall Library. I am grateful for the assistance of many staff in the departments of the museum for providing ideas for illustrations and information about them. Ralph Hyde, keeper of Prints and Maps at Guildhall Library and his colleagues gave additional help. David Challis coordinated this exercise, drawing upon his own considerable knowledge of the many sources of illustrative material about the three museums, greatly enhancing the visual presentation.

Alec Jolly of Jolly & Barber offered encouragement and practical assistance in the formative stages of the project. More recently, Bob Barnard of HMSO and Roger Tooke of Balding + Mansell have provided direct and constant practical support over the production of the book.

Lastly, and certainly not least, I am most grateful to Mr R M Robbins, Chairman of the Governors of the Museum of London, for much help and encouragement.

Francis Sheppard

FOREWORD

5 *The South Sea Company's plate, 1715.*
Silver-gilt cup, cover and salver engraved
with the coat of arms of the South Sea
Company. Made by Thomas Farren in
London (page 177)

In the mid-1980s the Museum of London was approaching a number of important anniversaries. 1986 marked the tenth anniversary of the opening of the Museum in its new home in the City of London, but it also commemorated 75 years of the London Museum and approximately 160 years of the Guildhall Museum. The Museum of London's history is unusual because, in 1975, two existing museums, the London Museum and Guildhall Museum, had merged to form the *new* Museum of London. With some manipulation of the figures, the Museum of London can lay claim to a history of the three museums covering over 250 years of significant museological activity.

However, it was apparent that, with the exception of some of those closely connected with the place, few people were aware of the complicated history of the Museum and its predecessors. Partial histories and surveys were available, but nothing comprehensive. In order to rectify this omission, the Board invited Dr Francis Sheppard, the distinguished historian and former member of the London Museum's staff, to write a definitive account. Neither the Museum, nor he, was aware of the ramifications of the task that he agreed to undertake but the result bears no sign of the difficulties that he encountered in its research and composition.

The story he has produced is a fascinating exposition of strong personalities, great if sometimes self-interested patronage, and the evolution of a type of museum illustrating the history of a place which is still rare both in Great Britain and abroad. The Museum of London uses its magnificent collections of archaeological, social and working history, fine and applied arts and documentary evidence to give a three dimensional context within which the history of London can be explored. The founders of the London Museum, impressed by Paris' history museum, the Musée Carnavalet, set out to foster this biographical approach. All subsequent trustees and directors, much assisted by the amalgamation with the Guildhall Museum in 1975 – whose collections of early material were of great importance – have followed this approach.

A great international city deserves a great historical museum, but Dr Sheppard's analysis indicates that this concept was one which took far too long to realise. For most of their joint histories the Guildhall Museum and the London Museum were peripatetic, never secure in their respective buildings, always making the best of cramped conditions. Today the idea of a genuinely peripatetic museum might seem imaginative, providing opportunities to present the history of the capital throughout the 600 square miles of Greater London. However, in the late nineteenth and early twentieth centuries, a major museum needed a secure, accessible, preferably central building of some consequence in which to curate and display its collections. The eventual achievement of this by the 1970s, and all the preliminary negotiations, form a major section within the history. By late 1987, when Dr Sheppard's history ends, there was, despite the abolition of the GLC in 1986, a mood of considerable optimism within the museum.

Much has happened since then, with the museum continuing to adjust skilfully to requirements for higher standards of care of collections and for greater self-sufficiency. The 'Support Centre', now called the Resources Centre, is well on the way to being realised, with generous assistance from the two funding authorities. A building has been acquired in Hackney which, when adapted to museum use, will be able to house existing collections and their expected growth over the next decade or so. By 1992 this major new centre for the study of London's history, planned for use by visitors of all ages and interests, should be up and running. The opportunities presented by this initiative are welcomed by staff, and by those growing numbers of visitors who have enjoyed pilot schemes of introduction to an existing out-store.

Greater self-sufficiency through partnership with developers has, for a number of years, characterised the work of the two archaeological departments. The reputation of the Museum of London as a centre of excellence in all areas of archaeological activity is acknowledged both nationally and internationally. Since the time of Charles Roach Smith (1806–90), the major importance of archaeology to the understanding of London's early history has been emphasized. In recent years the later period has also benefited from the results of excavation. The challenge of the 1990s will be finding a method by which the archive of archaeological material can be retained and adequately funded.

Developer-funding which allowed archaeology to grow at an unprecedented level in the 1980s was dependent on a buoyant property market and a strong national economy. Economic wealth and government encouragement also provided incentives for business sponsorship of a wide variety of museum activities. However, the uncertainty of such inter-dependence between the public and private sector has also been felt. Problems with the property market have delayed two museum development projects. An extension to the main building as part of a commercial development at the western end of London Wall now seems unlikely. The public will continue, therefore, to struggle with the complexities of the Barbican area stairways and highwalks to find their way into the museum. The City Corporation is introducing new signing schemes to make the area easier for visitors to understand but the wish for an identifiable and friendly street-level entrance to the museum is a desire shared by staff and visitors alike. The slow-down in redevelopment has also delayed the possibility of a Museum in Docklands. This project was to 'ride-on-the-back' of a commercial scheme but a site, and appropriate funding, has still to be found. It remains a long term goal of the museum to do full justice to the story of the people of London in their place of work, by displaying the remarkable port and industry collections assembled over the last decade.

Museums are sometimes accused of being too inward looking, too concerned with the small groups of users able to comprehend refined scholarship. Collections must be studied, new knowledge must be acquired but it is the responsibility of museums to attract and retain visitors by making ideas and collections accessible. Showmanship was always a feature of the London Museum, particularly when the charismatic Sir Mortimer Wheeler made it one of the most popular museums in the 1930s, with innovative public programmes. Popularity is an important element in the success of any public institution. All museum work will, however, need re-defining in the 1990s. 1993 will see the end of internal barriers to trade and movement in the European Community. The Channel Tunnel opens soon after. The nature of London and its relationship with the rest of Europe will change, affecting both the story we have to tell and the needs and perceptions of our visitors. The challenge of recording these changes and explaining London to a new European audience is one that the Museum of London is determined to meet. The remarkable history of the Museum, contained within this book, is a stimulus to further experimentation and change within an organization that has always risen to fresh challenges.

Max Hebditch
President of the Museums Association

6 *Fifteenth-century silver collar of SS, one of the museum's most important medieval acquisitions, here shown in association with other exhibits of the period, a document bag of white leather, a purse (partly restored), an inkhorn and a pewter candlestick*

The Treasury of London's Past

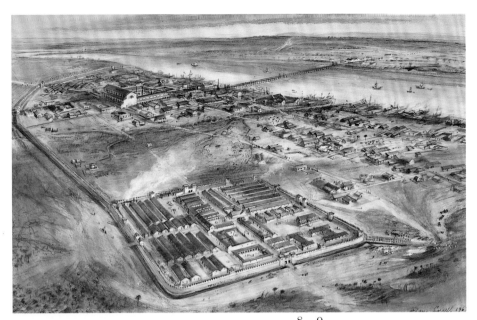

7 *Londinium, looking south east, during the building of the landward wall, c.AD200. Watercolour by Alan Sorrell, 1967*

8 *Unused new samian pottery, found in 1974 in the Thames at New Fresh Wharf (page 158)*

9 *Part of the Cheapside Hoard of Jacobean Jewellery (page 71)*

10 *The frozen Thames, looking eastward towards Old London Bridge, 1677: oil on canvas by Abraham Hondius (page 109)*

11 *Enamelled glass beaker, early fourteenth century, found in 1982 during excavations in Foster Lane in the City*

8   9

10   11

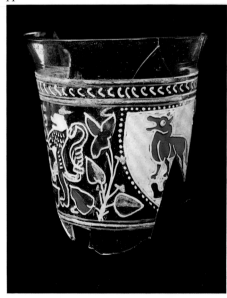

12 *Charles II's coronation procession, 1661: oil on canvas by Roderigo (Dirck) Stoop*

13 *Model of the Great Fire of London, 1666. J B Thorp's model was made for the London Museum in 1914 and paid for by J G Joicey (page 84)*

14 *'The Dancing Lesson', Chelsea porcelain group, c.1762–9. Given by Mrs W Salting (page 70)*

15 *The north end of London Bridge from Fresh Wharf, c.1762: oil on canvas by William Marlow (page 122)*

16 *French bisque doll,
c.1865–70. Fashionably
dressed in silk trimmed with
lace and beads*

17 *Georgian dolls' house,
c.1740. Given to the London
Museum by Miss Blackett, 1913
(page 69)*

18 *Blue brocaded silk dress
with contemporary ruffles, fan
and gloves, c.1765. Given by
Mr Joicey*

16

17

18

19 *Reconstruction at the Museum of London of a mid
seventeenth-century room. Panelling from Poyle Park,
Surrey, and virginal by Jacobus White of Old Jewry,
1656*

20

21 22

23

20   *Queen Victoria and her family at the Great Exhibition, 1851: oil on canvas by George? Wells*

21   *Dolls dressed by Princess (later Queen) Victoria and displayed at the London Museum in 1912 (page 66)*

22   *Parliament robe and surcoat worn by Queen Victoria to her coronation in 1838, and displayed in the London Museum in 1912 (page 60)*

23   *Suffragette banner of 1908, used in the campaign for women's right to vote (page 123)*

25

26

24 *Statue of Charles I at Charing Cross, 1835: watercolour by G S Shepherd. Given to the London Museum by P A S Phillips in 1915* (page 94)

27   28

29 'London's Flying Start' exhibition, 1981–2, a dramatic presentation of London's part in the early history of the British aviation industry

30 Robes and dresses worn at the coronation of George VI in 1937 by H M Queen Elizabeth (now the Queen Mother) and her daughters Princess Elizabeth (now H M the Queen) and Princess Margaret

25 Costume worn by Henry Irving as King Lear in 1892

26 Sketches of Henry Irving in various roles: watercolour by Tom Heslewood, after 1892

27 Watchmaker's workshop: photographic reconstruction, 1987

28 'Russian Dance' costume worn by Anna Pavlova, 1909–11. Presented to the London Museum after her death in 1931

31 Detail from Robert Dighton's watercolour of 'The Westminster Election of 1788' which was used for the poster advertising the 'Londoners' exhibition of 1987

32 A late Victorian schoolroom, as reconstructed in the museum

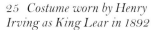

33 *The visitor centre of the Museum in Docklands project at 'W' Warehouse, Royal Victoria Dock, in 1986*

34 *Lloyd's – The Stairwell, 1987: acrylic on paper by Brendan Neiland. Recently purchased by the museum*

35 *Inside Lloyd's of London, Lime Street, photograph by Anna Fox, 1987.*
From a series of photographs of office life in London commissioned by the Museum of London in association with Camerawork

36 *Detail from 'Debarkation of the Lord Mayor at Westminster Stairs', 1830: watercolour by David Roberts.*
A picture that featured in the exhibition 'London Delineated', 1981, which was the result of collaboration between the museum and Guildhall Library and drew upon both collections to illustrate the changing face of London and artists' views of it between c.1740 and c.1900

HISTORICAL
CONTEXTS

37 *After making her speech which marked the formal opening of the Museum of London, H M the Queen toured the galleries.*

She is seen in the Roman gallery with the keeper, Ralph Merrifield (38) and inspecting a nineteenth-century grocer's shop, with Oliver Green (to her left), the keeper, Colin Sorensen, and the director, Tom Hume (39)

Chapter 1
HISTORICAL CONTEXTS

40 *The opening of the Museum of London, 2 December 1976.*
H M the Queen, escorted by Lord Harcourt, chairman of the Board of Governors, is introduced to the director, Tom Hume. She entered the building through the ceremonial double-doors at street level on London Wall

The Museum of London was opened by Queen Elizabeth II on 2 December 1976. The museum has no formal front entrance at ground level, and so Her Majesty alighted from her limousine outside the shuttered-steel doorway designed to provide access for the Lord Mayor's coach and to act as the ceremonial entrance. She was received by the Lord Mayor, accompanied by the chairman of the Greater London Council and by Viscount Harcourt, chairman of the governors of the museum, and Mr Tom Hume, the director, who escorted her upstairs to the main foyer. There a distinguished company of guests awaited her, and Lord Harcourt invited her to declare the museum open.

In a short speech Her Majesty referred to her 'considerable proprietary interest' in the old London Museum, and to the role of her grandmother, Queen Mary, in its foundation. She recalled that it had been one of the first museums she herself had ever visited and that it had twice had its home in the old royal residence at Kensington Palace. 'I am indeed glad', she continued, 'to see this "old friend of the family" at long last happily and respectably married to the Guildhall Museum! I am greatly looking forward to being shown round this connubial home which has been specially designed and built to house the "happy pair"!'

So despite its youth and the modernity of its architecture, the Museum of London has a long and distinguished pedigree. The Guildhall Museum was much the older of the two partners in the marriage which produced the Museum of London, the Corporation of London having resolved as long ago as 1826 to 'consider the propriety' of establishing such an institution. During the next eighty-five years the Guildhall Museum amassed a large collection of miscellaneous objects related in some way to London, chiefly to the City of London. In 1911, however, a pushy rival appeared, the London Museum, set up under powerful aristocratic auspices and supported by royal patronage, and privately financed in some mysterious and unexplained way. In general, the Guildhall Museum thereafter restricted itself to the collection of antiquities relating to the area of the City and its immediate environs, while the London Museum aimed to cast its net over the whole of the metropolis within twenty-five miles of Charing Cross.

So inevitably there had been rivalry, or at least 'mutual emulation',[1] between the two museums, for in its early days the London Museum had, by one means or another, acquired numerous valuable objects originating in or related to the City, which the Guildhall Museum regarded as its exclusive territory; and in 1915 the City Corporation even contemplated taking legal action against this tiresome upstart for breach of the Corporation's ancient chartered rights and privileges. Thereafter an uneasy truce had ensued, and it was not until 1959 that the first steps were taken which led ultimately to the amalgamation of the two collections to form the Museum of London. Old animosities began to fade away, the new building was erected in a mere three years, and in 1976, at long last, London acquired its own museum, worthy of its great past.

The existence of these two partly overlapping collections, each concerned with the history of London, and the distrustful relationship which for many years prevailed between them, was the result of an important event in that history itself – the refusal of the Corporation to accept as part of its domain the new suburbs which from c.1580 onwards grew up around the ancient walled city. The constitution of the Corporation of London, unlike that of all other local authorities in England, rests upon the ancient rights and privileges which its citizens have accumulated since before the Norman Conquest. Even William the

Conqueror, by the charter which he granted to the citizens, had tacitly acknowledged London's unique status. Five centuries later, when the new suburbs began to spring up outside the City's walls, it was perhaps this long and deeply engrained tradition of independence, coupled with their own commercial interests, which impelled the City Fathers to reject any territorial extension of their responsibilities. This 'Great Refusal', as it has been dubbed – a turning point in the history of London – was made on three separate occasions – firstly in 1633, when the Privy Council asked the Corporation 'whether they would accepte of parte of the suburbs into their jurisdiction and liberty for better government'; again in 1634, and lastly soon after the Restoration.[2] This is why the Corporation of the City of London to this day only rules over a tiny island in the centre of the metropolis, and why, several centuries later, two largely complementary collections of antiquities grew up, each purporting to illustrate the history of London but neither of them able to do so successfully until their union to form the Museum of London.

Yet despite their limitations, both the Guildhall Museum and the London Museum marked, at the time of their respective foundation, important advances in the development of museums in England. In the 1820s the British Museum was still the only public museum in all London, the Victoria & Albert and all the other great institutions of South Kensington being as yet far away in the future. So the Corporation could claim that it was ahead of the times in 1826 when it contemplated establishing its own museum. It was not until 1845 that town councils were empowered by Act of Parliament to provide museums, and even in 1850 there were not more than fifty museums throughout the length and breadth of the land, many of them still privately financed by local philosophical and archaeological societies. In the second half of the nineteenth century, however, the number quadrupled, the main fields of interest of these Victorian museums being natural history, ethnography, and archaeology. Numerous municipal art galleries were also founded, and in 1889 the Museums Association was established.[3] But even in the early twentieth century museums did not much concern themselves with the ordinary everyday things of the more recent post-archaeological past; and it was the great achievement of the London Museum to present social history for the first time to a mainly urban public largely deprived of its traditional roots. Today many local councils have followed the City Corporation's example in establishing their own museums, in nearly all of which the local past provides an important ingredient; and the Museum of London can now fairly claim to be 'England's Principal History Museum'.

41 *The interior of number 5, Liverpool Street, about 1850.*
These premises were occupied by Charles Roach Smith since 1840 and contained his extensive collection of antiquities acquired from sites in the City of London during public works programmes in the 1830s and 1840s

THE GUILDHALL
MUSEUM

1826 TO 1911

Building works in the City between 1869 and 1882.
Deep-level works, including those associated with the construction of the Underground just east of Blackfriars (42), revealed much evidence of London's early history. A Roman sarcophagus was found near Fleet Lane in 1873 (43), and a section of the Roman city wall in Pilgrim Street in 1882 (44)

Chapter 2
THE GUILDHALL MUSEUM
1826 TO 1911

45 *Richard Lambert Jones, 1783–1863: oil on canvas, by John Robert Dicksee. An influential member of the Court of Common Council from 1819 until 1852, Lambert Jones, as chairman, kept firm control of the Library Committee, under whose aegis the Guildhall Museum was established*

At a meeting of the Court of Common Council (the City Corporation's principal assembly, some two hundred strong) held on 8 April 1824 councilman Richard Lambert Jones proposed and carried a motion to set up a Special Committee 'to enquire and examine the best mode of arranging and carrying into effect (in the Guildhall) a Library of all matters relating to this City, the Borough of Southwark, and the County of Middlesex . . .'. At about that time popular education was receiving much public attention. This was the great age of cultural and scientific institutions of all kinds, and as recently as 1823 Dr George Birkbeck and others had founded the London Mechanics' Institution (now Birkbeck College in the University of London) – the first of some sixty such institutes to be founded in London alone during the next twenty years.

It was therefore in a very favourable climate that councilman Jones persuaded the Corporation to set up a library. Richard Lambert Jones (1783–1863) had started out in life as a working man – a plumber, painter and glazier living in Little Moorfields. In 1819 he was elected to the Common Council for the Ward of Cripplegate Without, which he continued to represent until his retirement from the Corporation in 1852. He was 'of a tall and commanding aspect' and (in his own words) possessed 'a certain firmness of character' and 'a resolute determination to discharge with fidelity every trust' reposed in him which very quickly made him 'a mighty man in the city'. In 1823 he was appointed chairman of the Bridge House Estates Committee, which was then about to start on the complex business of rebuilding London Bridge. Later he was also chairman of the Corporation's Public Improvements Committee and of the Committee for Rebuilding the Royal Exchange. In 1846, when these labours had mostly been completed, a public meeting was held at the Mansion House to congratulate him on his public services. After the sum of £1000 had been raised by public subscription, a marble bust of him was placed in the Guildhall, and he was presented with a gold medal. It was not for nothing that he was generally known as 'the City Dictator'.[1]

Despite all these multifarious activities Jones kept the library (one might almost say *his* library) firmly under his control throughout his chairmanship of the Library Committee, which lasted from 1824 until 1843. It was he – or very largely he – who found a first temporary home for the infant library within the cramped and crowded Guildhall, persuaded the Common Council to spend £500 on 'an Outfit' for it, plus £200 per annum for the purchase of books, and to appoint a salaried librarian, William Herbert. Both before and for many years after the opening of the library on 2 June 1828 he frequently attended auctions to buy books for the library (whether with or without the knowledge of Herbert, the librarian, is not clear), always carefully recovering the cost of his purchases afterwards; and it was he personally who bid £145 to acquire the Guildhall Library's most highly prized possession – the famous Shakespeare deed of 1612. By 1832 the library contained some 3600 volumes,[2] as well as a number of prints and drawings, and in the next two or three years some £2295 was spent in enlarging it by means of an extension over a ground-floor passage.[3] In 1839 Jones and his fellow committeemen were also busy classifying and indexing the ancient records in the Guildhall's numerous muniment rooms, which the Corporation had ordered them to examine.[4] Use of the library was, of course, for many years restricted to members and senior officers of the Corporation and occasionally to their nominees, and books could not be borrowed; but despite this limitation, Jones had got his library off to a very good start.

The establishment of the museum, by contrast, took much longer; and even when it had been established, it remained the poor relation of the library, unloved by the Corporation and often neglected by the Library Committee and the reigning librarian. For decades successive librarians kept the little museum firmly under their thumbs. They knew all about written records, whether in the form of books or prints or drawings or manuscripts, but they did not know about objects in the round, or how to deal with them, particularly when they were large and awkward in shape, as was often the case. So the museum was often un-cared for. It was not until 1907 that a qualified person was appointed to look after it, and even he and his successors remained under the heavy hand of the librarian until as late as 1966, when the then keeper, Norman Cook, a leading figure in the museum world and at that time president of the Museums Association, persuaded the Corporation that the museum must be a separate entity independent from the library. ▣

47 *Charles Roach Smith, 1806–90. Roach Smith was a chemist, with premises at first in Lothbury and later in Liverpool Street. His passion for Roman antiquities led him to assemble one of the great nineteenth-century collections, but ensured a stormy and controversial career of opposition to the City Corporation and other public bodies that he felt were neglecting archaeology in London (right)*

The story of the Guildhall Museum began on 19 January 1826, some two years after that of the library, when the Common Council requested the Library Committee 'to consider the propriety of providing a suitable place for the reception of such Antiquities as relate to the City of London, and Suburbs, as may be procured, or presented to the Corporation, and to report thereon'.[5] The word 'museum', it may be noted, was not used at all in this resolution, and in 1845, after the lapse of nearly twenty years, the Library Committee had still not presented such a report to the Common Council. Some progress had, nevertheless, been made, for in 1829 William Herbert, the librarian, felt able to tell the Library Committee that 'a foundation is laid for a Civic Museum or Collection of Metropolitan Antiquities and Curiosities'.[6] Amongst the more important items already in the collection were two large fragments of Roman tesselated pavement 'lately taken up near St Dunstan's Hill' – the very first items to be acquired by the museum. They were presented by the City Printer, Arthur Taylor, who was also a fellow of the Society of Antiquaries, and who, a few months after his gift had been accepted, suggested to members of the Library Committee (who were evidently rather nonplussed about how to cope with this unwieldly possession) 'the propriety of a Frame, or Box, being provided'.[7] There were also a few coins, 'several Roman and other Antiquities' discovered during digging the foundations of the new Post Office in St Martin's-le-Grand, 'various articles' found during the rebuilding of London Bridge, and 'several subjects of antiquity or curiosity from the late Guildhall Chapel, and other places'. All these, thought Herbert, 'though at present incon-siderable, will, when augmented by additional Donations and such subjects as must continually be discovered in the vast alterations and improvements of the Capital, form a Collection of Great Interest, and which it is to be lamented was not began [*sic*] many years since'.[8]

So at any rate a start had been made; and already the Guildhall Museum's principal later speciality is discernible – antiquities of all kinds discovered in excavations made during the ceaseless rebuilding of the City. This general drift continued during the 1830s, when there were several donations from the City Commissioners of Sewers of objects found during their extensive trenching operations. In 1835 the Library Committee made its first purchase for the museum, paying a few pounds for a collection of the seals of monastic houses formerly in the City or adjacent parts of Surrey, seals being conveniently small objects, and easy to store and classify.[9]

46 *Press interest in finds related to Roman London ensured both descriptive and illustrative articles. This engraving shows a Roman wall at Bread Street Hill revealed during the construction of the 'common sewers'*

48 *Roach Smith's premises in Lothbury. The chemist shop was Roach Smith's home from 1832 until 1840 when the site was compulsorily purchased by the City Corporation for road improvements*

Apart from the large objects, which were often kept out of doors in the City's stone-yard,[10] most of the collection was housed in a 'small room attached to the Library fitted up as a Museum';[11] but as the library's own accommodation at this time was later described as only a 'narrow and ill-adapted corridor',[12] the museum's 'small room' was probably little more than a large cupboard. In January 1840 chairman Jones and a sub-committee of his Library Committee were, however, considering the 'proper arrangement of the various Antiquities and curiosities' in their possession, and in May they recommended that suitable cases should be provided; but nothing was done.[13]

It was in this first half of 1840 that there occurred the first of those events which were to have important long-term results for the Guildhall Museum. This was the compulsory purchase and demolition by Richard Lambert Jones's Improvements Committee of a little shop in Lothbury occupied leasehold by Charles Roach Smith, a retail chemist.

Charles Roach Smith (1806–90), a life-long bachelor, was by far the most important figure in the nineteenth-century history of London's archaeology. His ancestors had been for centuries fairly prosperous tenant farmers in the Isle of Wight, but his father had died when he was still a boy. Having shown no aptitude for his first situation in a lawyer's office, his family persuaded him to apprentice himself to a chemist in Chichester. There a Roman coin found one day in the shop's till had inspired his first interest in Roman antiquities, which are particularly abundant in and about that ancient city. By about 1828 he had moved to London, and in 1832 he set up in business on his own account in Lothbury, in the centre of the Roman metropolis in Britain.[14]

There he had at once observed that many parts of the city were being dug up and generally cut about, mainly by two different organs of the Corporation – the Commissioners of Sewers and councilman Jones's Improvements Committee, or (to give it its full title) the Committee to Carry into Execution the Act of Parliament for the Rebuilding of London Bridge and for Improving and Making Suitable Approaches Thereto. The Commissioners were building a new system of huge, deep sewers which entailed making deep longitudinal cuttings, mainly along the centre of streets – digging down, in fact, to levels which at that time had not been touched or even seen since medieval or Roman times. The Improvements Committee, meanwhile, having completed the rebuilding of London Bridge in 1831, was 'making suitable approaches thereto', chiefly by the formation of King William Street (*c.*1829–35) and Moorgate Street (*c.*1838–9) and the widening of Princes Street, so providing greatly improved communication northward from the new bridge. These works did not entail digging down so deep, and were therefore not so damaging to Roman archaeological deposits (though of course they were very destructive of medieval remains) as those of the Commissioners of Sewers.[15] But above ground level they required the demolition of Wren's St Michael, Crooked Lane (1831), 'one of the handsomest of the City churches', according to Jones himself, who in a rapid series of interviews with the Duke of Wellington (Prime Minister 1828–30) and the Archbishop of Canterbury personally arranged for its destruction, much to his own satisfaction. Later, as chairman of the Committee for Rebuilding the Royal Exchange, he also managed to get rid of St Bartholomew by the Exchange and St Benet Fink, also by Wren. After this second success he 'came to the conclusion that it would be desirable also to remove some other of the City churches', but after another promising campaign in the ante-rooms of episcopal power he was finally thwarted, apparently by powerful remonstrances made in the press.[16]

If the loss of these Wren churches was a heavy price to pay above ground level for new and better roads in the city, the price paid below ground for the new system of sewers (and for the deepening of the bed of the Thames near London Bridge, which was also going on in the 1830s) was far higher. In the journals (now in the British Museum) which Roach Smith began to keep in 1835 he noted almost daily the precious objects uncovered and often destroyed by the picks and shovels of the armies of workmen employed by the Commissioners of Sewers – pottery, glass, coins, sculpture, domestic utensils, cinerary urns, wall paintings (sometimes 'still brilliant in colour') and, above all, mosaic pavements, of which he recorded the discovery of half a dozen in 1836–7 alone – the irreplaceable raw material, in fact, for the study of Roman and medieval London, much of it now lost for ever; or if not actually lost, deprived of most of its meaning through lack of records of its provenance.

He collected as much as he could of it, of course, often buying objects direct from the workmen who uncovered them, but he soon found that 'to succeed with the men it is necessary to be very alert and active and persevering in attendance',[17] and he could not always absent himself from his little business. So some of his best pieces came into his possession through the agency of 'the little band of juvenile watchers' which he organized.[18] They knew pretty well what he wanted, and were able to haunt the excavations or the dredgers in the river and pay spot cash for promising finds which they then sold on either to Roach Smith or to one of his rival collectors. In the summer of 1836, when a deep trench was being dug along Lothbury, he hardly had even to stir outside his own door to acquire fine pickings; and his 'museum', as he began to refer to his collection, was already beginning to attract visitors, including a reporter from one of the leading monthly journals.[19]

But he was much more than just another collector. He was constantly observing, describing, recording, drawing, comparing, conjecturing and attempting to explain the objects that were being unearthed in such profusion in the 1830s and 40s. So convinced was he of the importance of recording the circumstances of every excavation and of every find that he even noted down the recollections of workmen engaged three or four years previously in making trenches which he himself had not seen; and he gladly accepted a 'sketch of a Roman building' discovered in East Cheap, made in the untutored hand of one of his 'juvenile watchers'.[20]

In all these ways Roach Smith was, indeed, a pioneer. In the 1830s the Society of Antiquaries, which might have interested itself in the fate

49 *Engravings of works to improve London Bridge and its approaches, 1830.*
The extensive scale of public works in the City not only destroyed much evidence about Roman and medieval London, but also entailed the demolition of three Wren churches including St Michael, Crooked Lane (centre background), thought to be one of the finest post-Fire City churches

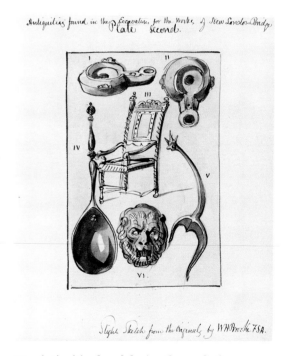

50 *Antiquities found during the works for London Bridge*

51 *'A few of the F.S.A.'s,' engraving of c.1832–3.*

Charles Roach Smith became a fellow of the Society of Antiquaries in 1836, and tried unsuccessfully to persuade them to establish their own museum in which antiquities from the City could be displayed

of London's archaeological remains, was still a lethargic and dilettante body incapable of effective action. There was no British Archaeological Association or Royal Archaeological Institute, the British Museum had no department interested in British antiquities, hardly any county archaeological societies had yet been founded (the London and Middlesex not until 1855), and successive governments were indifferent to the nation's antiquities. It was Roach Smith's misfortune perhaps (for he was a prickly and disappointed man) that in archaeological matters he was at least a quarter of a century ahead of his time.

For some years he did, however, try to stir up the Society of Antiquaries. From 1836 onwards he read a number of papers to the Society on Roman remains found in the City, and he often exhibited recent finds at the Society's meetings at Somerset House.[21] In 1836 he was admitted a fellow of the Society (only after some social prejudice against him caused by his being involved in trade had with difficulty been overcome). Soon afterwards he was agitating his fellow Antiquaries to establish their own museum,[22] and in May 1839 a petition signed by nearly eighty fellows was presented to the Council of the Society; but nothing was done.[23]

It is also certain that his archaeological activities in the City did not make him popular with the authorities there. He does not seem to have made any public criticism of the Corporation in the 1830s, but he is unlikely to have entirely suppressed his profound indignation as he repeatedly watched helplessly the wholesale destruction of many of the remnants of Roman London. 'Thus the remains of nearly 2,000 years', he noted in his journal on one such occasion, 'which might serve to illustrate the state of the arts at such a remote period, or give a lesson to progressing science, are annihilated for ever by the vulgar hand of modern barbarism'. The labourers were 'ignorant wretches', and a foreman with some choice specimens at his disposal was 'an ignorant and low-bred being' who (for whatever reason) was so exasperated with Roach Smith that he even ordered the deliberate destruction of all pottery finds – 'That's a good bit, but never mind, knock it to pieces – he (meaning me) shan't have it.' And later Smith declared, in clear reference to Richard Lambert Jones himself, that in these years he had been exposed 'to much vexatious interference urged by persons who had they improved in manners as they had risen in worldly power, ought to have known better'.[24]

But when the study of archaeology was in such an embryonic state it is hardly surprising that the City Corporation did so little about its museum in the 1830s – indeed it is much more remarkable that it had ever decided to establish such a thing at all. During these years prior to 1840 even Roach Smith himself seems to have tacitly accepted the situation. Within the privacy of his journal he did, in the summer of 1835, record, in reference to works near Bread Street, that 'most interesting discoveries might have been made had the Corporation of London possessed sufficient zeal of antiquities to cause the excavations to be made under the superintendence of some intelligent antiquarian'. But in 1835 he apparently accepted, unsceptically, the assurance of a building contractor that his workmen had been 'ordered to take all they discovered to the Surveyor's Office for the City Museum (I think he said) and they were always remembered [*ie paid*] for what they found'.[25] Similarly in 1836, some of the tiles found in Laurence Pountney Lane 'I hear have been preserved entire to the City Museum'; and in 1838, in reference to recent finds in Bloomfield Street, he noted without any adverse comment that the bulk of them 'up to the present time have gone to the Guildhall

Museum'.[26] At the Society of Antiquaries he even seemed to be defending the City Corporation, for after he had exhibited some recently found antiquities there, the Bishop of Bath and Wells ('an old gentleman with wig and apron') had asked 'whether there were no place for the depositing them, the British Museum for instance. I replied that any attempt on the part of the City Authorities to monopolize the antiquities would be fruitless, as there was no possible way to hinder the men from secreting them, and that if antiquaries were restricted from purchasing, that most probably in such a place as London where so many people are passing the sites of excavation, that whatever was found would either be sold directly to people who perchance may throw down a shilling or half-crown to secure something ancient merely as a curiosity of the day, or that the things would be secretly taken away and sold to Jews etc. In either case the public would be the losers.'[27]

This almost acquiescent attitude changed altogether, however, in 1840–1. By 1839 the City Corporation's Improvements Committee had completed the new northward street from London Bridge to Moorgate, and had applied to Parliament for power to make an improved east-west route, starting at the north end of Princes Street, near Roach Smith's premises, and extending westward to St Martin's-le-Grand and beyond. The Act authorizing this work contained (as was usual in such cases) a schedule of those properties which the Corporation could compulsorily purchase; and in addition to the properties to the west of Princes Street the schedule also contained half a dozen others to the east of Princes Street and situated on the north side of Lothbury. Amongst these was Roach Smith's little shop.[28]

Roach Smith regarded his ensuing expropriation as the 'terrible revenge' of the 'City Authorities'. Street improvements, he claimed very soon afterwards, 'found an excuse for my expulsion from Lothbury and the overthrow of my business with a pitiful allowance not yet equal to half my expenses in moving to a third rate street to begin the world and all its cares again'.[29] His enforced removal from his excellently situated premises in Lothbury, in the centre (as he put it) of 'the most opulent part of the first City of the World', and his resultant separation from a medical neighbour who had provided him with much business, were certainly severe blows indeed. It is very probable that the compensation which he received from the Corporation (£583) left him out of pocket, but he had only a short lease of his shop, and all the adjacent tenants who were also bought out were treated on a similar basis.[30] It is also likely that, when he appeared in person before the Improvements Committee at Guildhall, with Richard Lambert Jones himself in the chair, to request that he might be reinstated as near as possible to his existing premises, he was derided and humiliated.[31] But all this does not amount to the 'revenge' which he claimed was taken upon him. The City Corporation had been buying up land for public use in Lothbury by voluntary agreement before it had even obtained compulsory purchase powers;[32] and the setting back of the street frontage to the line of that of the church of St Margaret Lothbury was a natural sequel to the very recent formation of Moorgate Street. The truth seems to be that while Jones and his fellow councilmen, who 'were laughing and joking' when Roach Smith came before them, may have regarded his archaeologizing activities in the 1830s as a tiresome nuisance and were probably glad to see him in difficulties, he was not (in their eyes) important enough to merit any deliberate revenge.

By October 1840 Roach Smith and his two assistants had removed to larger but much less advantageously situated premises at No 5 Liverpool

*52 Green glazed medieval jug, made
at Mill Green, Ingatestone, Essex,
late thirteenth century.
Recovered from the site of the Royal
Exchange during digging for the new
foundations in 1840*

Street,[33] where his constantly growing collection of city antiquities was to be housed for the next sixteen years. But in the very next month there occurred the first of a series of events which were to lead to a further sharp deterioration in his relations with the Corporation. In January 1838 the Royal Exchange, which had been founded by the great Elizabethan merchant Sir Thomas Gresham and which belonged jointly to the Mercers' Company and the City Corporation, had been destroyed by fire. Soon afterwards none other than Richard Lambert Jones became chairman of the Royal Exchange and Gresham Trusts Committee charged with its rebuilding, and in due course (Sir) William Tite was appointed architect. Digging for the foundations of the new building began in the autumn of 1840, and in November one of the workmen brought a piece of Roman samian pottery found there to Roach Smith's house in Liverpool Street. A day or two later Smith applied to Tite for an order permitting him to enter the site, and a week later he made his first visit.[34]

As it had been expected that interesting objects might be discovered in course of digging for the foundations of the new building, a clause in the agreement between the Royal Exchange Committee and the contractors had required the latter to hand over all such objects to the Committee – a very early instance of such a provision, which in later years was to become common form; and the labourers were ordered to bring all antiquities to the clerk of works, who would 'remunerate' them.[35] During his occasional visits to the site in January 1841 Roach Smith was therefore scrupulously careful not to acquire anything whatever; but he was of course known to many of the labourers as a collector, and one evening, when he was away from home, one of them brought to Roach Smith's house a fragment of a statue of Charles II which he had somehow managed to abstract from the building site. When the man returned the next morning, expecting to be paid, Roach Smith ordered him to take it back, and even paid for the hire of a barrow to enable him to do so. But, being ignorant and probably confused, he evidently took his unwanted and incriminating burden to either the Guildhall or the British Museum. Thence the news of its abduction from the Royal Exchange was passed back to the Corporation authorities, and on the next day, when Roach Smith visited the site, he was turned off in the most offensive way. 'You sir! – Mr Smith! – Stop! Go back, Sir. You are not permitted to come here', shouted the foreman, 'a stout ill looking man' with whom Smith had previously had a clash. 'If you don't go, I'll get ye kicked off. . . . Didn't ye bribe the men to bring ye an image the other day? And then didn't ye bribe em to take it away somewhere else?' Even the authority of Tite's *laissez passer* was of no use, for another (more civil) person in authority at the site declared that 'we have orders from the Gresham Committee to prevent your coming on the ground'.[36]

Nor was Tite himself of any use, for when Roach Smith met him at the Exchange the following day, he in effect refused ('in a cool, stolid manner, peculiar to himself') to enforce the authority of his own order; whereupon Smith rashly replied that this being so he would on future visits 'feel it necessary, in self defence, to come armed'; and if the Committee's agent were 'to lay hands or feet upon my person, he might run the risk of being shot'.[37] He then returned home and wrote a long letter of complaint to the Committee, describing the events at the Royal Exchange, 'in which I am the sufferer and you are the aggressors through persons in your employ',[38] and adding for good measure that over the years he had been 'struck with the indifference with which remains of antiquity was regarded' by 'the City Authorities'. He never received any answer.[39]

Despite the ferocity of this war of words he did, however, visit the Royal Exchange site on one or two subsequent occasions.[40] But in late February or early March 1841 he must have given fresh offence when he declared in a paper read at the Society of Antiquaries (of which Tite was also a Fellow) that 'no provision is made by the body corporate of our venerable city to turn aside the axe and spade at the approach to a frescoed wall, or a rich mosaic pavement; the hand of unchecked ignorance in a few minutes destroys what time had spared, and often before it is possible for the antiquary to make even a memorandum of the fact'.[41]

In the latter part of 1841 there was more rancour when Richard Lambert Jones (chairman of the Royal Exchange Committee) was infuriated by an article published in *The Westminster Review* which severely criticized his role in the recent street improvements in the City, and of which he wrongly assumed that Roach Smith was the author.[42] And in December 1841 Tite, with better reason, was much annoyed by censorious remarks made by Roach Smith when reading another paper at the Antiquaries. An abbreviated version was published a few weeks later in *The Gentleman's Magazine* with the comment that 'we were very sorry to hear the writer state that his exertions to rescue these objects [*found at the Exchange*] . . . were opposed by persons who alleged they were instructed to do so by the United Gresham and City Improvements Committees, to the great destruction of his researches'.[43]

Early in 1843 mutual animosity between Roach Smith and the 'City Authorities' must have deepened still further when he successfully prevented their destroying a very well-preserved fragment of the Roman and medieval city wall at Tower Hill. In April he was informed by Mr Thomas Lott, a solicitor, a member of the Court of Common Council and a valuable ally of Roach Smith's, that the Corporation intended to surrender to the Church Building Society the land upon which this section of the wall stood in exchange for a piece of Church land near St Paul's. He immediately wrote to Sir Robert Inglis, a High Tory MP who had unwittingly got himself involved in this deal, and sent a paragraph to *The Morning Post* and other newspapers. He denied that the Corporation had any right to pull the wall down at all – they 'were appointed Conservators of the City, but not Destroyers'. After Inglis had seen the wall for himself and had been presented with a well-supported petition from the Society of Antiquaries, he promised that 'his best energies should be devoted to the preservation' of it.[44] This piece of the wall still survives, and is now a protected ancient monument.

Later in 1843 Roach Smith produced the first number of a series of essays entitled *Collectanea Antiqua*, which he continued to write and edit for many years, and which eventually extended to seven volumes. In an article upon the (so one might suppose) harmless subject of bronzes and pottery found during recent excavations at Etaples, near Calais, he contrasted the enlightened efficiency of the French in matters antiquarian with 'the general apathy of municipal authorities in England in the preservation of antiquities and formation of public museums'. He then went on to deliver an insult of such devastating rudeness that, if it had come from anyone else, one would have at once assumed that it had been deliberately designed to give offence: 'While every town in France has its museum, in no town or city in England is there so contemptible an apology for one, as in the City of London; at the same time, it must be allowed, that nowhere in the kingdom is there to be found a corporation composed of people more unintellectual and uneducated'.[45]

This is not the way to make friends or influence people. Nor was the bitter altercation which Roach Smith had with William Tite in November

53 *The Roman and medieval city wall at Tower Hill. From an engraving in Roach Smith's 'Illustrations of Roman London', 1859.*
The partial demolition of Bastion 2, shown here, revealed fragments of the Classicianus tombstone (see page 141)

and December 1845 in the columns of the new and already authoritative weekly periodical, *The Builder*. Tite, who had with some justice been much annoyed by the reports in *Archaeologia* and *The Gentleman's Magazine* of Roach Smith's critical remarks, started this new feud at a meeting of the Institute of British Architects at which the foundation of a collection of national antiquities, either at the British Museum or elsewhere, had been discussed. In defending the 'City Authorities' from accusations that 'they looked after nothing but turtle and railway shares', he said that during the excavations at the Royal Exchange 'Mr Roach Smith had given much trouble by his efforts to elude the regulations and purchase for his own collection'; but despite this, all the finds made there were now safely in a temporary home at the London Institution, and the only question was whether they should finally 'be placed in the City Library or the British Museum'.[46]

Roach Smith replied at some length, and Tite then accused him of having somehow improperly acquired a bell and a leaden medalet found at the Exchange. Angry strokes and counterstrokes continued, and Roach Smith even challenged Tite to a disputation at a public meeting of the British Archaeological Association in Leicester Square – an invitation which was, however, refused. The British Archaeological Association passed a resolution in support of Smith, who finally seems to have been victorious in his verbal joustings with Tite – at all events he certainly had the last word.[47]

One of Roach Smith's letters to *The Builder* (extending in all to over three columns of closely printed matter) contained the following passage: 'That the "City Authorities" have hitherto ever had the least regard for their ancient monuments is an absurd notion, disproved by the known fact of their never having attempted to preserve them, either in former times or during the last twenty years, when so many which were extant have been destroyed, and so many discoveries made to no useful purpose, as far as "City Authorities" were concerned. On the contrary, I can bear personal evidence, confirmed by dates and indisputable facts, that for a long series of years, they have directly countenanced a wholesale and indiscriminate system of destruction. Had they ever possessed a feeling for the works of ancient art, which illustrate the history of old London, they would not in the year 1845 be talking and disputing about fitting up *one room* for their reception; they would have possessed a mansion solely devoted to them, an entire building for such a museum as might have been formed, and such as the valuable monuments now irrevocably destroyed, demanded. No; let it be frankly and honestly owned, that the "City Authorities" have done nothing for, but much against their antiquities, and then charity may listen to a plea of ignorance on their behalf, and a promise of better behaviour for the future.'[48]

Whether in the long run Roach Smith's habitual use of vehement and agitated language of this kind advanced or retarded the cause of the museum for the City is uncertain. Equally uncertain was the effect of his reference during this controversy to the alleged embezzlement by 'a servant of the corporation' of thirty or forty medieval gold nobles found during the rebuilding of London Bridge many years previously.[49] There are several references to this bizarre story in Smith's private journals,[50] but this was the first occasion on which he mentioned it in print. The 'servant of the corporation' was none other than Richard Lambert Jones, who was said to have impounded the coins on behalf of the City, sold them to a gold refiner in Old Jewry and never accounted to the Corporation for the proceeds.[51]*

* Roach Smith repeated this accusation in much the same terms in 1854,[52] but it was not until 1883, twenty years after Jones's death, that he publicly mentioned Jones by name as the alleged villain.[53]

Roach Smith himself, at all events, seems to have been oblivious to the possibility that his words and writings might be counter-productive. All through the 1840s this remarkable man presented miscellaneous antiquities and copies of his written works to the Corporation whose alleged sins of omission he was at the same time so constantly attacking – he even presented the library with a copy of his essay about the excavations at Etaples! In 1841 his gifts included 'Two parcels of Antiquities (mostly Roman) found in excavating for approaches for the Railway in Southwark'; in 1843 came a 'very early English spade', found near Liverpool Street; in 1844 ten specimens of Roman frescoes from various parts of London;[54] and in 1845 some medieval items recently uncovered in Whitechapel. This last gift was, however, accompanied by a characteristically abrasive letter to the chairman of the Corporation's Library Committee which demonstrates his extraordinary capacity for antagonizing the very people upon whose sympathy and benevolence the success of his archaeological work most depended. 'Sir', he began, 'As I understand the Library Committee has at last resolved to wipe away from the City of London the reproach of having no museum for its antiquities, I present these remains for the embryo collection.' It is hardly surprising to find that although the gift was accepted, no customary letter of thanks was sent to the donor.[55]

In this same year the Library Committee did, however, briefly bestir itself on behalf of its museum. By 1845 several important changes in public attitudes had taken place since the 1830s. In the field of antiquities both the Numismatic Society (1838) and the British Archaeological Association (1843) had been founded (the latter by Roach Smith with his friend Thomas Wright) out of dissatisfaction with the Society of Antiquaries and the (Royal) Archaeological Institute; and the British Museum was in leisurely fashion contemplating the formation of a collection of national antiquities.[56] The establishment of such weekly periodicals as *The Builder* and *The Illustrated London News* had greatly added to the power of the press, and ever since 1837, when a Royal Commission had published a critical report on its affairs, the City Corporation had been on the defensive. More particularly, William Ewart's Museums Act of 1845 had authorized municipal councils to levy a halfpenny rate for the establishment of 'museums of art and science'.[57]

Museums were, in fact, news; and this is perhaps why early in 1845 Roach Smith's ally, councilman Thomas Lott, moved that the Common Council's resolution of 19 January 1826 requesting the Library Committee 'to consider the propriety of providing a suitable place for the reception of such Antiquities as relate to the City of London, and Suburbs', should be revived. On the first occasion when Lott proposed this motion, there were not enough members present to form a Court, but after *The Builder* had commented that 'The apathy thus evidenced is really disgraceful to the City of London and cannot be sufficiently reprobated',[58] a quorum was found and the matter was in due course referred to a sub-committee of the Library Committee. This found that the existing 'small room adjoining the Library' fitted up as a museum was 'inappropriate' and recommended that part of the beautiful medieval crypt beneath the Guildhall should be used instead.[59] But nothing came of this, and in the end it was decided that 'the Ante-Room of the Library should be fitted up to contain Antiquities and Works of Art'. J B Bunning, then Clerk of the City's Works, reported that 'the several Antiquities belonging to the Corporation . . . can be very well arranged in Two Glass Cases' placed in two recesses, with another in the centre of the room. He also proposed, 'The Room being somewhat dark for the purposes of a Museum', to paint the woodwork a very light colour; and he estimated that the total cost of this and a few ancillary works would amount to £450. This was, however, too much for the Corporation, which in March 1846 sanctioned the expenditure of only £200.[60]

In the same month the chairman of the Library Committee wrote to the Royal Exchange Committee and asked that the antiquities found in 1841 at the Exchange might now be deposited in the Corporation's museum; and in the autumn of 1846 Tite sent over two cases of 'curiosities' from the London Institution, where they had *pro tempore* been housed, one containing samian pottery and the other various domestic implements.[61]

The Library Committee's burst of activity was resumed early in 1847, when it expressed concern about the disastrous effect which digging deep new sewers was having upon the study of Roman London. Acting on the Committee's instruction the town clerk wrote in February to the Commissioners of Sewers that 'The recent formation of a Museum in the Library, which already contains many interesting specimens presented to the Library by the Gresham Committee from the foundations of the Royal Exchange and by other donors, renders the preservation of similar specimens more important to the Corporation of London'. As, he continued, 'a precise account of the locality and depth at which such articles are found might lead to an interesting development of the Ancient Roman City', the Library Committee wished 'to urge upon the attention of the Commissioners [*of Sewers*] the expediency of giving directions to their Officers and those employed under them to give immediate information to the Officers of the Commissioners of any Antiquity being discovered, and for its careful preservation until it has been inspected'. And finally he requested that he, the Town Clerk, should be immediately informed of any such discoveries.[62]

One or two minor items were, indeed, handed over by the Commissioners of Sewers, but an important fragment of Roman sculpture found in the course of digging for a sewer in Hart Street only reached the museum (after a long sojourn in an outhouse in the Corporation's stone-yard) because councilman Lott made a fuss about it. No system of inspection of sites would, in fact, ever be effective without the energetic support of the librarian, and this was still lacking. William Herbert, the first holder of the post, had retired in 1845, old and ill, but his successor, William Turner Alchin, who reigned from 1845 to 1865, seems to have been quite indifferent to the museum, and to have had little idea of what its purpose might or ought to be.[63]

And so when, in December 1847, Roach Smith presented some miscellaneous Roman and other objects recently found in London, the Library Committee, after hearing Alchin's advice, decided to refuse them. A letter was accordingly sent to Smith, informing him that the articles were 'not in the opinion of this Committee adapted for the Collection contemplated by the Corporation of the City of London'. A few days later, and probably before he had received this letter, he sent over 'for the incipient Museum of the Guildhall' a number of fragments of samian ware, some having potters' marks on them; and these too were promptly rejected.[64]

The identity of the donor rather than the relevance of the object seems, indeed, to have been at this time the Library Committee's main criterion in deciding whether to accept or reject gifts. In 1846 the librarian's uncle, a baronet, successfully offered 'the jaw and thigh bone of a gigantic animal from the Brazils, A fine specimen of Rock Crystal' from the same quarter, and several pieces of agate; and Alchin himself chipped in with 'A Chinese Compass, An Egyptian China Mummy, [*and*] Specimen of

Egyptian Stone'. Two years later 'a young Elephant's head' from Carpenters' Hall and 'Specimen of Coal Formation from Merthyr in Wales' from the Commissioners of Coal Whippers were all gladly accepted, as also in 1853 was Alderman Thomas Finnis's gift of a large marble slab 'from the ruins of Nineveh', Sir Henry Layard's recently published accounts of his excavations there having made Assyrian antiquities all the rage at about that time.[65]

Meanwhile in 1849 there had been renewed skirmishing between Roach Smith on the one hand and both the Corporation and William Tite on the other. In February the Commissioners of Sewers summoned Roach Smith before the Lord Mayor's Court to answer a charge of having received stolen property – to wit, a substantial fragment of a Roman stone statue (now in the British Museum) which had been discovered by the Commissioners' workmen in Bevis Marks and carted away beyond the precincts of the City. There Roach Smith had recovered it, 'at some trouble and cost' to himself, and (supported by the evidence of the navvies involved) was able to prove his innocence.[66]

This paltry little case was reported at some length in *The Times*, and in a manner very favourable to Smith.[67] A few months later *The Times* was also the scene of renewed hostilities with Tite, the *casus belli* being a notice of Tite's long-awaited *Descriptive Catalogue of the Antiquities found in the Excavations at the New Royal Exchange*. In April 1849 the 'greater part' of Tite's finds had been transferred to the Guildhall by Richard Thomson, one of the librarians at the London Institution and the real author of most of the catalogue. There they had been placed in the glass cases provided, but (according even to Tite, never a man to criticize such a powerful patron as the Corporation) 'for want of space this is yet done in a very imperfect manner'; and according to Thomson, 'Other articles remain for the present unopened, until some further accommodation of shelves shall be provided.' Tite had, however, provided a long bland introduction to the *Catalogue*, and in it he had referred to the 'inconsiderate injustice of those gross attacks on the Corporation and its officers' for their alleged neglect of local antiquities.[68] This had produced a fierce letter from Roach Smith (over the signature of 'A London Antiquary') pointing out that the provision of the single room now devoted to the City's antiquities was entirely due to Thomas Lott, 'the only member of the corporation who, through a series of repulses and oppositions which would have daunted a less enterprising man, at last prevailed upon the corporation to allot this space'; and (after a feeble answer from Tite) demanding to know 'what has become of the antiquities discovered since 1841? . . . Where are they? Has the City Museum acquired any of these? No! Scarcely a single object has been added, found since 1841. . . .'* And so on and so forth, at great length.[69]

Yet despite this renewed acrimony, and despite the insulting rejection of his proffered gifts to the museum in 1847, this strange man was so devoted to the well-being of the antiquities of London that in June 1850 he actually offered to present more items from his collection. He did so through his friend Thomas Lott, who informed the Library Committee of Roach Smith's intention, and expressed his own opinion that the 'pieces of Norman and Early English Sculpture' in question were 'well worthy of a place' in the museum. And so they were accepted, and a letter of thanks was sent out.[70]

There can never, however, have been any serious possibility of the Corporation agreeing to purchase the whole of Roach Smith's great collection. His arch-adversary, Richard Lambert Jones, who would certainly have opposed any such idea, had, it is true, retired from the

* The lost 'antiquities discovered since 1841' included those which must have been found at the Roman bath during excavations for the foundations of the Coal Exchange in Lower Thames Street. Not a single object from this site was acquired by the Guildhall Museum, despite the fact that Lott was chairman of the Corporation's committee for building the Coal Exchange and that Bunning, the Corporation's architect, was soon afterwards elected a fellow of the Society of Antiquaries. The Corporation did, however, preserve the bath (thanks evidently to the efforts of Lott and Bunning), which still exists beneath the new offices of the Trustee Savings Bank and which may one day be opened to the public.

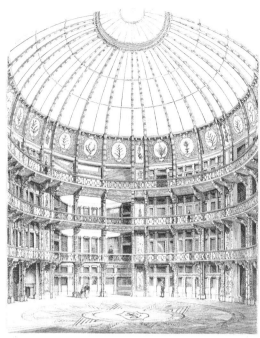

54 *Roman bath discovered in Lower Thames Street in 1848 on the site proposed for the new Coal Exchange.*
This is one of the earliest examples of a major ancient structure being deliberately retained because of its antiquity

55 *Interior of the new Coal Exchange: engraving, c.1850.*
The Roman bath was preserved below this new building, now the site of the Trustee Savings Bank. Since 1987 the City Corporation has undertaken conservation work which should lead to the bath and associated 'domestic' building being opened to the public

Corporation around the end of 1852 (he died, full of years and municipal honours in 1863, leaving a very large fortune of some £80000).[71] But by 1854 Smith's business was no longer so prosperous as previously, his health was 'impaired' and the lease of his house in Liverpool Street was nearing its end. He began to realize that he and his collection 'must soon part', and so he prepared and published by subscription a detailed *Catalogue of the Museum of London Antiquities* in his possession. It was profusely illustrated, contained over a thousand entries, and covered the whole range of the collection – Roman sculpture, bronzes, coins, pottery and terracotta, glass, tiles, pavements, wall paintings, personal ornaments, leather sandals and utensils of many kinds; and from the Anglo-Saxon and medieval periods there were sculptures, weapons, coins, pottery, leatherwork, pilgrims' badges, seals and lead tokens. There had never before been a collection of metropolitan antiquities of such importance, and (in the words of a petition later presented to the Treasury) there was 'no probability that such a collection will ever be made again'.[72]

Because he felt that it was his duty to keep the collection together, and if possible to provide it with a permanent home, which only public custody could guarantee, he offered it simultaneously to the City Corporation and to the Trustees of the British Museum. The offer to the former was made on 22 January 1855 in a letter written on his behalf to the Lord Mayor by three fellows of the Society of Antiquaries, of whom Thomas Lott was one. The matter was, of course, referred to the Library Committee, members of which went to inspect the collection on 12 March, when the asking price of £3000 was freely mentioned. But they made no recommendation as to what should be done, and on 26 March the Library Committee came to no decision either.[73]

The Corporation and the Trustees of the British Museum (the latter having by this time decided not to purchase the collection) now found themselves in an awkward predicament.[74] Both of them were being severely criticized for their lethargic attitude towards, respectively, metropolitan and British antiquities.[75] The Corporation, of course, probably never intended to buy Roach Smith's treasures. In 1852 an antiquary who had offered his London specimens to the Guildhall for a mere £30 had been informed that it was 'not in the power of the [*Library*] Committee to purchase the articles', nothing had ever been bought for the Guildhall Museum for more than about twenty pounds, the Guildhall Library's annual purchase grant for books was still only £200, and even the Corporation's lavish and enlightened expenditure on the repair and indexing of its own archives amounted to only £2350, spread over more than four years.[76]

But a plausible excuse for not taking up Roach Smith's offer was nevertheless needed, and fortunately for the Corporation this was ready to hand in the form of the Bill going through Parliament in the spring of 1855 'for establishing Free Libraries and Museums in all large Towns'. All this measure did when it became law later in the year was to authorize municipal corporations to spend a one penny rate on libraries and museums, subject to the previous adoption of the Act by a special poll of the ratepayers.[77] For the City Corporation's Library Committee this was enough – there might be heavy expenditure in the offing if the City ratepayers decided to adopt the Act; 'the sum required for the purchase' of the Roach Smith collection had not actually been specified in the original letter to the Lord Mayor (although it was perfectly well known to the Corporation); and so, on 7 May, the Library Committee decided that 'the question [*of purchasing*] should not at present be entertained'. And four weeks later, nearly five months after the original offer had been made, the town clerk informed Roach Smith of the Corporation's decision.[78]

In July Mr Gladstone presented a very powerfully supported petition to the House of Commons emphasizing the importance of securing the collection for the nation, and a similar memorial was sent to the Treasury. Eventually, after much cheese-paring about the price, the Trustees of the British Museum offered £2000, which Roach Smith accepted in March 1856; and soon afterwards the collection was transferred to Bloomsbury, where it still remains. Meanwhile the City Corporation had organized a public meeting of ratepayers to decide whether to adopt the new Libraries Act. It was held in the Mansion House on 5 November 1855, and according to Roach Smith many members of the Corporation urged their constituents to vote against adoption. At all events, the proposal was rejected by an immense majority,[79] and the Corporation did not, in fact, provide any public lending library for over another hundred years – until 1965, when recent legislation obliged it to do so.

The failure of the Corporation to purchase Roach Smith's collection did irreparable damage to the Guildhall Museum. At the British Museum it is, of course, admirably looked after, but only a very small proportion of it can be exhibited at any one time, and it has been distributed amongst no fewer than four different departments. Even now, however, after well over a century, the Department of Prehistoric and Romano-British Antiquities 'still counts its part of the collection as its major single acquisition'. But for the Corporation there was to be no second chance, for after his departure there was nobody of Roach Smith's stature to cope with the immense volume of archaeological discovery which could have been made in the City in the second half of the nineteenth century.[80] He himself retired to a small property which he bought at Strood, near Rochester, where he lived for many years with his sister, and where he eventually died in 1890, aged eighty-three, leaving a very small estate of under two thousand pounds and a reputation for archaeological vision and scholarship which, after the lapse of nearly a hundred years, is still continuing to grow.[81]

56 *Decorated limestone slab, c.1030. Found in St Paul's churchyard in 1852, this slab probably formed part of a tomb, perhaps of one of King Cnut's Scandinavian nobles*

57 *Insignia of the London and Middlesex Archaeological Society, founded in 1855. From the title page of John Edward Price's 'On a Bastion of London Wall or, Excavations in Camomile Street, Bishopsgate', 1880*

58 *Railway works at Dowgate Hill during the construction of Cannon Street Station, 1864.*
Contractors' excavations revealed numerous massive walls, one of which was 200 feet long, 10 feet high and 12 feet wide. The Roman masonry was so hard that some stretches had to be blown up with dynamite in order to remove them. As a result of excavations and observations by Peter Marsden on the station and adjacent sites in the 1960s, the walls were interpreted as being part of the Roman governor's palace. The construction of a massive office building above the station platforms in 1988–9 has involved the Department of Urban Archaeology in further excavation of the 'palace' and has revealed two massive Roman waterfronts

For some years after Roach Smith's removal from London in 1856 the Guildhall Museum was largely ignored by the City authorities. In 1857 members of the public were allowed to use the library for the first time, and members of the Corporation only were even allowed to borrow certain books,[82] but in 1860 Thomas Lott's request that a catalogue of the contents of the museum should be made was rejected on grounds of expense.[83] Yet this seventh decade of the nineteenth century was to be a period when (to borrow Sir John Summerson's phrase) 'London was more excavated, more cut about, more rebuilt . . . than at any time in its previous history'.[84] And in the City itself the excavations made for new offices, warehouses, banks, hotels, insurance company palaces, railways, markets and other public works were certainly on a far greater scale than anything done in the 1830s and 40s. The extent of the loss to metropolitan archaeology is impossible to estimate.

Nevertheless the library and museum did have two valuable new champions in the 1860s; and for perhaps the only time in its history the museum benefited from being merely an adjunct of the library, for without the library the museum would certainly not have acquired its new premises, built by the Corporation in 1869–72. The first of these new friends was Charles Reed (1819–81), later Sir Charles Reed, chairman of the London School Board, and proprietor of a printing business. He was deeply interested in popular education and had immediately made his mark in the Court of Common Council, to which he was elected in 1855, by the publication (shortly before the public meeting at the Mansion House in that year) of a pamphlet entitled *Plea for a Free Public Library and Museum in the City of London*. In 1858 and again in 1865 he had been chairman of the Library Committee, and there he had encountered a kindred spirit in Dr William Sedgwick Saunders, MD, an authority on cholera, and chairman of the committee in 1866 and 1869, who was almost as critical of the Corporation as Roach Smith had been, but who was rather more skilful in getting it to do what he wanted. And in 1865 the efficiency of both library and museum were much enhanced by the death of the now old librarian, Alchin, and the appointment (no doubt engineered by Reed and Saunders) of William Henry Overall, of whom even Roach Smith had a good opinion.[85] It was this efficient trio which extracted £200 from the Common Council to buy a private collection of Roman and medieval antiquities found in London in recent years from Mr Thomas Gunston of Islington Green. And in 1867 Reed and Saunders successfully rescued for the museum a Roman column bearing a touching inscription of conjugal affection which had been found some sixty years previously near Ludgate and which was now lying forlorn and uncared for in the yard of a nearby coffee-house.[86]

But their most lasting and important achievement – particularly in the case of Dr Saunders – was to persuade the Corporation to build proper accommodation for the library, and hence, of course, for the museum too. By the early 1860s the library was bursting at the seams, its treasures (in Saunders' words) 'literally stowed away like so much lumber' in its 'miserable accommodation'. In 1861 Common Council had voted £3000 for the adaptation of a few rooms over the Comptroller's office, but this work was not done, for, to quote the same source again, it was 'not by tinkerings like these that we can hope to meet our present needs'.[87] Two years later Dr Saunders suggested to the Library Committee that a completely new building should be provided for the library, and that this should contain a 'Chief Apartment' a hundred feet in length for the library and museum, a reading room for the public, a committee room and a strong-room. This was certainly not ideal from the museum's point of view, for its principal accommodation was to have been a double row of cases extending down the centre of the 'Chief Apartment'; but it was at least a step in the right direction, and the matter was referred to the Guildhall Improvement Committee.[88] This in December 1866 recommended the building (at a cost of £25000) of a new library and museum on the site actually later used, between the east end of Guildhall and Basinghall Street, with the museum occupying the whole of the lower floor beneath the library.[89] But part of the legal business then still done in the law courts in another part of the Guildhall complex would, it was thought, soon be transferred to the new Royal Courts of Justice later built in the Strand; and (in the opinion of some members of Common Council) the rooms thus to be vacated would in due course be very suitable for the library and museum.[90] So in May 1867 the Library Committee was once again glumly discussing ideas for adapting the rooms over the Comptroller's office.[91]

By this time, however, the Corporation was being frequently criticized for its neglect of its library. In 1866 the existence of free public libraries in many cities abroad was contrasted with the situation in London, which stood 'degraded and disgraced for its apathy in this matter'. The *City Press* lamented the loss of the Roach Smith collection to the British Museum, and early in 1869 *The Illustrated London News* proclaimed that 'The Corporation library and museum are, it is notorious, ill-housed in what may be almost called a strip of a building on the south side of the Guildhall, and a most inefficient depository it is for such treasures as are from time to time added to the collection'.[92] These were years in which the Corporation was also being frequently criticized on many other grounds. Hardly a year passed without a House of Commons Select Committee prying into some aspect of the City's affairs, and Bills for the reform of metropolitan government were frequently pending in Parliament. So when, to the accompaniment of much publicity, a Roman tesselated pavement was unexpectedly unearthed near Bucklersbury during the construction of Queen Victoria Street by the Metropolitan Board of Works in the spring of 1869, Dr Saunders realized that a great opportunity had presented itself.

He also knew well how to use the situation to the best advantage. As chairman of the Library Committee he got the Metropolitan Board of Works to promise to present the pavement to the Corporation, and then arranged for it to be seen by the public *in situ*. 'By letting the visitors enter at one door, pass round the excavation, and out at another, all confusion was avoided', *The Builder* reported, and during the three days in May that it was on view, 33 000 people inspected the hole where it lay, 'fresh and bright as when it was first put down'.[93] . . . In an interview with *The Illustrated London News*, Dr Saunders admitted that the Corporation was ashamed of the existing accommodation for the museum. But he was sanguine, he continued, that 'that reproach will be speedily removed, and an edifice erected worthy alike of its importance and the dignity of the first city in the world'.[94] Then, at the meeting in June at which he reported the successful removal of the pavement to Guildhall, he also persuaded the Library Committee to resolve unequivocally 'That it is not desirable to expend any further sums of money in the adaptation of buildings which are totally inadequate to the wants and requirements of the Library and Museum.'[95] He followed this up with an able and very diplomatically phrased pamphlet entitled *Guildhall Library: Its Origins and Progress; being an Appeal to the Corporation of London for its Reconstruction*, which was circulated to all the aldermen and councilmen; and at its meeting on 22 July 1869 the Court of Common Council at last

59 *First-century Roman monumental tombstone found in 1867 near Ludgate during railway excavations.*
Translated, the Latin inscription reads 'To the spirits of the departed and to Claudia Martina, aged 19, Anencletus, slave of the Province, set up this to his most devoted wife. She lies here'

60 *The Bucklersbury Pavement. This tesselated floor was found in Bucklersbury near to Mansion House in 1869 and excited much public attention*

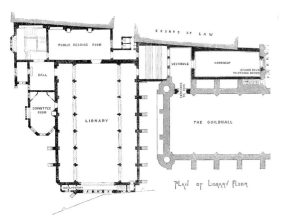

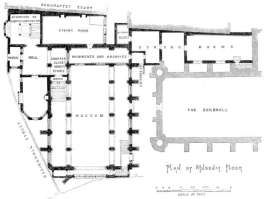

61 *Floor plans for the new library and museum built in 1870–2. Horace Jones, architect*

62 *View of the proposed building from Basinghall Street*

63 *View of the library*

agreed to the building of a new library and museum.[96] A special committee for the erection of the new building was set up, of which Dr Saunders was chairman throughout the five years of its existence. Members of the committee inspected a large number of libraries in London, Oxford and elsewhere, some of them even venturing as far afield as Munich and Vienna; the Corporation's architect, Horace Jones, produced plans, and in July 1870 the tender of George Trollope and Sons for £21 360 for the building only was accepted.[97]

The new building, built in stone in a handsome Perpendicular Gothic style, stands upon the site of some old houses on the west side of Basinghall Street, at right-angles to the Guildhall. It consisted mainly of two arcaded halls placed one over the other, the library having the upper floor, and being connected to the Guildhall itself by a wide flight of stairs and a vestibule – a very important point, for the Corporation intended that the library should also serve, on state occasions, as a reception hall or robing room for the main chamber itself. The principal entrance was from Basinghall Street by means of a fine stone staircase which led up to the public reading room and a small hall, where the Company of Clockmakers' collection of ancient clocks and watches was soon to be housed. On the east side of the library itself there was a fine committee room, also used by successive librarians as their office.

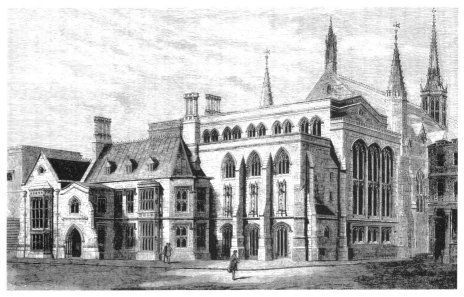

Downstairs was the museum's new home, an impressive chamber, divided by massive stone piers into nave and aisles, measuring 83 feet in length and 64 feet in breadth, and flanked on the south side by several fireproof muniment rooms. It was, however, so far below ground level that the southern end of the hall was said to have been 'plunged in almost total darkness'. Attempts were made to get borrowed daylight by means of brass grilles and 'glass bulls' eyes' inserted in the floor of the library above. But the main illumination was by gas lights, which were needed in such numbers that even before the opening of the museum there were problems of ventilation, aggravated, no doubt, by the nearby furnace of the hot-water heating system.[98]

In addition to the cost of the building itself, another large sum was spent upon the fine oak bookcases, tables, desks, chairs, cases and other fittings, all supplied by Messrs Cooper and Holt, the City upholsterers; and the total cost of the building and all its fittings eventually amounted to no less than £57 870.[99]

On 5 November 1872 an evening reception was held for over two thousand people to celebrate the opening of the library. Lord Chancellor Selborne was the guest of honour (after both the Prince of Wales and his younger brother Prince Arthur had proved to be unavailable), the band of the Coldstream Guards played suitable music, and tea, coffee, ices, biscuits, sherry and light claret were served. A gigantic temporary exhibition of a very heterogeneous nature was provided, and afterwards tickets of admission were sent to all members of the Corporation 'for distribution among the working classes in their respective Wards'. The total cost of this glittering entertainment was £1500.[100]

The museum was not, however, opened until nearly two years later. In 1871 the Building Committee had been concerned that the Corporation's existing collections were 'of a small character and insufficient to make an adequate display in the New Museum', and had asked to spend £500 on the purchase of plaster casts 'from the Antique and other large subjects'. Nothing seems to have come of this, but a little later alderman Finnis came to the rescue with the gift of two more 'massive and finely sculptured slabs from Nineveh', and early in 1872 Common Council did vote £500 'for the purchase of such objects of antiquarian interest as may be considered desirable for furnishing the Museum recently erected'. Some of this money was spent on the erection in a vertical position against the north wall of the east aisle of the Roman pavement found at Bucklersbury (now restored to horizontality in the Museum of London), and on the provision of 'a stout wooden frame' for the Assyrian slabs.[101] The museum was finally opened without any ceremony on 15 June 1874.

This tenebrous chamber was the museum's home until 1939, while the library remained upstairs until 1974, when it removed to its new quarters to the west of the Guildhall. The museum was open (free) on weekdays from 10 am to 4 pm (or 5 pm in summer), but it was always closed when the library was closed, and the library was always closed whenever there was an important event in the Guildhall. For a really important occasion such as the award of the freedom of the City to Lord Beaconsfield and Lord Salisbury in 1878, for instance, the library and museum were closed for several days, and these interruptions usually occurred on about thirty weekdays a year.

65 *The museum displayed important Roman finds such as the Bucklersbury pavement, the statue of a Roman soldier and a monumental tombstone, which jostled for attention alongside Assyrian sculptures*

66–68 *The museum in the late nineteenth century: watercolours by H E Tidmarsh*

Gradually the museum filled up. The six glass cases which were all that it possessed prior to 1874 were added to as the collection grew; but even now the Library Committee laid down no criteria about what the museum should or should not collect, and some decisions which it took are hard to understand now. In 1884, for instance, the offer by the late alderman Finnis's niece to present two Assyrian sculptures representing 'the God Nebo and the Goddess Astarte' was accepted, although in 1875 the Commissioners of Sewers' offer of 'an ancient Stone Coffin' unearthed in Bishopsgate had been refused owing to 'the limited space in the Museum'. But a large Roman coffin found a few years later during the extension of Liverpool Street Station was accepted from the Great Eastern Railway Company[102] – one of only a very few acquisitions from railway companies, whose operations in the City must have uncovered quantities of archaeological material. On the other hand a gun recently salvaged from HMS *Lutine* (wrecked off the coast of Holland in 1799) was welcomed, and so too was a model of the chapel of King's College, Cambridge. More important than the Committee's acceptance of these oddly inconsequential objects, however, was the Committee's failure to buy such outstanding items as the sword of alderman Sir Barnard Turner, commander of the London Foot Association during the Gordon Riots in 1780, or even the steelyard (ie weighing balance) of Sir Thomas Gresham – both of which were later acquired by the London Museum and now ornament the Museum of London.[103]

In the 1870s a slow change in the Corporation's attitude to archaeology in the City, and hence to the museum, was, however, beginning to become apparent. Ever since the foundation in 1855 of the London and Middlesex Archaeological Society, the Corporation had been increasingly aware of the existence of this highly respectable and very distinguished 'pressure group' dedicated, inter alia, to 'the careful observation and preservation of antiquities discovered in the progress of works', to the encouragement of 'individuals and public bodies in making researches and excavations', and even to the foundation of a museum of its own.[104] It was difficult for the Corporation to resist the polite but firm pressure applied by such an eminent society, and in 1870 it therefore cooperated with the LAMAS in the publication of a well-illustrated and scholarly *Description of the Roman Tesselated Pavement found in Bucklersbury*, to the printing of which it contributed £135.[105]

The author of this work, John Edward Price, a fellow of the Society of Antiquaries and sometime honorary secretary of the LAMAS, was the leading authority on City antiquities in the 1860s and 1870s. A 'City man', in business in Cowcross Street, he watched building sites and, in marked contrast with Roach Smith's example, made a point of cultivating good (almost sycophantic) relations with the Corporation, and particularly with William Overall, the librarian. In 1873 he was the author of another scholarly work, this time produced at the sole cost of the LAMAS, on the *Roman Antiquities . . . Recently Discovered on the Site of The National Safe Deposit Company's Premises* to the west of the Mansion House. He used this opportunity to 'review' many of the previous discoveries made in Roman London, thereby promoting more general interest in the subject, and he even pointed out politely that in 'the chief city of the empire, sufficient interest has never yet been manifested to induce a properly organised investigation of any given site'.[106] The Corporation responded, in 1875, by successfully inviting the National Safe Deposit Company to present its 'very interesting collection of Roman Antiquities' to the museum.[107]

In the following year Overall, the librarian, was informed that 'certain architectural fragments' had been found in Camomile Street, Bishopsgate, during the removal for redevelopment purposes of what proved to be one of the bastions of the City wall. Overall passed this news on to Price, who persuaded the LAMAS to pay for 'a complete investigation of the site', and the site owner's architect agreed to a delay in his rebuilding operations. For nearly a month two or three navvies hauled out 'upwards of fifty massive fragments of sculptured stone', evidently originally deposited there as rubble for the foundation of the bastion. The owner readily consented to present them to the museum, and the Corporation, after being reminded that in 1869 it had spent £135 on printing Price's account of the Bucklersbury pavement, voted an exactly similar amount – £45 for the transport of these 'very large blocks' to Guildhall, plus £45 for the cost of placing them on exhibition in the museum, and another £45 towards the cost of producing, again in association with the LAMAS, an illustrated account of the whole event. All this was duly done, *On A Bastion of London Wall, or Excavations in Camomile Street, Bishopsgate,* by Price, being published in 1880; and today the statue of the Roman warrior, the figure of a lion in combat, and the massive head of (apparently) a negro, all found in the Camomile Street bastion, form some of the most important items in the Museum of London's Roman collection.[108]

69 *Sculptured blocks of stone in course of removal from Bastion 10 of the Roman city wall at Camomile Street, Bishopsgate, 1876*

In 1881 more Roman architectural remains – mostly pieces of cornices, spandrels, columns and sepulchral monuments – were unearthed in another bastion, close by in Duke Street, Houndsditch; and these too were presented to the museum and brought to Guildhall at the Corporation's expense. Roman archaeology was, indeed, for a while all the rage within the Court of Common Council, and so the offer for sale of the late Walker Baily's collection of Roman and medieval antiquities, made by his executors in April 1881, came at an extremely opportune moment.[109]

John Walker Baily (1809–73) was the head of a successful firm of ironmongers in Gracechurch Street. During the last decade or so of his life he had collected City antiquities, which he displayed at his large house at Champion Park, Denmark Hill. This collection 'accumulated so fast and to such an extent that every corner, shelf, landing and lobby of the house became crowded with it, and constituted, to use Mr Baily's own words, "a perfect nuisance to its indwellers"', so in 1869 he had added a special wing to house it all. It consisted principally of Roman pottery, coins, lamps, glass, leather, bronze and other metalwork, together with some medieval objects of the same kind, and a great number of spurs and daggers, almost all of them found within the walls of the City. Walker Baily had formed his collection by purchasing from the touts who haunted all the building sites; and because he was known to be easily accessible at his centrally-placed business, and particularly because he always paid the touts just 'for the sight of what they had to sell, whether he purchased or not, they naturally went first to him, being sure of something for their trouble'. So he generally had the first choice, and between 1863 and 1872 he got the pick of anything on the market.[110]

The two most remarkable things about the Walker Baily collection were, however, first, the beautiful manuscript catalogue of it which Baily himself had compiled, and which is now deposited in the Guildhall Library. It extends to nearly four hundred pages, and contains hundreds of extremely accomplished watercolour drawings of each object, each drawing accompanied by precise information about the topographical provenance and the dimensions of the object. And second, the Corporation agreed, with very little trouble, to buy the collection for the asking price of £650. One councilman did venture to query the authenticity of the objects, but another, more in touch with the new mood within the Corporation, deprecated 'any attempt to beat down the price. To chaffer over a question of this kind like an ordinary huckster was utterly unworthy of the Corporation.'[111]

70 *The antiquities found on the site occupied by the National Safe Deposit Company on display in the Guildhall Museum*

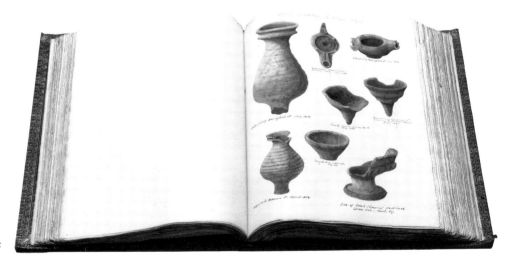

71 *John Walker Baily's manuscript catalogue of his collection of City antiquities*

So gradually an increasingly valuable accumulation was being put together in the museum. As long ago as 1850 H B Hanbury Beaufoy had presented his valuable cabinet of seventeeth-century London tradesmen's tokens, of which a catalogue had been published in 1853. Tokens were conveniently small objects, easy to store and to classify; and so to them had been added badges and medals used among the City Guilds, and the commemorative medals struck in Victorian times by the Corporation itself. The Walker Baily precedent of paying for the acquisition of archaeological material was followed from time to time with small purchases, but in 1893 the Corporation provided the substantial sum of £400 for the acquisition of the collection of James Smith, a Whitechapel workman devoted to archaeology; and later there was £100 for selected items formerly belonging to the Reverend S M Mayhew, FSA.[112] There was also a steady stream of donations, mostly of small objects. In 1899, however, an enormous blazon of the Royal Arms from the church of St Michael Bassishaw (demolished in that year) was attached to the south wall of the museum, and numerous shop and inn signs were fastened to other parts of the walls, those of the Boar's Head in Eastcheap (a tavern well known to readers of Shakespeare's plays) and the Bull and Mouth (the coaching inn in St Martin's-le-Grand) being the most arresting.[113]

72 *The museum collected material of later periods and several inn and shop signs, including this one from the Bull and Mouth coaching inn in St Martin's-le-Grand, were displayed on the walls*

In 1888 the Library Committee felt that the time had come to prepare a catalogue of its museum, which in due course should be printed and published. William Overall, librarian since 1865, had recently died and been succeeded by his assistant, Charles Welch, and the production of a new edition of the catalogue of the library had just been completed.[114] By this time the Library Committee had a fine record for the care of ancient archives. Much money had been spent over the years in putting the Corporation's own records in order, in 1876 a new post of clerk of the records had been created, and a long series of printed calendars was in progress. From the 1860s, too, the library had provided a secure home for the records of other City institutions, such as the wards, parish churches and livery companies – a policy far ahead of its time, and much later to be followed by many other libraries and by local record offices. As recently as 1885 the Corporation had, moreover, established its own art gallery, and the inauguration five years later of a series of loan exhibitions there drew very large attendances. Only the museum still needed a little stimulation; and the provision of a catalogue was clearly the first step to take. But in the event this operation was to take fifteen years to complete.

When work began in 1888 most of the collection seems to have been little more than a great jumble of unsorted, unlabelled and unnumbered objects.[115] Welch did not possess the knowledge or the inclination to do the cataloguing himself, and spent much of his official time on outside work. So four temporary assistants, each possessing some degree of archaeological expertise, were successively employed as museum cataloguers under the librarian, with the Corporation periodically doling out a hundred guineas for the payment of their fees.[116]

The first of these assistants was none other than John Edward Price, who in 1883 had been commissioned by the Corporation to compile what proved, on its publication three years later, to be a magisterial *Descriptive Account of the Guildhall of the City of London: Its History and Associations.* For the more prosaic work of compiling a catalogue of the museum, he proved, however, to have too many irons in the fire, for in the summer of 1890 he allowed his other interests to take such precedence over his official work that Welch was obliged 'to have his seat removed from the Museum [*downstairs*] to the table near my desk in the Library [*upstairs*]'. This produced 'an improved diligence and a more conscientious discharge of duty', but soon afterwards it was found that Price had been selling museum objects to private collectors (and actually doing so in the museum), and so his services were discontinued. This distressing event marked the end of an otherwise distinguished and valuable life's work, for the unhappy man died early in 1892.[117]

Price's successor was Arthur G Wright, who was originally employed for three months at two guineas a week. In February 1891 Welch had been unwise enough to say that another hundred guineas for the payment of a whole-time assistant for one year would 'suffice to complete the arrangement and the preparation of the catalogue for the printer', but

73 *Staff of the Guildhall Library and Museum, late nineteenth century*

74 *G F Lawrence 1862–1939. Lawrence, who later joined the London Museum, was a temporary assistant at the Guildhall Museum from 1901 until 1904. His work included the revision and condensation of the manuscript catalogue of the collection*

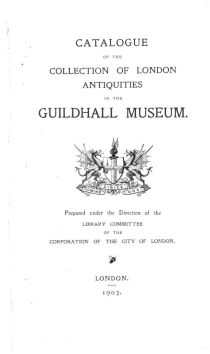

CATALOGUE
OF THE
COLLECTION OF LONDON
ANTIQUITIES
IN THE
GUILDHALL MUSEUM.

Prepared under the Direction of the
LIBRARY COMMITTEE
OF THE
CORPORATION OF THE CITY OF LONDON.

LONDON.
——
1903.

75 *Guildhall Museum catalogue, title page, 1903*

Wright seems nevertheless to have been continuously employed for several years. When at last the Library Committee sought authority to have the first section of the catalogue printed in a grand quarto form, heavily illustrated, the Court of Common Council refused, commenting in January 1898 that over £1000 had already been spent on fees for the compilation of the catalogue, that this expenditure should now stop, and that the catalogue should be produced in a much less elaborate way.[118]

This decision evoked a petition of protest from the Royal Society and other learned bodies. Ultimately Common Council authorized the expenditure of £400 on the printing of a much cheaper, though still comprehensive, catalogue in handbook form. This, however, required the production of a condensed version of the now complete manuscript catalogue.[119] As Wright's services had by now been discontinued, Allan S Walker became for a short while the third assistant to work on the catalogue; but on 1 April 1901 he was succeeded by G F Lawrence, who was engaged as a temporary assistant 'to render occasional services in the Museum', and was to be paid at the rate of one shilling and sixpence per hour.[120]

George Fabian Lawrence (1862–1939), or 'Stoney Jack', as he was known to every navvy in the City, was later to be one of the founder members of the 'staff' of the London Museum, which he faithfully served in his own unique way for many years. He had been brought up in the Barbican, where his father had had a pawnbroker's shop, and for decades he frequented the building sites of the City and the inner suburbs, quietly (or even surreptitiously) buying finds direct from the workmen. He occupied the twilight area of the dealer in archaeological antiquities where exactly what was or was not stolen property was often not at all clear, and his little shop in Wandsworth was a place of pilgrimage for both navvies with something to sell and collectors in search of something rare or curious to buy. In 1891 he had successfully sold to the Library Committee for £10 a small collection of objects found in the Thames at Wandsworth, and in the 1930s he was still happily making deals with Dr (later Sir) Mortimer Wheeler, a fellow archaeological swashbuckler who was then keeper of the London Museum. Without him countless objects of great value would have been lost; but like Roach Smith before him, he laid up no treasure for himself, his effects being valued after his death at only £1035.[121]

Lawrence was employed at the Guildhall Museum part-time, and perhaps only intermittently, from April 1901 until at least 1904. His main job was the revision and condensation of the manuscript catalogue, to which he brought an expertise probably greater than that of any of his three predecessors. Early in 1903 the members of the Library Committee were thoroughly exasperated by the librarian's endless delays in the production of the printed catalogue and consulted Lawrence direct. Welch, being then 'invited to make a statement', confessed that 'the Museum was not a credit to the Committee or himself; he admitted his negligence in the preparation of the catalogue', and asked for a little more time. He was nevertheless deprived for nearly a whole year of his position as librarian, to which he was not reinstated until March 1904. During this period he was instructed to devote his entire time to the catalogue, but the Committee seems to have paid more attention to Lawrence, who stated that 'he was not satisfied with all the sections of the catalogue' and was authorized to make the necessary corrections in the printer's proofs. Copies of the great work – one of the first museum catalogues to contain photographic illustrations – were at last delivered in July 1903.[122]

After all this the Library Committee was determined that 'some definite steps be taken for the future proper management and control of the Museum', and a permanent Museum Sub-Committee was therefore established. But it was Lawrence more than anyone who pulled the Guildhall Museum together and put it on something like a professional basis. In 1893–4 electric light had been installed, which 'for the first time permitted the entire extent of the Museum to be satisfactorily seen'.[123] In 1903 the Assyrian slabs presented by alderman Finnis and his niece were offered to and accepted by the British Museum, the appearance of the museum being much improved thereby, and also, added the acting librarian, 'the amount of light gained should result in a saving in the charge for electric light'.[124] The three crying needs of the museum were still 'more space, better light, and less heat', but with Lawrence in 1904 still beavering away one day a week in describing and labelling everything, the museum was becoming a more worthwhile place to visit. So, at least, the public evidently thought, for between 1905 and 1910 annual attendances rose from 108 000 to 153 000.[125]

In 1906 Charles Welch retired, and was succeeded as librarian by his assistant, E M Borrajo, who during his short reign (for he died in 1909) achieved one crucial thing for the museum.[126] Having seen Welch struggling with museum duties for which he had no qualification, Borrajo was determined that there should be a museum clerk, who, under the direction of the librarian, 'should devote the whole of his time to the maintenance of this valuable and important collection in a manner creditable to the Corporation; he must be a person interested in archaeology, especially that of London, prepared to conduct parties over the museum and explain its contents, watch all excavations within the City, and previous experience or training in the work is therefore indispensable'. The Library Committee was convinced and so too, after at first refusing, was Common Council,[127] and in 1907 Mr Frank Lambert, a young Cambridge graduate, took up his post at a salary of £120 per annum.[128]

So at last, more than eighty years after its establishment, the Corporation had provided its museum with a qualified person to look after it. Lambert set to work at once, acquiring such basic equipment as dust sheets, 'an outfit for printing descriptive labels' and protective 'blouses' for his own use. But he had hardly had time to make any impact before in April 1911 disquieting news was conveyed to the Library Committee about 'the proposed institution of a London Museum'. Prudently, it was resolved that 'the consideration of the matter be adjourned for the present'.[129]

76 *Building excavations exposed part of the Roman city wall at Newgate Street in 1903. This work included the site of the former Newgate prison. 'Relics' from the prison were auctioned in February of that year (77), and some later found their way into the London Museum's collections*

78 *Guy Laking, first keeper of the London Museum, directing the removal of a Roman Boat found in 1911 during excavations near Westminster Bridge for the building of County Hall*

FOUNDATION OF THE LONDON MUSEUM
1910 TO 1912

79 *The Roman Boat in situ, 1911.
Excavations for the foundations of County
Hall revealed remains of a craft which could
be dated to the late third century AD.
Although damaged it measured about 60 feet
in length and weighed over 20 tons*

80 *The Roman Boat ready to be moved.
Guy Laking (left, wearing bowler hat)
discussing the logistics of moving the boat
from Westminster to Kensington Palace
(New Scotland Yard in the background)
(above left)*

81 *The Roman Boat on the ramp up to
Belvedere Road*

82 *The Roman Boat on its way to
Kensington Palace (St Thomas's Hospital
and the Palace of Westminster in the
background).
The tarpaulin covering the catafalque
provided excellent advertising space for the
unopened new London Museum. The
progress of the procession was watched by
large crowds*

Chapter 3
FOUNDATION OF THE LONDON MUSEUM
1910 TO 1912

83 *Lewis, first Viscount Harcourt, 1922, co-founder with Lord Esher of the London Museum: oil on fibreboard by S J Solomon*

ABRIDGED PEDIGREE OF THE
HARCOURT FAMILY

Sir William Harcourt
1827–1904
Statesman
|
Lewis Harcourt
1863–1922
cr. Viscount Harcourt 1917
=
Mary Ethel Burns (*d.*1960)
niece of J Pierpont Morgan
|
William, second Viscount Harcourt
1908–1979

The most remarkable thing about the London Museum is that it ever came into existence at all. All museums have three basic requirements – exhibits, a building in which to house them, and money to pay for their security. When Lewis Harcourt and Lord Esher put their heads together in 1910 to establish a museum which, they intended, should ultimately illustrate the whole vast panorama of the history of London, they had none of these things. Yet within only two years they had gathered a collection together, found it a home (although only a very temporary one) and even conjured up some money from somewhere or other to pay for everything. One year later – in 1913 – the infant museum acquired another, slightly less precarious, home, and the Government agreed to pay for all the running costs. So within three hectic years of its conception the London Museum had become a national institution; and if some of the clandestine means by which all this was done were a trifle unusual, nobody's interests suffered thereby, and the public had at negligible cost acquired a real bargain of lasting cultural value.

Lewis Harcourt (1863–1922, latterly first Viscount Harcourt), First Commissioner of Works from 1905 to 1910, was the true progenitor of the London Museum. Over six feet four inches in height, with fair hair and an aquiline nose, and by temperament never ruffled, he had 'a genius for organisation and a super-genius for making things run smoothly'.[1] Like Winston Churchill, his colleague in Asquith's Liberal Government, he was a member of a cadet branch of an ancient landed aristocratic family. There have been Harcourts at Stanton Harcourt, five miles west of Oxford, since the middle of the twelfth century. In 1756, however, Simon, first Earl Harcourt, began to build himself a new house on another part of his estate, at Nuneham Courtenay, five miles south of Oxford. Nuneham Park stands in a beautiful natural landscape above the Thames, with commanding views over the river and towards the distant domes and spires of Oxford. Many of the best architects of the day had a hand in these and later extensive building operations; and in the 1830s another Harcourt, Edward, Archbishop of York, had made substantial additions to what was already a substantial pile.

Thanks to the early death of a childless cousin and the unexpected terms of his will, Nuneham Park became Lewis Harcourt's property in 1904. By that time he was rich, for in 1899 he had married a niece of Pierpont Morgan, the American financier, and he (or to be more accurate, his wife) already had a London House in Berkeley Square.[2] But Nuneham was his home, where throughout the rest of his life he spent as much time as his public life permitted, and where he loved to entertain his friends and political colleagues. At first there were drains and plumbing and 'the heating apparatus' to be seen to; then the building of new servants rooms,[3] a new lodge and even (with characteristic boldness) a gallery at first-floor level extending across the original Georgian façade of the house. But above all there were the gardens, where he constructed a series of formal terraces, the planting of whose shrubberies and herbaceous borders he personally directed, accompanied by his gardeners and a barrow-full of plants, and assigning to each its safe and carefully-chosen home.[4] He was in fact a Whig grandee of the old school, one of the last and not the least distinguished of a dying breed.

But there were other sides to him. His mother had died immediately after his birth in 1863, and he, the only surviving child, had been brought up by his father, Sir William Harcourt, the great Liberal statesman, now best remembered for being the originator of death duties. At his town house in Stratford Place, at his country house at Malwood in Hampshire, and on holidays in Scotland and abroad, Sir William and his little son

were inseparable; and it was only after Loulou (as Lewis Harcourt was known throughout his life to both family and friends) had been reluctantly sent away to Eton that his father had remarried. Five years later, in 1881, Lewis's ill health (in the words of Sir William's biographer) 'interfered with the idea of a Cambridge career'; and so, without even going to a university, he became at the age of eighteen his father's private secretary, an association which lasted for over twenty years, until the end of Sir William's career in 1904.[5]

During this period Sir William was Home Secretary (1880–5) and twice Chancellor of the Exchequer (1886 and 1892–5). Working in the closest intimacy with his father, Lewis Harcourt was thus able to learn at first hand how power and influence could be gained, and how they could be privately employed for the public good. By 1892 he was, indeed, already so expert in these delicate operations that his father entrusted to him the negotiations with Mr Henry Tate, whose offer of an art gallery and the gift of his own collection of modern pictures to the nation had previously come to nothing when Goschen had been Chancellor of the Exchequer (1887–92).[6] With the Harcourts in charge, however, there were no more mishaps, and these negotiations led a few years later to the building of the Tate Gallery (at a cost of £80000) and to a baronetcy for Mr Tate. They also provided Lewis Harcourt with his first experience of (to use his own words) 'endeavouring to make public generosity supplement official parsimony'[7] – a field in which, as First Commissioner of Works, he was later to become a virtuoso.

It was also to his father that Lewis Harcourt owed his first encounter with Reginald Brett, later second Viscount Esher (1852–1930), who was to become a close friend and his principal coadjutor in the foundation of the London Museum. Both Harcourt and Esher had charge of the infant museum until their deaths, at first, until Harcourt's death in 1922, in a partnership in which Harcourt was very much the leader, and thereafter with Esher in solitary command until he died in 1930. But this was far from being the end of either the Harcourts or the Eshers in the history of the museum. Lord Esher was immediately succeeded on the Board of Trustees by his son, Oliver Esher, the third Viscount, who later served as chairman from 1947 until 1961. His successor as chairman was none other than Lewis Harcourt's only son, William Harcourt, the second Viscount, who had been a Trustee since 1958 and who remained chairman for the rest of the London Museum's days (*ie* until 1975). In 1962 he also became chairman of the Interim Board of Governors of the proposed Museum of London, and from 1975 until his death in 1979 chairman of the permanent Board. Working in very different circumstances, William Harcourt was, indeed, almost as much the progenitor of the Museum of

London as his father had been of the London Museum. Certainly, anyone who has ever spent a happy hour in either of these museums owes much to these two distinguished men.

Reginald Brett was the eldest son of the first Viscount Esher, an eminent judge and ultimately Master of the Rolls, whom he succeeded as second Viscount in 1899. The Bretts, like the Harcourts, were of ancient lineage, but they were not so grand, or so rich. Throughout most of his long life Reginald Brett remained detached from the main stream of politics, yet he was for ever at the centre of events, advising, influencing, persuading. He enjoyed the friendship and confidence of three such different sovereigns as Queen Victoria, Edward VII, and George V. Successive Conservative and Liberal Prime Ministers entrusted him with the leading role in the far-reaching reorganization of national defence which began soon after the end of the Boer War; and later he was active in the creation of the Territorial Army. He was also an exceedingly skilful committeeman, an ubiquitous *eminence grise* and an invaluable ally in any project in which the possession of influence in high places might be useful. For him, the London Museum was always a relatively minor interest, and it was certainly never so important as it was to Harcourt; yet it would never have come into being without him.

Sir William Harcourt, in the days when he was professor of International Law at Cambridge, had known young Reginald Brett as an undergraduate at Trinity, and lent him rooms there;[8] and it was perhaps as a sequel of this kindly act that Brett and Lewis Harcourt first met. Later, Sir William had introduced Brett to the Liberal Unionist leader, the Marquis of Hartington, whom Brett served as private secretary for seven years (1878–85), three of them at the War Office.[9] Thus Lewis Harcourt and Reginald Brett occupied similar positions in the background of the political scene, and an intimate, lifelong fellowship quickly sprang up between them, Harcourt, still a bachelor, being a frequent visitor to Brett's houses at Tilney Street, Mayfair, Orchard Lea, near Windsor, and (after 1897) the Roman Camp at Callander in Perthshire.[10]

Both of them were still learning the arts of political management and the uses of patronage, and for many years they worked together hand in glove. Brett, indeed, seems to have owed his appointment by Lord Rosebery to the full-time salaried position of secretary to the Office of Works (a post which he held from 1895 to 1902) at least in part to Lewis Harcourt, who a few weeks before the appointment was asking 'won't you let me try to get the Office of Works for you?'.[11] And they were also already conspiring together in the getting of titles and honours for appropriate recipients. As early as 1892, when both were still insignificant figures on the political landscape, Brett wrote to Harcourt that 'I hear Mr. Gladstone [*then Prime Minister*] won't make our [*unnamed*] friend a Baronet. So I have written to ask him whether he will be a Knight?' And a little later, in reference to another gentleman 'who is *most anxious* to have a Baronetcy', he was urging Harcourt 'will you manage it? That's a dear.'[12]

During the next ten years or so the power and influence of both Harcourt and Esher greatly increased. Sir William Harcourt's retirement and death in 1904 at last enabled his son to start his own political career, first as a Member of Parliament and then in 1905 in the Cabinet as First Commissioner of Works – an appointment which Lewis Harcourt attributed to the influence of Brett (now Lord Esher). 'I am "Works"' he wrote. 'I am very happy and most grateful to you. I consider myself your nominee and am delighted that we shall have some work to do' – as indeed proved to be the case. And, on the other hand, Lord Esher had by this

85 *Reginald Brett, second Viscount Esher, c.1910–14.*
Lord Esher was Lewis Harcourt's partner in the foundation of the London Museum. A consummate courtier, his links with the Royal Family ensured the patronage of King George V, Queen Mary and Queen Alexandra for the new project

ABRIDGED PEDIGREE OF THE
BRETT FAMILY

William Baliol Brett
First Viscount Esher
1815–1899
Master of the Rolls
|
Reginald Baliol Brett
Second Viscount Esher
1852–1930

Oliver Brett   Maurice Brett
Third Viscount Esher   1882–1934
1881–1963
|
Lionel Brett
Fourth Viscount Esher
1913–
Architect

time become the trusted confidant and friend of the new monarch, and, in 1902, a member of the Honours Committee.[13]

As First Commissioner of Works, Lewis Harcourt now had a great opportunity to engage in his much favoured pursuit of making 'public generosity supplement official parsimony'. In 1907–8 he personally conducted the negotiations with Alfred Mond, acting on behalf of his father, Ludwig Mond, the industrialist and founder of Brunner, Mond and Company, which resulted not only in the bequest of the latter's great collection of pictures to the National Gallery (subject to his wife's life interest) but also of a large sum of money to pay for the building of rooms there for their accommodation.[14] Ludwig Mond died soon afterwards, in 1909, and Alfred Mond received a baronetcy in 1910.

'What a splendid success you have had with the Monds', wrote Sir Schomberg McDonnell, Lord Esher's successor as permanent secretary at the Office of Works, and went on to encourage Harcourt to concern himself with funds for the enlargement of the Tate Gallery.[15] He was, in fact, already doing so, for, as he had previously written to Sir Hugh Gilzean-Reid (an influential journalist of the day), 'If you could find a millionaire friend who would give me £30,000, I would start [building] at once.' Reid had replied suggesting one or two possible names, and adding that he himself would 'try' Andrew Carnegie.[16] He was, therefore, greatly impressed to see in *The Times* in May 1908 an announcement that Harcourt had just concluded the formal arrangements for the presentation by Joseph Duveen senior (1843–1908) of a new wing at the Tate Gallery, to be built (at a cost of at least £25000) for the accommodation of the famous Turner Bequest pictures.[17] So he wrote to Harcourt to present his 'heartiest congratulations. . . . Your statement in the Newspapers was simply astounding. What a splendid triumph. . . . It will realise the highest aspirations, and be to you an everlasting recompense.'[18] Six weeks later Duveen, now a very sick man, was awarded a knighthood – but only after a little difficulty. The original honours list had been so long, so Esher (writing from Windsor Castle) informed Harcourt, that the Prime Minister had been asked to cut the number of projected knights and baronets. 'It is impossible, I fear', added Esher, 'for poor old Duveen to live to another "honours list" date', so he ought to receive priority; and it was fortunate that he did in fact receive such special treatment for he died only five months later.[19]

It was, however, one thing to persuade potential benefactors, anxious, perhaps, to enjoy the approbation of a grateful nation, to give money or works of art to an existing Government-funded national institution; but quite another to find someone willing to hand over in the utmost secrecy a large sum for the creation *de novo* of a brand new museum, as yet homeless and financially unsupported from any other source. The establishment of the London Museum by what might now be appropriately termed the old firm of Harcourt and Esher was in fact a much more ticklish business than securing benefactions for the National Gallery or the Tate; and as in the case of Duveen's knighthood, unforseeable difficulties arose along the road.   ◨

In one of his opening moves Lewis Harcourt stated in a letter addressed in April 1910 to King Edward VII's Private Secretary, Lord Knollys, that 'It has been the dream of my life to establish a London (Carnavalet) Museum.'[20] The Musée Carnavalet presents the history of Paris – all of Paris. It occupies a fine seventeenth-century *hotel* in an ancient *quartier* of Paris, and was first opened in 1881.[21] In the early days of the London

Museum it was frequently cited as a model to follow, and in a trip which they made to Paris in 1890 Harcourt and Esher may well have visited it together.[22] At all events they must both have inspected it at some time or other; and Harcourt may well have compared the enlightened concern of the Ville de Paris for the whole history of the whole of the capital city of France with the attitude of the Corporation of London, satisfied with a museum which ignored the history of nine-tenths of the capital of Britain and the British Empire, then at the mighty peak of its power and prestige.

By 1910, however, London did have the London County Council to take a broader view of metropolitan affairs. Under the auspices of its oddly-titled Local Government, Records and Museums Committee, the LCC already managed the Horniman Museum at Forest Hill, which had been presented to it in 1901 by a successful tea merchant, complete with a brand new building and collections mainly devoted to anthropology and natural history; and in 1906 the Council had obtained wider statutory powers for the provision of art galleries and museums.[23] But the thinking of the Council seems to have been greatly influenced by C R Ashbee, who in the preface to the first volume of his *Survey of London* (published in 1900 at the expense of the LCC) had advocated 'a number of small municipal museums in different parts of London . . . set in some historic house and surrounded by the garden that is already in existence'.[24] Early in 1910 – at exactly the moment when Lewis Harcourt was opening his campaign for a museum for the history of all London – the Council was in process of buying the Geffrye almshouses in Shoreditch, and when it soon afterwards decided to use them as a museum of furniture and cabinet making it added that 'in London the principle of special independent museums at suitable centres is the right one upon which to proceed'.[25]

So the LCC was certainly busy about museums in 1910, but not in the way envisaged by Harcourt. He was keenly aware of the existence of a number of private collections of antiquities or of prints and drawings relating to the history of London which would sooner or later be dispersed unless previously acquired by some public institution. There were, for instance, those of Mr F G Hilton Price, a partner in Child's Bank, comprising a wide variety of London objects of all periods, and of Mr Seymour Lucas, RA, consisting of costume from the sixteenth century onwards, both of which Harcourt was afterwards able to buy for the London Museum, thereby defeating a very substantial offer made for the latter by the Metropolitan Museum of New York.[26] Above all, there was the vast collection of London prints and drawings formed by John Edmund Gardner, consisting of some 60000 items and probably the largest collection of London topographical material ever assembled anywhere.[27] After Gardner's death in 1899 his son had eventually decided to sell it all, and the announcement to this effect which had appeared in *The Times* in June 1909 had no doubt been read with concern by Harcourt.[28]

On the other hand he had been involved, as First Commissioner of Works, in the gift by Charles Edward Jerningham, a rather excitable journalist[29] who for many years wrote a regular 'chat' column in *Truth*, of his collection of prints and drawings illustrating the Royal Parks in London. These had been exhibited at Kensington Palace in 1906, and after Edward VII had inspected them there Jerningham had wanted to make a personal present of them to his sovereign; but the king had insisted that they should not be given to him but to 'The Nation', and they were later incorporated into the London Museum.[30] Royal interest, and a public exhibition in a Royal Palace could be used as powerful

86 *Seymour Lucas, RA. Oil on canvas by John Singer Sargent*

magnets for the acquisition of valuable material for a museum of London, as Harcourt no doubt began to realize. And although he did not move so easily in the field of civics as he did in the ante-rooms of courtly power, Harcourt was probably also aware of the sociologist Patrick Geddes's ideas for a 'Civic Museum'* in London which should be 'an instrument in the process of creating what is so largely lacking still – a civic consciousness among citizens . . . which has been lost in the vastness of modern London . . .'.[31] Civics, town planning and enthusiasm for 'research' into cities were, in fact, very much in intellectual vogue in 1910 when Lewis Harcourt, dimly realizing what was being so much talked about (as politicians often do), first began to feel his way towards the establishment of his London Museum.[32]

In the spring of 1910 it became known that Sotheby's were intending to sell the whole of the Gardner collection of London prints and drawings on 23 May and the following four days.[33] Harcourt, of course, wanted to acquire it somehow for the nation, and probably discussed with Lord Esher the possibility of finding another rich benefactor like Mond or Duveen. At all events, on 14 March 1910 he wrote from his house in Berkeley Square to Esher to say 'Please tell me about Mr Harry Waechter.'

Harry Waechter was the only son of Sir Max Waechter (1837–1924), a German immigrant of ancient lineage who had settled in England as a young man and who had in due course amassed a vast fortune, though by what means nobody now seems to be sure. *The Times* obituarist referred knowingly to his firm, Bessler, Waechter and Company, as metal, chemical and general merchants and coal, coke and firebrick exporters, and family tradition has it that Sir Max's shipping interests included tankers for the transport of oil. They certainly included several large private yachts, and by 1914 he boasted that he was worth £12m. He was also a notable philanthropist, and as the tireless exponent of European federation he had personally explained his ideas to the heads, both crowned and otherwise, of almost every European state. Nearer home, he was the friend of Edward VII and the financial adviser of the somewhat impoverished Duchess of Teck (the mother of George V's consort, Queen Mary), who was a neighbour of Sir Max's on Richmond Hill.[34]

87 *Sir Harry Waechter, first (and secret) benefactor of the London Museum*

But Sir Max had one great disappointment – he had no legitimate son, for Harry (1871–1929) had been born out of wedlock, his mother being a Yorkshire innkeeper's daughter.[35] A hereditary title was therefore useless to Sir Max, so he had refused a baronetcy and a peerage,[36] and contented himself with a knighthood, conferred by Edward VII in 1902. But Sir Max's wish to found a titled dynasty was nevertheless strong and was concentrated upon young Harry, who evidently shared it to the full. When Sir Max had realized that his wife was not going to bear him a son, Harry had been removed from his unprotesting Yorkshire mother's arms, provided with a solitary private education of the utmost rigour and in due course sent to Cambridge. Thence he had reluctantly entered his father's business, of which at one time he was managing director. But his heart had never been in it, and in due course he had set up as a country gentleman in Surrey, lavishly supported, no doubt, by his domineering father. Endowed with a beautiful house at Chiddingfold (and later, after his disastrous marriage in 1911, with a beautiful wife), he had energetically set about doing all the right things – Master of the Chiddingfold Foxhounds, a generous supporter of the Territorial forces both in Surrey and London, commandant and financial sponsor of the West Surrey Cadet Battalion, and in 1910, when he had not yet reached the age of forty, High Sheriff of Surrey – an honour usually reserved for old County buffers twenty years his senior.[37]

* Already achieved by Geddes in Edinburgh in the form of the Outlook Tower, which still exists today.

This was the man about whom Harcourt wrote to Esher on 14 March 1910 as follows:[38]

'My dear Reggy,

Please tell me about Mr Harry Waechter. Is he in "Finance" and is he a Company Promoter, and if so, what are the companies with which he is connected? Also, what relation is he, if any, to Sir Max Waechter? The reward could hardly come immediately upon the announcement of the gift, but would have to be delayed until it was nearing completion; but we may be out of Office by that time. Would this amount of uncertainty be satisfactory to him?

Yours ever, Loulou'

This letter shows that it was Esher who first produced Harry Waechter. The sentence 'The reward could hardly come immediately upon the announcement of the gift, but would have to be delayed until it was nearing completion' shows that at this first stage of the negotiations Harcourt was envisaging a public announcement that Harry Waechter had given a large sum for the construction of a new museum, and that when the building was 'nearing completion' his public generosity should be publicly rewarded with a title – all in much the same way as Harcourt had previously arranged matters with Henry Tate and Joseph Duveen. Finally, the letter refers to the difficulty caused by the unstable political situation of 1910, when the rejection of Lloyd George's Budget by the House of Lords in 1909 was leading on to the Parliament Act crisis of 1910–11. There had already been one general election in 1910, in January, and there was to be another in December. Would Mr Waechter be satisfied, Harcourt wanted to know, with a promise of reward from a Government with such an uncertain hold on the levers of power?

A month later, on 16 April, Harcourt was still hoping that Waechter would pay for a building and that somebody else might pay for the Gardner prints and drawings. 'I am told that the Gardner collection would cost £17,000', he wrote to Esher. 'If bought, . . . where could it be housed? We ought to have a London Carnavalet [*Museum*], but how to get it and where to put it is the puzzle. But it seems to me we ought not to lose the Gardner collection. If someone else would buy it Mr. Waechter might give the building to hold it!'[39]

The price which Harry Waechter was in fact willing to pay (despite the uncertain political outlook) for his 'reward' seems to have been agreed upon a day or two later, the sum being £30000. But by 26 April a great misfortune had befallen – the Gardner collection had been privately sold *en bloc*, a month before the advertised auction sale, to Major Edward Coates, a stockbroker and Conservative MP, who was now refusing to part with it, despite being told that it was in the national interest that he should do so.[40]

Harcourt was not, however, the man to be defeated by a setback of this kind, for he immediately sought an audience with the King. His letter (already quoted in part) to Lord Knollys,[40] Edward VII's Private Secretary, stated that:

'It has been the dream of my life to establish a London (Carnavalet) Museum. I find myself at this moment in a position to secure £30,000 for this purpose. It is to be spent thus: £18,000 for the Gardner Collection of prints and drawings etc. of old London. £2,000 for the Hilton Price collection of old curios of London. £10,000 for the building of the Museum which the County Council would be willing to erect alongside of their great new offices near Westminster Bridge. It would be one of the biggest things done for London and would develop rapidly and enormously by gift and bequest.'

But, he continued, Major Coates had bought the Gardner material a few hours before he, Harcourt, had been in a position to purchase it. 'The result is that the whole scheme falls to the ground and I shall not get my Museum or the other collection. My friend [*ie Harry Waechter*] will give the money for the *whole* but not for a part.' So could he (Harcourt) 'see the King for 5 minutes... to tell him the whole story and to ask him to authorise you [*Knollys*] to put personal pressure upon Major Coates to surrender his purchase for this national purpose'.

Harcourt's request for an audience was granted, the King presumably being told nothing about either the source of the £30000 or the reward which was to accompany it. He was, however, told that both Asquith (the Prime Minister) and of course Esher supported Harcourt's scheme, the former being 'warmly in favour of it'. But unfortunately the King did not know Major Coates, and felt unable to intervene in the matter.[40]* Ten days later he died, on 6 May 1910.

The death of Edward VII, coming only a few days after the Gardner collection had been snatched away by Major Coates, might well have tempted Harcourt to abandon any further notion of a 'London Carnavalet' museum. But his enthusiasm had been renewed by a recent visit to the Carnavalet (he was actually in Paris when the King died),[42] and he still had the promise of £30000 from Waechter. So, even though he knew very well that the LCC (despite what he had told Knollys) had not yet really committed itself to the support of the museum, he was determined to press on. In July, accordingly, he was getting down to brass tacks with Harry Waechter in 'a very pleasant interview' which he later described in a letter to Esher. 'I told him', he wrote, 'that I had an absolute assurance of the "recommendation" for the January [*Honours*] list. Mr. Waechter mentioned a sum of "from £20,000 to £30,000" for the London Museum. Will you please make it clear that the amount is £30,000 and would you suggest that £10,000 might be paid *now* and the remaining £20,000 in January. There is one London collection I should like to buy *now*.'[43] And Mr Waechter duly did what he was told, for by October Harcourt had already bought the Hilton Price collection[44] – five months before the public announcement that the museum was to be formed, and at a time when Harcourt's ideas about where it was to be housed were still vague in the extreme.

Because it came at just the moment when the foundation of a new museum was being privately discussed but before any firm plans had yet been made, the death of Edward VII – or rather, its aftermath – did nevertheless have a profound and lasting influence upon the nature of the London Museum. It introduced Royalty, or (to use the words already quoted of Queen Elizabeth II when she opened the Museum of London in 1976) that 'considerable proprietary interest' which she herself and other members of the Royal Family, particularly Queen Mary, felt for the London Museum throughout its life. And it was largely through Lord Esher's efforts that, for better or worse, Harcourt's idea of a 'London Carnavalet' was fused together with the royal idea of a permanent exhibition of royal costume and other relics to form that happy and extraordinary amalgam, the London Museum.

The idea for such a royal exhibition originated with Edward VII's widow, Queen Alexandra, as she herself explicitly claimed and as Harcourt and Esher both acknowledged.[45] Some weeks after the King's death she seems to have discussed with Lord Esher, as an old and trusted friend, how certain personal relics of both Queen Victoria and Edward VII, which she wished to give to the nation, might best be exhibited; and on 26 July 1910 Esher sent her the following memorandum:[46]

88 *Bellarmine jug with the arms and cypher of Queen Elizabeth. From the Hilton Price collection*

* After Coates's death in 1921 his collection was sold by auction in a series of sales in 1923–4 which realized £20966. Small parts of it were bought by the City Corporation and the London County Council.[41]

'In accordance with Your Majesty's wishes I have carefully thought out [41]
the best mode of exhibiting the profoundly interesting relics of
H.M. Queen Victoria and of His Late Beloved Majesty which it is the
gracious intention of Your Majesty to present to the nation.
'The Victoria and Albert would be unsuitable as it is entirely devoted to
art in connection with education. Indeed there is no Museum at present
in existence which is altogether suitable. Of course Queen Victoria's
things could be exhibited at Kensington Palace, but I think a great
opportunity would be lost if advantage were not taken of your Majesty's
offer to at once bring into existence a Museum for London on the
principle of the Carnavalet Museum in Paris.
'Of all the interesting things in Paris that museum is in the opinion of
many the most interesting, and many have regretted that we have
nothing to show in London at all comparable to it.
'Your Majesty's proposed gifts would produce a great effect and would
stimulate the generosity of others who possess objects of art and of
public interest to contribute towards a museum so auspiciously
inaugurated.
'A munificent donor has already offered £30,000 towards the foundation
of such a museum in London.
'If Your Majesty approves of the idea and will allow me to speak to the
Prime Minister and to the First Commissioner of Works [*Harcourt!*]
I feel quite sure that it will be possible to found a museum of Your
Majesty's gifts.
'The museum would contain everything which could be collected of
historic interest connected with London from the earliest times;
pictures, china, costume, arms, engravings, miniatures, snuff-boxes and
manuscripts.
'Your Majesty will realise that under proper guidance and arranged
with knowledge and good taste, a collection of this kind ought at least
to equal in interest and beauty any similar collection in the world.'

Queen Alexandra was delighted by the interest which Esher was
'taking in my scheme' and hoped that 'we can soon start the Museum'.[47]
But Queen Mary and King George V were much surprised, for Queen
Alexandra had not spoken to them about her idea and, as Queen Mary
wrote to Lord Esher a few days later, 'I understand that both Queen
Victoria's and the late King's things are not in the power of Q.A. [*sic*]
to give away'. Queen Mary herself 'had rather hoped that the Kensington
Palace staterooms [*later to become the first home of the London Museum*],
which already contain some of Queen Victoria's souvenirs, would be
utilised as a family Museum . . .', but the King was opposed to this on
account of the danger of fire; and anyway he was much averse to anything leaving Windsor, where many of the Royal Family's most valuable
possessions were kept, even though, as Queen Mary had pointed out to
him, there were also there 'many souvenirs which are not very ornamental
which *would* be of great interest to the public in general as a collection
and could well be spared…'. With regard to Harcourt's 'London
Carnavalet' scheme, of which she had known nothing, both she and
King George wished to reserve their opinion until they had had an
opportunity to discuss the matter with Esher.[48]

At much the same time as these events were taking place, Lord Esher
had stayed for a few days with Harcourt at Nuneham, and then Harcourt
visited Esher at the latter's house in Perthshire. Towards the end of
August Esher had been bidden to Balmoral for several days, whence he
reported to Harcourt that 'The Queen is warmly in favour of Kensington
Palace and keenly anxious you should keep control of the Carnavalet.

He [*the King*] has never seen Kensington Palace and will not commit himself yet. You will have to take him to Kensington.'[49] In July and August 1910 there was, therefore, plenty of opportunity for Harcourt and Esher to concert their tactics, and then for Esher to bring the King and Queen round to his idea that the 'London Carnavalet' and the 'Royal treasure box' could and should be combined in a single institution.

Lord Esher was much helped in this by the current deliberations as to the form which London's memorial to Edward VII should take. Early in August the Lord Mayor had, at Asquith's request, set up a large committee to consider the matter and organize a public appeal for contributions;[50] and either Harcourt or Esher had hit upon the bright idea that the establishment of their proposed museum would be an admirable way for the metropolis to commemorate the late monarch. By early October Esher was able to inform Harcourt 'that the two Queens are in favour of the King Edward Memorial taking the form of a Carnavalet Museum', while Harcourt had 'arranged' that both he and Lord Esher should be on the Lord Mayor's executive committee, which was to consider the numerous suggestions already made for the memorial.[51]

This adroit little *coup de main* did not in fact succeed, and Edward VII was eventually (in the early 1920s) commemorated in London by an equestrian statue in Waterloo Place and by a small but much needed public park in Shadwell. But the episode is of importance because it enabled Harcourt and Esher to float their 'London Carnavalet' proposal publicly for the first time; and as their museum was, they hoped, to be London's memorial to the late King and to bear his name, royal interest in it was thereby assured. The form of the London Museum as it eventually emerged was already beginning to take shape.

Thanks no doubt to Harcourt and Esher's persuasiveness, the Lord Mayor's executive committee had by the latter part of October narrowed the choice down from well over a hundred ideas to just two – Lord Avebury's proposal for a central building for the University of London, and what *The Times* referred to as Lord Esher's proposal – which were to be presented on 7 November to the general committee for final decision.[52] Lord Esher was in fact the 'front man' throughout this operation, for it would have been unseemly for a Minister of the Crown to throw his weight about publicly in such a matter. It was at Harcourt's request, however, that Esher (acting on Harcourt's detailed instructions about what he should and should not say) addressed a long explanatory letter to the Lord Mayor, printed copies of which were sent to all two hundred and fifty members of the general committee, and the text of which was published in *The Times* on the morning of the vital day, together with a long personal interview with Esher. But it was all to no avail, for the upshot of the meeting on 7 November was that while there should certainly be a statue of the King, the proposals for the main memorial should be given further consideration.[53]

Nevertheless, readers of *The Times* now knew that Esher and Harcourt had for many years wished 'to see London possess, as Paris does in so remarkable a degree, a museum dedicated to the historical record, in archaeology, in art, in decoration, in costumes, and in historical and artistic manufacture, of the metropolis'. They also knew that Harcourt, thanks 'to the splendid munificence of an anonymous donor', had already begun to use the 'very large sum of money' placed in his hands for the purchase of objects for the museum. Finally they were told that 'the promoters of the scheme have in view a site on which to build the museum, and that, whether the Memorial to King Edward takes this particular form or not, it is the intention to proceed with its erection'.[54]

89 *H M Queen Mary, consort of George V, 1867–1953.*
From the earliest discussions about the proposed London Museum in 1910 until the end of her life, Queen Mary took an active interest in, and was a frequent benefactor to, the museum

90 *Staple Inn, High Holborn, c.1900*

To make this last statement required considerable courage on the part of Harcourt and Esher. The only building site ever mentioned at this early stage was the one beside the LCC's new County Hall (the construction of which was just then beginning), referred to by Harcourt in his letter of the previous April to Lord Knollys. By now, six months later in November, they can have been under no illusion that the Council was going to build them a museum there or anywhere else. And Harry Waechter's 'munificent donation' was by itself nothing like big enough for them to start building on their own.

This lack of funds had not, however, prevented Harcourt from starting on his long quest to buy Staple Inn for the museum – 'a perfect solution if we could get the money for it and the present owner was willing to sell'. Staple Inn is now best known as the row of picturesque old timbered and gabled houses on the south side of High Holborn, but it had formerly been one of the Inns of Court, and behind the shops and houses was a small enclosed quadrangle with a fine dining-hall on the far side. It would certainly have made a fitting home for the museum, but neither the owners, the Prudential Assurance Company Limited, nor the principal tenants, the Institute of Actuaries, really wanted to sell; and the price would have been 'somewhere from £80,000 to £100,000'. Harcourt nevertheless continued negotiations with dogged persistence from October 1910 until well into 1913; and it was only when the museum was provided with the offer of another home at Stafford (or Lancaster) House that he finally abandoned this idea.[55]

After the Lord Mayor's Committee had postponed making any decision about the form of the main memorial to Edward VII the museum project seems to have 'gone dead' for several months, though no doubt the matter was frequently discussed privately in influential or powerful places. In a Cabinet re-shuffle made early in November Harcourt had been transferred from Works to be Secretary of State for the Colonies. This was, of course, political promotion, but it nevertheless removed him from his key post, as First Commissioner of Works, in the world of royal palaces and museums; and Esher recorded that Harcourt was at first 'rather frightened and depressed by his new responsibilities'.[56] It was, in fact, a worrying winter for the museum's well-wishers; and the only one who must really have enjoyed it was Harry Waechter, whose baronetcy was announced in the New Year Honours list on 2 January 1911. 'Has given generous support to the Territorial Force and Cadet Corps in Surrey', said *The Times.* 'High Sheriff of Surrey in 1910 and Master of Chiddingfold Foxhounds.'[57] But Sir Harry had still only handed over the deposit of £10000; and a day or two later Harcourt wrote to Esher to remind him that £20000 was still to be paid – as no doubt it was soon afterwards.[58]

The circumstances of the origins of the Waechter baronetcy, and the use of the fund of £30000 which arose therefrom to establish the London Museum, have hitherto remained virtually unknown. The money was secretly paid to Lewis Harcourt, who kept it in his private 'London Museum Account' at Child's Bank, and who administered it for the sole benefit of the museum until his death in 1922.[59] Even Guy Laking, the museum's first keeper, did not know anything about these matters until Sir Harry himself told him about them in January 1912[60] – although of course, like all the public, he did know that Harcourt held a large sum presented by an anonymous donor. Equally in the dark was such a superior and usually well-informed public person as Lord Curzon, who was most interested in the museum and (as Laking later reported a dinner-party conversation with him to Harcourt) very 'inquisitive as to its financial standing, on which point I did not enlighten him'.[61] Amongst the staff of the museum it was generally known, in later years, that Sir Harry Waechter had been an important benefactor, because in 1913–15 he did openly make a number of donations, notably a valuable collection of antique firearms; and it was also known that originally there had been a secret fund to finance the museum's early purchases. But nobody seems to have been aware of the connection between Sir Harry, his title, and the fund. Similarly, later generations even of his own family, while assuming almost as a matter of course that Sir Harry had paid for his title, did not associate this presumed transaction with the London Museum. So his secret was well kept.

However peculiar more virtuous later generations may regard such arrangements, neither Harcourt, nor Esher, nor Sir Harry had any qualms about what they had done, for only a few months later, when the Parliament Bill crisis was at its height and a large creation of new peers was being contemplated, the three of them were plotting together again to do another similar deal, once more for the benefit of the London Museum. Sir Harry was 'willing to be one of the Peers', Harcourt reported to Esher on 1 August 1911, but he 'would like a K.C.B. as well so as to take him out of the common ruck! . . . What I should like to know', Harcourt added, 'is whether he would give £100,000 towards the purchase and reconstruction' of Staple Inn.[62] This interesting question was, however, never answered, for shortly afterwards the Lords accepted the Parliament Bill and consequently no new peers were required. Had the Lords rejected the Bill, the London Museum might have gone to High Holborn, and remained there to this day. ▣

When Harcourt wrote to Esher on 5 January 1911 to remind him that Sir Harry had not yet paid up in full he also said 'when the King's at Windsor I wish you would take an opportunity of talking over with him again our ideas about the London Museum and get from [him] a definite expression of his willingness for it to be accommodated at all events temporarily in the State Rooms at Kensington Palace'.[63] The Lord Mayor's Committee was still shilly-shallying about the Edward VII memorial, there was no rich successor to Sir Harry in sight (yet), and so Kensington Palace was now the only feasible option left to Harcourt and Esher, who were of course already publicly committed to establishing a London Museum somewhere, somehow. The King's consent for the State Apartments there to be used temporarily for this purpose seems to have been given early in March 1911, Queen Mary having at last persuaded him to do so. On 19 March King George was wanting to see the Hilton Price collection, which (as previously mentioned) Harcourt had already bought and was then in store at the British Museum, and which was soon to form the nucleus of the London Museum's display at Kensington.[64] At about the same time Queen Alexandra wrote to Esher to express her pleasure that 'George has proposed to use Kensington Palace' for the exhibition of royal robes and treasures,[65] while Queen Mary, in also conveying her satisfaction at this new use for Kensington Palace, added 'Some day we must arrange a visit there to view possibilities' – a portent of the active interest which Her Majesty was to take in the London Museum for the rest of her life.[66]

The official announcement of the formation of the museum was made in *The Times* on 25 March 1911, under the cautious heading 'The King and a London Museum'. It was as follows:
'The King has appointed Mr. Harcourt, Viscount Esher, and the First

Commissioner of Works for the time being to be Trustees of the projected London Museum.

'His Majesty has graciously placed the State Apartments at Kensington Palace temporarily at the disposal of the Trustees for the exhibition of the collections already and hereafter to be acquired.

'It is hoped eventually to obtain some permanent and suitable building in which the Museum can be housed.

'The King and Queen and Queen Alexandra have promised a loan of some objects of London interest to the Museum.

'Mr Guy Laking has been appointed Keeper and Secretary to the Trustees.'

This inaugural announcement marks the public emergence of the London Museum in its eventual form as a fusion of the 'London Carnavalet' and the 'Royal treasure box' ideas – two compatible and indeed to a large extent complementary ideas which, despite their separate origins, were to co-exist within the museum in reasonable amity throughout the whole of its life. It may also be noted that the appointment of the three Trustees was made (as Harcourt later had occasion to remind the Treasury) by the King himself and not by the Government, though doubtless the Prime Minister was informed of it. As neither the City Corporation nor the LCC was even mentioned in the announcement, the London Museum was therefore established without any public funding whatever, and in a home provided by the King on a strictly temporary basis. It was a precarious start.

Lewis Harcourt was, however, a perennial optimist, and he did at this time receive some encouragement from at least the LCC. Hitherto his dealings with the Council had probably taken the form of private discussion with its able clerk, Sir Laurence Gomme, who had wanted the new museum to have its permanent home within the projected new County Hall complex; but the Council itself had not given any promise to this effect, and had merely 'offered the use of some rooms'.[67] For the ever-hopeful Harcourt, however, this had evidently been enough for him to refer to the Council's attitude in wildly optimistic terms in his letter of April 1910 (previously quoted) to Lord Knollys. And now, on the basis evidently of only some private assurance, Harcourt felt able to tell Esher on 3 April that 'I have got the L.C.C. to give me the *whole* of their London collection [*of antiquities*]! Isn't it splendid?'[68] He was not, however, disappointed, for four months later the Council confirmed this commitment[69] and the permanent loan (not gift) of its chiefly architectural antiquities was soon to provide one of the mainstays of the museum's display at Kensington Palace.

But from the Corporation of the City of London there came only silence. One Common Councilman who was also a Member of Parliament did say crossly that there was 'no likelihood of the Corporation parting with its remarkable collection of London relics';[70] and even the sensible idea that the new museum should have its permanent home in the Tower, amalgamated with the Guildhall Museum, evoked no official response from the Corporation which (according to one well-informed City gentleman) was 'rather sore at being ignored'.[71]

The inaugural announcement of 25 March also stated, in its last paragraph, that 'Mr Guy Laking has been appointed Keeper and Secretary to the Trustees'. With Harcourt, Esher and Waechter, Guy Laking (1875–1919) was one of the four cornerstones of the London Museum. He alone of this quartet had nothing to do with the events leading up to the public announcement of the establishment of the museum, so he was the last of the four to make his entrance. He was also the youngest of

91 *Sir Guy Laking, 1875–1919.*
Guy Francis Laking was appointed keeper and secretary to the Trustees of the London Museum in 1911. He owed his appointment to the patronage of Lord Esher, and proved an inspired choice

them, and the first to leave the scene, by his premature death, aged forty-four, in 1919. He was the first and some may think the greatest keeper of the London Museum.

Guy Laking was almost ideally qualified for the extraordinary post which he was now to take up. His father, Sir Francis Laking, Bart, was the family physician and trusted friend of Queen Victoria, Edward VII and George V, and a regular guest at Windsor, Balmoral and Sandringham. Brought up almost literally within the shadow of royalty (for his father's house in Pall Mall faced both St James's Palace and Marlborough House), young Guy had been sent to school at Westminster. But 'a boyish escapade with a pony he had bought, and leave that was taken in the French fashion' led to his being invited to withdraw from the school at the early age of fifteen,[72] when his formal education came to an end. By this time his lifelong passion for antique arms and armour had already become apparent. He was a frequent visitor at Christie's auction rooms (near his home in Pall Mall), where he attracted the attention of one of the partners, Mr T H Woods, who took him in hand as a kind of pupil. Thus began the connection between Laking and Christie's which became closer and more important as the years went on.

In 1891 he also made the acquaintance of Baron De Cosson, the foremost connoisseur of arms and armour of his generation, who became a lifelong friend. By 1897, at the age of only twenty-two, he compiled the first of many sale catalogues for Christie's, and in 1900 he was appointed honorary inspector of the armouries at the Wallace Collection, where he was already cataloguing the European part of the collection. Two years later he became keeper of the King's Armoury at Windsor, a post specially created for him by Edward VII. He was thus able to combine commercial activity with numerous museum appointments in a way which in more recent years would have been impossible. He was himself a great collector – his arms and armour were sold after his death for over £34000 – he advised his friends (including both Esher and later Lewis Harcourt) on sales and purchases, and haggled privately on their behalf. It was by these means, evidently – for (so far as is known) he drew no salary from his official appointments – that he was able to live in some style, after his marriage in 1898 for several years in rooms in Ambassadors' Court within St James's Palace itself, then from 1911 at No 3 Cleveland Row directly facing the Palace, and finally at No 16 Avenue Road, Regent's Park, a handsome double-fronted detached house where the neighbours included such people of ample means as Mrs Ludwig Mond, still enjoying her life interest in her late husband's pictures. He became a popular member of London society, a favourite companion at the Marlborough Club and elsewhere of Edward VII, for whom his 'inexhaustible fund of scandalous anecdotes about the medieval nobility' had a great appeal. He is said to have 'spent his money like one who has a store of gold angels and gold nobles in an iron chest rather than as one who draws cheques on a bank account'; and like his royal patron he is widely reputed 'to have indulged to the full in the escapades associated with the Naughty Nineties'.[73]

But he was not just a fashionable playboy. He also had a tremendous capacity for hard unremitting labour, and between 1903 and 1907 he produced catalogues of the Armoury at Windsor, the Furniture at Windsor, the Sèvres Porcelain at Buckingham Palace and Windsor, as well as of the Armoury of the Knights of St John of Jerusalem in Malta. Later came his catalogue of Oriental Arms and Armour at the Wallace (1914) and finally his great four-volume Record of European Armour and Arms, published posthumously in 1920–2. Some of these works have stood the test of time better than others – his Oriental Arms and Armour at the Wallace, for instance, was reprinted as recently as 1978, but on the other hand the chapters in the Record dealing with armour have now been largely superseded. Much of his work was handicapped by his ignorance of German, and even apparently of French and Spanish; for whenever letters in any of these languages arrived for him at the London Museum, he used to send them along to Christie's to have them translated.[74] Nor was his knowledge of Latin always reliable. Nevertheless he was in his own day a formidable scholar with a formidable record; and in 1911, aged thirty-six, he was at the height of his powers.

In January of that year he was, however, deeply depressed, for despite the efforts of his friend Lord Esher on his behalf, he had failed to get the post of keeper of the Wallace Collection, to which Asquith had instead appointed D S MacColl. And at the same time he had been asked to vacate his rooms in St James's Palace. 'I am gradually losing ground and being passed over', he had told Lord Esher. And then suddenly, out of the blue, had come the invitation – it must have been Lord Esher's idea, for as yet he did not even know Harcourt – to take charge, without salary or any other inducement, of a non-existent museum without a permanent home; and he had jumped at it. 'Lord Esher, my dear friend', he wrote on 26 March, 'to you do I owe it all. I look forward to seeing you either tomorrow or Tuesday. May I meet you Savoy lunch either day? Affectionately yours, Guy.'[75]

Kensington Palace is a large rambling brick mansion which, as Nottingham House, was bought by William III in 1689 and greatly enlarged to designs by Wren. No reigning sovereign has lived there since the death of George II in 1760, but both Queen Victoria and Queen Mary were born and brought up there, and in 1911 other members of the royal family still lived in parts of the Palace. The State Apartments, which had been open to the public since 1899, consisted of about a dozen rooms on the *piano nobile*, and contained appropriate furniture and pictures, none of any great note. The main staircase leading up to the Apartments was not allocated to the museum, the entrance to and exit from which were therefore by a subsidiary but still substantial staircase at the north end of Queen Mary's Gallery. All visitors to the museum had to walk through Kensington Gardens for a distance of about a quarter of a mile from the nearest public thoroughfares, Bayswater Road or Kensington High Street. The rooms, mostly panelled, varied greatly in size, ranging from the imposing King's Gallery on the south side, well over a hundred feet in length, and the stately King's Drawing Room and Cupola Room to the more domestic scale of Queen Mary's Gallery and the adjoining privy chambers.* In 1911 there was still neither gas nor electricity in any of the rooms – there was, in fact, in Laking's words, a total absence of lighting in any form whatsoever.[76] The fabric of the Palace, and the furniture in the State Apartments, were looked after by the Office of Works, but the pictures came within the province of the Lord Chamberlain's Department; and Queen Mary also interested herself in the developments about to take place in her childhood home.[77] The keeper's lot was, indeed, to prove an extremely testing one.

Laking's first step was to employ a typist, Maurice Read, aged seventeen. The first letters on museum business were posted on 28 March 1911, only two days after the public announcement of the museum's existence, and by the end of April over three hundred had been sent out, all from the keeper's new flat in Cleveland Row or from his office at Christie's.[78] Until the following August there was no other 'in house' staff, but from April onwards G F Lawrence (whom we have previously

* The names of the rooms used here are those used in 1912, and can be identified in the plan (*figure* 111, page 62). Some of the names have subsequently been changed.

encountered at the Guildhall Museum) was paid a retaining fee of £5 a week to acquire newly discovered archaeological material on site for the museum. 'Do come and see me some time on Tuesday at Christie's', Laking had written to Lawrence on 3 April. 'I want to talk to you on several subjects.'[79] Hitherto Lawrence had been in the habit of offering his archaeological acquisitions to the British Museum or to private collectors, but a year later, in April 1912, Laking told Harcourt that 'everything that has been found in London since the foundation of the Museum has come to us ... there has not been a building demolished, or an excavation of any kind made within the London area, that he has not visited for this Museum'.[80]

It was almost certainly from Lawrence that Laking made the very first purchase for the London Museum, for on 4 April he informed Harcourt that he had 'bought a good many trifling though interesting objects' dug up in Horseferry Road, Westminster – the first of thousands of objects bought from Lawrence by Laking and (to a much lesser extent) by his more impoverished successors during the next twenty years. Because Lawrence was sometimes (or perhaps frequently) a party to the removal of some of these newly found objects without the site owners' consent, the provenance of many of them was not precisely recorded; and the early accessions registers of the museum abound with such vague entries as 'found in Bishopsgate Street', or 'found in Horseferry Road', or even 'found in London'. Nevertheless Dr Mortimer Wheeler, who, when keeper of the museum in later years, himself took part in some of these semi-clandestine dealings with Lawrence, wrote in 1937 that 'but for Mr. Lawrence, not a tithe of the objects found during building or dredging operations in the neighbourhood of London during the past forty years would have been saved to knowledge. If on occasion a remote landowner may, in the process, theoretically have lost some trifle that was his just due, a higher justice may reasonably recognise that, but for this irregularity, that trifle would in a vast majority of cases never have been preserved at all. The representative and, indeed, important prehistoric, Roman, Saxon and medieval collections of the [London] Museum are largely founded upon this work of skilful salvage.'[81]*

Lawrence's weekly retaining fee, Laking's purchases from him, and very soon numerous other purchases from other sources, and all sorts of miscellaneous expenses, all had, of course, to be paid for. So a London Museum account in Laking's name was opened at the London Joint Stock Bank in Pall Mall. This was replenished by Lewis Harcourt as occasion arose out of his secret London Museum account at Child's Bank where Sir Harry Waechter's £30000 had been deposited. Harcourt's first cheque, for £100, was paid into Laking's Pall Mall account towards the end of April[82] – the first of scores of such payments, always most promptly made by Harcourt in response to Laking's requests, and soon for very much larger amounts than £100. In the late summer of 1911, for instance, when expenditure was in full spate, Laking wrote on 18 August, 'I think if from your funds you can afford to send me a cheque for £400, I will pay Joubert [for showcases], and it will leave me a little in hand'. Ten days later he wanted another £100 'before you go away ... to wipe off certain expenses that we have incurred', and within less than another week he was asking apologetically for £1100: 'I hate to appear always greedy for money, but do you think I can pay for the Seymour Lucas collection [of costume] by next Saturday ...'. Detailed accounts of 'how I have spent the various sums of money that ... you have placed to my museum account', and quarterly balances, were subsequently submitted to Harcourt by Laking.[83]

92 *Roman wine jug, AD70–90. Inscribed 'Londini ad Fanum Isidis', this jug was found in Southwark and was presumably used in a votive offering at a temple of the goddess Isis. This notable acquisition was made for the London Museum by G F Lawrence in 1912, and provides the earliest piece of writing containing the name of London*

93 *Sixth-century brooch from the Saxon cemetery at Mitcham, also acquired for the London Museum through G F Lawrence*

* Notable among Lawrence's acquisitions for the London Museum were the Roman Jug inscribed 'Londini ad Fanum Isidis' (bought in 1912), several hundred items from the Saxon cemetery at Mitcham (1918), and a substantial proportion of the museum's famous collection of bronze age material.

94 *Guy Laking at his office in Kensington Palace, 1911*

Laking's first step towards taking possession of the State Apartments at Kensington Palace was to go and see Sir Schomberg McDonnell, the secretary of the Office of Works, at his office in Storey's Gate. Sir Schomberg, a man of discriminating and artistic taste who in his younger days had been principal private secretary to Lord Salisbury and who was later killed in France in 1915 aged well over fifty, proved 'most kind, and anxious to help us'. He happily lent the museum some old office furniture, he agreed that Laking might use two extra rooms which were not part of the State Apartments as an office and ante-room, and at Laking's request he moved furniture about within the Apartments, or even carted some of it off to Buckingham Palace or Holyrood in order to make room for the museum's new showcases.[84] But through his staff he kept a very strict eye on the museum's doings at Kensington, and not so much as 'a small screw or even a tintack' could be inserted into the panelling without producing a thunderbolt from Storey's Gate. And it was doubtless at Sir Schomberg's insistence that not even Harcourt was able to persuade the Office of Works to agree to close the State Apartments to the public, even for a few days, during the preparation of the museum's displays. So much of this work had to be done under the intrusive stare of inquisitive members of the public who had come ostensibly to view the State Apartments.[85]

Exhibits very soon began to pour in. On the day of the public announcement of the formation of the museum (25 March), the three Trustees (Harcourt, Esher and Lord Beauchamp, then First Commissioner of Works) had written a letter to *The Times* to appeal for contributions, either by gift or loan. 'We wish to acquire objects of historic and local interest to Londoners', they said, 'and to exhibit many things which would find no place at the British or the Victoria and Albert Museums, but which, nevertheless, are of value and cannot fail to appeal to Londoners and visitors to the metropolis'.[86] At first the objects which immediately began to arrive in considerable quantities were stored either at Laking's flat in Cleveland Row or at Christie's, but by early May he had installed himself at Kensington Palace. Only a month later, when everything except the Hilton Price collection had been transferred there, he told Lord Esher that 'we have an astonishing amount of property, already much more than we can show . . .'; and he hoped 'in August and September to be able to put some real hard work in, as regards arrangement and classifying our possessions'.[87]

In the meantime Laking was laying the curatorial foundations of the museum. After consultation with the V&A he inaugurated four different numerical sequences for the registration of accessions; he made arrangements for the printing of descriptive slips for each object, and for the painting of showcase labels and of the accession number on each object – a task performed by Mr E T Steele or his brother for some forty years;[88] and he placed a first order for showcases with Felix Joubert, an ingenious but not always reliable Frenchman whose varied business at the Pheasantry in King's Road, Chelsea, included the provision of all manner of museum requirements. Early in June he (Laking) went to Paris and made 'a most careful and thorough inspection of the Musée Carnavalet . . . Alas', he told Harcourt, 'they have got a long way ahead of us, and I fear it will be some years before we shall catch them up. But we will.'[89]

During the first four months of the museum's life (April to July 1911) Laking was very much on his own. He tried repeatedly to arrange a meeting of the Trustees to decide such fundamental matters as whether the exhibits should be arranged chronologically or by subject; but all three of them were extremely busy, particularly before King George's

Coronation, on 22 June. Earl Beauchamp was not very interested anyway, and Lord Esher was happy to leave things to Harcourt. So in practice the decisions were taken by Harcourt in conjunction with Laking, who closeted themselves together from time to time, either at Harcourt's house in Berkeley Square or at his room at the House of Commons.[90] Harcourt, indeed, involved himself almost too actively, corresponding with potential donors without telling Laking, and on one occasion even bidding at Christie's, unbeknown to his keeper, for a collection of London knives which Laking had intended to buy. Once again, however, Harcourt's gifts of persuasion served the museum well, for it was (as we have already seen) he who induced the LCC to deposit their mainly architectural material with the infant museum. It was Harcourt, too, who successfully played such an important fish as Dr Frank Corner, a peppery physician who lived at the Manor House, Poplar, and was an active collector of London antiquities; for on a Sunday afternoon early in April the Secretary of State for the Colonies found the time to go down to the East End to see Dr Corner, and was afterwards able to claim that 'I think he will lend or give me anything I want out of his collection'. (And this, to a large extent, proved to be correct.)[91]

Whatever sense of isolation Laking may have felt in his first few weeks at the museum must have been relieved early in August, when (no doubt with Harcourt's agreement) two new men joined the staff. The first was Herbert W Murray, an impecunious Scot, then in his twenties or thirties, who claimed to have been at school at Eton and who was certainly a friend of Laking's, having previously worked with him at the Wallace Collection. He joined as a 'technical assistant', and was paid £2 6s a week out of museum funds.[92] The other was Frederick Arthur Harman Oates (1863–1928), a friend of Laking's, who came as Laking's secretary and in due course succeeded him as keeper. He was already aged nearly fifty, and for the first year of his time at the museum Laking paid his salary of £200 out of his (Laking's) own pocket – a sum subsequently reimbursed to Laking by Harcourt out of the museum Fund. Previously he had been a commercial traveller in the timber trade, and his hobby had been the study of finger rings. It is said by one usually reliable authority that he and Laking had first met in a railway carriage. Harman Oates was wearing an ornate ring which Laking kept eyeing; and eventually Oates had said, 'I see you are looking at my ring. That ring belonged to Joan of Arc.' Whatever the truth of all this, his 'excellent business capabilities' enabled Harman Oates to take charge of much of the clerical and business side of the museum, and to stand in for Laking during the latter's frequent absences. Soon he was writing all the routine letters, bringing to them, in the use of such phrases as 'your goodself' or 'will you kindly do the needful' a friendly taproom flavour of his own. He was totally devoted to Laking, for whom he provided all manner of services outside the normal duties of a secretary, and to whom, despite his being twelve years older than Laking, he always referred as 'The Chief'. He was also totally loyal to the museum and to the Trustees, and very discreet; and it was for these qualities rather than for any distinction as a scholar that he became the keeper after Laking's death in 1919.[93]

So with this much enlarged but still tiny staff Laking began in early August the serious work of classifying, cataloguing and arranging such material as had already arrived; and Lawrence was summoned to Kensington Palace from his peregrinations of the metropolitan building sites, to help with the archaeological material. Within a few weeks the printing of the first catalogue slips had begun, the museum had experienced the first of its many agitating muddles over accession numbers, and by the end of

95 *King George V and Queen Mary, 1911. The King and Queen were crowned at Westminster Abbey on 22 June. Their robes were later lent to the London Museum for display in the museum's second home, Lancaster House*

96 *The London Museum office at Kensington Palace, 1911. The figure on the left is probably Herbert Murray*

97 *Harman Oates at work in the office at Kensington Palace, with the typist Maurice Read, 1911*

98 *Doeskin coat of c.1680-90. From the Seymour Lucas collection*

September five or six cases had actually been arranged and placed in position, each one being on completion shrouded with a holland cloth cover 'so that the public will not see the museum in driblets, but arranged as a whole'.[94]

All this time more exhibits were 'pouring in so fast' that Laking took over a small unused closet next to his own room. 'We have such an enormous amount of packages and exhibits to go through carefully', he explained to Sir Schomberg McDonnell, that 'I can barely turn round in the rooms I am now using'. Offers came from as far afield as Tiflis in the Caucasus, whence a school friend of Laking's promised old prints of Sadler's Wells Theatre. Not all offers were, however, accepted, and much time had to be spent convincing such well-intentioned but ill-informed people as Mrs Parbury that 'the London Museum cannot accept the gift of your daughter's water colour drawings of Cashmir'. Sometimes, too, there were misunderstandings, as when Laking went to Drummond's Bank at Charing Cross to view some prehistoric remains found on the bank's site – 'bones of the elephant, mammoth, rhinoceros, red deer, lions, horse, in fact an entire Bostock Menagerie' – which he would very much like to have had for the museum ('We are very short of Mammalian objects'), but which he was later told Mr George Drummond had no intention of either giving or lending.[95] (They do nevertheless seem to have eventually ended up in the museum.) And on one occasion a leading West End dealer had to be sharply reprimanded, in the light of information supplied by the ever-knowledgeable Lawrence. 'I was somewhat surprised to ascertain', Laking wrote to this firm, 'amongst the items purchased from you last week for the London Museum, the Samian Bowl was charged to the Museum at £7 10s, whereas it cost you the sum of 30/–, and was purchased from the Arnold Sale, Lot 416. Surely this is a very excessive profit to charge one of the National Museums? This incident I fear will make my Trustees somewhat chary of dealing with your firm.' And he went on to ask for 'further particulars of the Flint Arrow Head described as found in Epping Forest, as I am assured by experts [*ie Lawrence*] that it is a well known South American type, and hardly likely to have been found as alleged?' The unfortunate dealer quickly replied with an excuse about the samian bowl, the true value of which seems to have been about £2; and as regards the arrowhead it was 'just possible' that the one in question had 'got shifted off its ticket at stocktaking and been replaced by an American specimen'. Laking accordingly returned the offending object, curtly adding 'You can either send me a credit note or the Epping Forest one'; and soon afterwards a credit note arrived at Kensington Palace. With Laking and Lawrence around, the London Museum was not to be defrauded.[96]

Early in September Laking persuaded Harcourt to spend £1000 on buying the famous costume collection of his old friend Seymour Lucas, RA, and was ordering showcases and dummies for its display at an estimated cost of £450, having previously told Harcourt that this was 'not going to be a very expensive item'. In the same letter he also mentioned that he was in process of buying two wooden cells from an ancient prison in Wellclose Square, Stepney – 'the most admirable thing for our Chamber of Horrors'. And a week or two later he had the entire Hilton Price collection, hitherto temporarily stored at the British Museum, brought to Kensington Palace, the British Museum authorities, who had been cataloguing the material, having proved 'so slow that had I to wait for their descriptions to the various objects, I believe a year would have elapsed before I should receive the entire catalogue'.[97]

It was at this busy stage of the museum's development that there supervened the bizarre episode of the Roman Boat. During excavations for the foundations of the LCC's new County Hall at the south end of Westminster Bridge, the battered remains of an ancient craft had been uncovered, and coins and other relics found in or on it had securely dated this interesting object to the latter part of the third century. By the summer of 1911 half of it had already been 'cut-off' during builders' excavation, and what was left seems then to have measured about sixty feet in length and twenty in breadth, and to have weighed over twenty tons. It was variously described in the newspapers as a 'barge', a 'Roman ferry boat', 'London's Roman War Galley', a 'Roman Dreadnought', and 'one of the saucy ships that flouted Imperial Rome in the Channel'. Not to be out-done, Laking himself described it as 'a single-decker war galley propelled by oars and sails', and built in Gaul.[98]

At the beginning of April, when Harcourt had received private assurances from the LCC that the Council would hand over all its London antiquities to the museum, the Roman Boat had been specifically included.[99] But little thought was then given as to where this bulky exhibit might be displayed at Kensington, for the Council did not finally make up its mind to part with the Boat until 2 August.[100] By that time its removal from the County Hall site had become a matter of urgency, for, as Sir Laurence Gomme, the Clerk of the Council, told Laking, unless it was speedily taken away 'it will be built around, and next to impossible to remove'. Over at the Office of Works, however, Sir Schomberg McDonnell rose to the occasion and at once provided the museum with a perfect site for the erection of a large temporary shed at Kensington. It was inconspicuously situated near the Palace, behind a high wall, 'in no way an eye-sore, and in a position most handy for the entrance and exit of the public' to the museum.[101] Here during the next few weeks there rapidly arose under the auspices of the LCC's Architect's Department and the Office of Works, a commodious Annexe over a hundred feet in length, where in addition to the Roman Boat numerous other large objects were later displayed – notably a 'prehistoric' dugout found at Mortlake by the Port of London Authority, the Wellclose Square prison cells and other penal relics, all the architectural oddments from the LCC, and several models of Old London.[102] It was here in the Annexe that Laking was able to give the freest play to his great flair for showmanship; and in terms of popularity with the public the Annexe proved a huge success. Its total cost, paid for out of Harcourt's precious museum Fund, was just over £1000, including an addition run up in 1912 by Felix Joubert for storage purposes; and when the museum left Kensington Palace shortly afterwards, the Office of Works bought it for half its cost price.[103]

Back at the County Hall site, however, there were problems, for the condition of the Boat itself was already deteriorating. When first discovered, it was 'so waterlogged that it was the consistency of a mushroom', but it had then been soaked to repletion with glycerine and coated with tar – all presumably by the LCC. By August the timbers had become so shrunken and dry that the wood was extremely brittle, and it was therefore thought to be of vital importance that the Boat should not be jolted. A wooden cradle was accordingly built underneath it, and ten men worked all night on 23 August with chains and pulleys and jacks to raise it, one-sixteenth of an inch at a time, up a long ramp twenty feet high extending from the level of the riverbed to that of the modern road above. Laking had originally intended that his precious cargo should cross Westminster Bridge by 6 am, 'or we shall be jolted in a stream of traffic', but in fact it was 3.45 pm before his stately cortege passed Big

99 *The Annexe at Kensington Palace, showing the 'prehistoric' dugout, embellished by Laking with the figure of an ancient Briton*

Ben, all other traffic having been halted, temporarily. Laking led the way, an imposing figure on horseback. The Boat itself was borne on an eight-wheeled catafalque covered with a tarpaulin bearing the legend 'Roman Boat, London Museum', and drawn by twelve powerful cart-horses. Half a dozen policemen marched alongside, and 'the rear was brought up by a motor-car conveying officers of the London Museum and of the County Council'. The procession went by way of Birdcage Walk, Grosvenor Place, Hyde Park Corner, Park Lane and Bayswater Road, and finally reached Kensington Palace at 5.30 pm, 'the arrival of the unique treasure being witnessed by a large crowd of the public'.[104]

At its new moorings in the museum Annexe there were more problems for Laking and the poor old Boat. The timber was now evidently in a very bad state, so Felix Joubert was employed to put matters right and to display this ancient but expensive relic in the best possible manner. He replaced a substantial part of the perished wood with painted plaster, while what remained was, according to an expert from the Museums Association who inspected the Boat a few months later, 'transformed into some sort of gluey composition'. And this visiting pundit concluded prophetically, 'We cannot regard its future with equanimity.'

But at least the method of exhibition was magnificent, as the same gentleman agreed. Laking decided to display the Boat exactly as it had been found. He had a large pit dug within the Annexe, so that visitors could look down from above, and lined this hole with river sand. The remains of the Boat rested on this bed, the bottom lying in pools of water represented by rolled glass. A few seashells were scattered about, and a stuffed seagull was placed on jaunty guard. 'We cannot praise too highly the present method of exhibition', said the man from the Museums Association. But he was not so happy about the prehistoric dugout from Mortlake, in which Laking had placed a hairy life-size standing figure of an ancient Briton, clad only in a bear-skin, 'a very inappropriate introduction of realism'.[105]

Laking at any rate was happy. Joubert's work, he thought, had been 'admirably carried out, and I do not know who else could have assisted me to fake it in the manner I directed'. But enough was enough, and after all the bills had been paid he told Harcourt with relief in January 1912

100 *The Roman Boat and prison relics as exhibited in the Annexe, 1911*

that 'We have now finished with the Roman Boat. Another is not likely to be found, we will take good care of that. This echoes the sentiments of all the officials of the London County Council who have been bothered with this white elephant.'[106]

The Annexe at Kensington was not, however, to be the Roman Boat's anchorage for long. Two years later it was moved – very quietly this time – to the museum's next home, at Lancaster House, St James's, where it was bedded down in a corner of the basement and became once more a very popular attraction for the public. But during the war of 1939–45 members of the War Reserve Police, who used this part of the basement as a dormitory, bowled down a number of large stone cannon-balls which had been exhibited nearby into the ancient vessel, or what was still left of it, and used the remainder as a rubbish pit. When all this refuse was removed after the war, it was found that all the wooden ribs had been piled up at one end, and that the sides, less damaged by the cannon-balls, consisted largely of lath and plaster. The director, Mr W F Grimes, instructed the museum's own conservation expert, Mr Arthur Trotman, to reconstruct the Boat as far as possible, and three-quarters of a ton of Keen's cement (a household wall plaster) was used to make prefabricated sections of the plankings. In this cosmetic but at least presentable condition it remained until 1978, when the Government authorities at Lancaster House requested the Museum of London either to remove it or to build a movable steel floor over it. Either course would have been vastly expensive, so it was eventually decided to scrap it, all ancient material being, of course, retained; and a few odd strakes, carefully wrapped in polythene, are all that now remains of Laking's twenty-ton Roman Boat. A large model of it, as it was when first discovered, is, however, on show in the museum's Roman Gallery. The 'prehistoric' dugout, by contrast, survives largely intact, but it has suffered the indignity of being subjected to a Carbon 14 test which has revealed that its origins were not prehistoric at all, but medieval.[107] ◨

The progress of the Roman Boat through London attracted widespread public attention – 'surely the strangest procession ever seen in London's chequered history', thought *The Morning Post.* Its journey had been 'an excellent advertisement for the London Museum', Laking wrote to Harcourt. 'We have received scores of press notices, and . . . it appears nightly at the cinematograph pictures at the Empire.'[108] Illustrated weeklies like *The Graphic* and *The Illustrated London News*, for instance, carried pictures as well as lengthy articles, and most provincial papers from Aberdeen to Plymouth noticed the event in some way. The London Museum had in fact captured the public imagination six months before it had even opened, and Laking saw to it that henceforth it was seldom out of the public eye for more than a week or two. A few days after the Boat episode he was able to announce the purchase of the great Seymour Lucas collection of costume (previously referred to), fine pieces of which he immediately had photographed, some of the dresses being actually modelled by beautiful young ladies of his acquaintance; and soon the prints which he distributed to the press were being published in such papers as *The Queen, The Lady's Pictorial, The Gentlewoman,* and else-where.[109] 'It is the notoriety thus obtained through the agency of the press', he wrote to Bruce Ingram, the editor of *The Illustrated London News,* to whom he also sent some photographs, 'that is getting the London Museum known to the general public'; and by this means, he added, 'we

101 *Costume from the Seymour Lucas collection, modelled and photographed for Laking outside Kensington Palace, 1911*

are receiving many gifts and loans'.[110] He also frequently invited journalists to come and view the progress being made at the Palace – come 'early in the day as the light fails', he told a man from *The Times* whose 'scholarly pen' he was particularly anxious to attract;[111] and on the frequent occasions when he was interviewed by the press, he always had the appropriate story for the appropriate paper. 'We had a very narrow shave of missing this splendid collection', he brightly told *The Daily Mail* in reference to the purchase of the Seymour Lucas material. Mr Lucas had been approached by the Metropolitan Museum of New York 'with an extremely advantageous offer'. This, however, he had 'patriotically declined, and offered the collection to us for a much smaller sum in order that it might remain in England. . . . And so we bought it.'[112]

Having spent the whole of his life within or on the fringes of the magic circles of the royal Court, Laking also knew precisely how to conduct himself with the museum's royal benefactors. As the youthful keeper of the King's Armoury at Windsor he had originally been a protégé of Edward VII, but he very soon won the esteem of Queen Mary, who years after Laking's death still spoke of him with the highest regard.[113] Through the agency of Lord Esher such valuable royal relics as Queen Victoria's collection of wooden dolls (from Windsor) had already been arriving at Kensington since May,[114] but towards the end of August Laking wrote to the Queen to ask for an audience. 'Considerable progress has now been made in the organisation of the Museum', he told her, 'and we are anxious to get the loans and possessions of the Museum together'; and after his interview, which took place on 1 September, a considerable number of royal objects were removed from Buckingham Palace on loan to the museum.[115]

Soon afterwards both Laking and Harcourt stayed with Esher at the latter's house at Callander in Perthshire, perhaps at the same time; and all three certainly discussed the museum's affairs. A little later, when he had fully recovered from a recent operation for appendicitis, Esher went to stay at Balmoral, where he discussed the same subject with his royal hostess. Back home at Callander he was able to tell Laking early in October that 'The Queen quite agreed with what we arranged when you were here, that is to say the importance of exhibiting in the first instance objects which will interest the majority'; and he added that Her Majesty might very probably visit the museum early in November before her departure to India for the Delhi Durbar.[116] Fortified by these signs of royal approval, Laking then sent to Buckingham Palace proofs of the labels 'to be placed on Your Majesty's exhibits' and successfully asked for another audience, which lasted 'nearly three hours, looking out her dresses and her mother's dresses, that she is going to lend to the Museum'.[117] When the date for the Queen's projected visit to Kensington had been fixed for 8 November, Harcourt made a hasty tour to make sure that all was well;[118] and on the great day itself – for however private, this was nevertheless the first royal visit to the London Museum – both Harcourt and Esher (and of course Laking) were at the Palace to receive Her Majesty. With characteristic skill Esher had also invited Sir Douglas Dawson, a tremendous swell from the Lord Chamberlain's Office, to be present. 'You are quite right in asking Sir Douglas Dawson', the Queen had commented, 'the more *they* see I am interested the better'. But another suggestion of Esher's had been firmly rejected. 'I think that on the whole I would prefer meeting Sir Harry Waechter another time when fewer people will be at the Museum, and there will not be so many things to discuss. . . .'[119] The visit was evidently a great success, and three days later Her Majesty set sail with King George for India.

To have the support of royalty was, however, one thing, but to have the good offices of the Lord Chamberlain's Department was quite another, as Laking was now to discover. The royal pictures in the State Apartments at Kensington were within the Lord Chamberlain's province, and under the immediate supervision of the Surveyor of the King's Pictures, who in 1911 was Lionel (later Sir Lionel) Cust. Towards the end of September, accordingly, Laking wrote to Cust (who was an old friend) in the most amicable manner to ask for the removal of 'some of the larger pictures' in the Queen's Gallery in order to make room for the museum's showcases – 'dear friend', he had rashly added, 'I will fall in with whatever views you have in the matter'. Two weeks later he received a 'rather stuffy' answer from Cust, which he passed on to Lord Esher, after politely reminding Cust that 'It is at Kensington Palace the King has chosen for the exhibition of the London Museum treasures, and certain alterations must perforce be made in the present arrangements.' To Esher he pointed out that the removal of only about twenty-five pictures was required, and 'I wonder whether you with your power could get the King's authority for this to be done'.[120]

But after the lapse of nearly another two precious weeks a deputation from the Lord Chamberlain's Office arrived at Kensington to hold a parley. The deputation consisted of Sir Douglas Dawson, his aide (a Major Crichton), and Cust. Brigadier General Sir Douglas Dawson, GCVO, CMG (who later collected a KCB and a CB and was also the holder of half a dozen foreign decorations), was in 1911 Comptroller in the Lord Chamberlain's Department; and both at Kensington and later at Lancaster House he was to be a formidable adversary of the London Museum. The colloquy in the State Apartments did not prove friendly; and the two letters which Laking wrote to Esher on the same day show that he had been thoroughly upset. 'I do wish I had one of my Trustees behind me', he began, 'as I had to fight them single handed. They had strong views about the London Museum, and so had I, and at first affairs assumed a gloomy and bellicose aspect. Sir Douglas Dawson was just, but obdurate. . . . We have talked hard for two hours. They have just gone.'

What Laking wanted, and finally got, was the rehanging of all the pictures in the Queen's Gallery on the walls of the staircase at the north end of the Palace; but he only got these 'concessions' from Dawson and his acolytes 'by diplomacy on my part in pretending, in the first place, I wanted more pictures moved than inwardly I knew was really necessary'. In return, he promised, unwisely, 'in the names of the Trustees that if they let us have the Queen's Gallery to ourselves we will not disturb the other pictures in the Palace'. And he begged Lord Esher to advise the King 'to fall in with' the recommendation to be made by the Lord Chamberlain's Office. King George evidently complied. The Queen's comment, made a few days later in a letter to Esher, 'I wish Cust and others *would* not be so tiresome' – showed where her sympathies lay.[121]

This would have been the end of the episode, if Laking had not unexpectedly acquired some more pictures for the museum in November and December; and by that time the King and Queen were far away in India, leaving Sir Douglas Dawson to make his own decisions about what might or might not be done at Kensington. Earlier in the year 1911 the Whitechapel Art Gallery had held an exhibition on 'Old London', and this was now nearing its end. In mid-November Laking and Harcourt therefore went to have a look, and soon afterwards Laking was busy inveigling the owners of various pictures exhibited at Whitechapel into giving, or lending, or even selling their possessions to the London Museum.[122] His famous charm worked its usual magic, of course, and before long Sir Douglas received a request for more wall space at Kensington. Three days before Christmas, however, Laking was becoming worried. 'Sir Douglas Dawson is silent as to the picture question here', he wrote to Harcourt. 'A van load of pictures will arrive here tomorrow from the Whitechapel Art Gallery, and on their arrival we shall be very seriously congested, so that I glance with eagerness at every post that arrives, hoping to see a letter bearing the insignia of the Lord Chamberlain's Office'. The blow fell on 3 January 1912 – Sir Douglas had decided that 'we can have no more wall space'; and the newly acquired pictures therefore had to be displayed on makeshift screens instead. 'I was so disappointed', the normally ebullient Laking confessed to Lord Esher.[123]

This was far from the end of the London Museum's dealings with Sir Douglas and the Lord Chamberlain's Office – dealings of markedly different tone from those with Sir Schomberg McDonnell at the Office of Works. During the winter of 1911–12 Sir Schomberg was giving helpful thought to the problems of security which would arise in the State Apartments when the museum opened to the public. At Laking's request he laid 'what I believe is called cork lino' down the gangways of the Queen's Gallery, and in the installation of turnstiles at the museum entrance he was, Laking thought, 'most kind and very obliging'.[124] ◨

Despite Sir Douglas Dawson, however, most people fell gladly enough under Laking's spell, particularly if they were potential benefactors whom he was courting; and very soon the young sorcerer found that he had skilful apprentices in Lawrence and Harman Oates. 'I approach you hat in hand as a beggar on behalf of my Museum . . .', Laking wrote in September 1911 to one such benefactor, Dr Frank Corner, the rather irascible physician whom Harcourt had visited in Poplar in the previous April. Dr Corner had collected miscellaneous London antiquities for many years, but he had no love for either the Guildhall or the British Museum, and found the less orthodox ways of the London Museum more congenial. Soon he was being visited by both Laking and Lawrence, and in February 1912 a van was sent down to Poplar for 'the removal of Dr. Corner's Collection' – but strictly on loan only. 'Your Museum will easily be the best of its kind, as it is fitting it should be', he had told Laking reassuringly; but he was always unpredictable, and the autumn of 1912 found him for some unknown reason in Moscow, 'having quite a good time', as he told Harman Oates, who had by now taken over his 'management' from Laking. Later it was Oates who got a flea in his ear from the doctor for supposed delay in sending out the printed green tickets of acknowledgement for the loan of some valuable stoneware pottery – 'Don't you think you had better change your printers?'. But despite such occasional contretemps Dr Corner nevertheless converted all his loans to gifts early in 1914, at the specific request of Lewis Harcourt. Harcourt, Laking, Harman Oates and Lawrence, at their very different levels and in their very different ways, were, indeed, a formidable team.[125]

The greatest benefactor in the whole history of the London Museum (apart from Sir Harry Waechter, of course) was Mr John George Joicey (1863–1919). He was a first cousin of the first Baron Joicey, colliery owner, and his own considerable wealth evidently came from the Joicey family's numerous coal-mining and other industrial interests in County Durham and Tyneside. He had been born in Gateshead, but in 1911 he was living, as a lifelong bachelor, at the Junior Carlton Club in Pall Mall, attended by his Italian valet and secretary, Luigi Mezzavilla, who hailed from Bassano, not far from Padua.[126] Laking said of Joicey that he was 'really a very modest and retiring man', and – most significantly – that 'unlike most donors of Collections he expects nothing in return'.[127] He certainly got nothing in the way of honours or decorations. But he did get genuine warmth and gratitude from both Laking and Harman Oates, and even (more distantly) from Harcourt. They gave him a feeling of personal involvement in the fortunes of the infant museum, which he showered with gifts and money throughout the rest of his life, and to which he finally bequeathed the residue of his considerable fortune.

Joicey's association with the museum began on 25 March 1911 when, having read in *The Times* the announcement of the intended museum's formation and the Trustees' appeal for gifts and loans, he wrote from the Junior Carlton Club to Laking offering to lend a few pieces of Bow and Chelsea porcelain and Battersea enamel. With characteristic diffidence he added that if these things were not considered suitable, he would send them 'to join my other collection at the Victoria & Albert Museum'. Laking, who had never previously even heard of Joicey, at once accepted this offer, but they did not actually meet until September, when some sixty pieces of Chelsea and sixty pieces of Bow porcelain, mostly of very fine quality, and some Battersea enamels, were delivered to Kensington Palace. It was evidently then that Laking realized Joicey's potential importance, for in November he was telling Joicey that his collection (all still on loan) exactly filled two cases 'in that small room by itself as I promised you. Please when you have time, come up and see it.' This friendly, easy-going treatment evidently pleased Joicey, for in December he transferred his Bow, Chelsea and Battersea pieces at the V&A to the London Museum; and soon after Christmas Mr Mezzavilla arrived at the Palace bearing, if not exactly gifts, at least more loans, this time of valuable London watches.[127]

There was then a three-months' pause in the Joicey story (which will be continued later), probably because he and Mr Mezzavilla were wintering on the Continent in warmer climates, as they often did.[127] Joicey was, however, by now firmly under Laking's spell, so there was no danger that he would escape for long. So far as is known, indeed, only one important potential benefactor, having once entered Laking's web, ever managed to get entirely free again. This was Mrs Gabrielle Enthoven, the great collector of historical material relating to the theatre, who for years had dreamed of a theatre section in one of the national museums, but who had always been confronted by indifference at both the British Museum and the V&A. In November 1911, however, Laking – himself a keen theatre-goer – discussed the matter with Harcourt and Esher; and with their authority he wrote to such great theatrical figures as Sir Herbert Tree and Sir George Alexander[128] to inform them that the London Museum would include 'a fine and comprehensive section dealing with the drama', and suggesting that this museum should in future be regarded as 'the proper and permanent home for all objects that illustrate the history of the Thespian art'.[129]

This idea, which was immediately published in the newspapers, met with widespread acclaim in the world of the theatre, and Mrs Enthoven became a prime mover in Laking's support. 'We are now to have for the first time a recognised theatrical section in a national museum', she wrote in one of numerous letters to the press. 'What is now of moment is that owners should give or lend what they can to make the beginning of the institution worthy of its aims.' And early in January 1912 she actually added a clause to her will, bequeathing 'to the London Museum for the National Collection in that Museum my collection of theatrical

102 *Theatrical portrait sheet advertising Mr Ducrow's equestrian performance at Astley's Amphitheatre, Lambeth, in 1817. From the Jonathan King collection, given to the museum in 1912.*
Printed sheets of this type were often available within days of a new performance; they were the immediate precursors of the Juvenile Drama (Toy Theatre) sheets for young people which were so popular in the mid nineteenth century

103/104 *Theatrical portrait sheets from the Jonathan King collection.*
The actors and actresses portrayed in such sheets were identified formally as Mr or Mrs, but their roles, often in melodramas, had such colloquial and blood-curdling names as Walder the Avenger or Black Ralph

programmes, playbills, books, pictures and engravings, relics and portraits', which she desired should be known as the Gabrielle Enthoven Theatrical Collection.[130]

In the letter to Laking in which she informed him of these testamentary dispositions she also suggested that he should write to the actress Ellen Terry and her daughter inviting them to give or lend material from their theatrical collection. Both ladies, she knew, would be 'willing to lend, ... but I think both would like the "Honour" of a letter from you asking them'.[130] Most unfortunately, however, Laking never did write to Miss Terry. During the three months before the opening of the museum (on 12 March 1912) he was frantically busy, and there was in any event no space for the 'fine and comprehensive section' which he and the Trustees had rashly promised to provide. In response to increasingly impatient letters from Mrs Enthoven, Harman Oates accordingly supplied what were intended to be soothing answers: 'He [*Laking*] has been so pressed with work preparing for the opening of the London Museum, otherwise he would have written you (*sic*) earlier. He is not yet quite ready for the miniature theatre, he had by no means forgotten it ...' etc.[131]

All that Laking managed finally to provide was a single case of mostly inferior relics – a 'scanty, mediocre and careless assortment', according to a letter in *The Pall Mall Gazette*; and the wrath of the *grandes dames* of the theatre was terrible. Laking, besides pleading lack of space, replied that the paucity of material exhibits was 'due entirely to the poor response made to the appeal for relics'; and by the end of June he did put on show some splendid crimson costumes worn by Tree and Samuel Phelps in the character of Cardinal Wolsey. Ellen Terry was implacable, however. 'I signified my intention of lending many relics of interest', she told *The Daily Telegraph*, rather pompously, 'and only waited an official request before sending them. That request, however, never came. I happen to know that others besides myself were placed in the same predicament.' Mrs Enthoven publicly accused Laking of failing to exhibit numerous offerings which he had received, and wanted to know 'whether or not you mean, after all, to use my friends' and my own contributions'. Privately, Laking managed to smooth her down a little, admitting that the theatrical section was 'poor';[132] but she nevertheless changed her will, for after her death her vast collection went (perhaps fortunately) to the V&A. The theatre section of the London Museum was, indeed, the one great failure of Laking's keepership;* and it was not until the 1930s that matters were put right by Martin Holmes, the museum's own theatre scholar, under the aegis of Dr Mortimer Wheeler. ▣

* One great theatre acquisition was, however, made during the hectic weeks before the opening of the museum. This was the gift by Mr Jonathan King (shortly before his death in April 1912) of forty large scrapbooks containing theatrical prints, scenes and figures for toy theatres; and there were also valentines, Christmas cards, pictorial calendars and over a hundred framed tinsel pictures. In the 1930s Jonathan King's son made important additions to the collection, which is now world famous amongst enthusiasts of the juvenile drama.

In the spring of 1912 life was hectic at the London Museum. More exhibits, more showcases and fittings were all arriving, and by April the catalogue entries for some eight thousand items had actually been printed. Purchases were being made too, and with increasing frequency after Sir Harry Waechter had personally assured Laking, in January 1912 when he had 'confessed', that it would be 'a long time before the fountain is dried that fertilises this museum'.[133] The Hughes collection of needlework had been acquired for £750, purchases of costume at the Ernest Croft sale amounted to £400 (including three 'buff coats' which the Metropolitan in New York had wanted), and £300 had been paid to John B Thorp for five models of Old London. 'This large outlay is not likely to be repeated', Laking optimistically told Harcourt in asking for a cheque for £1800.[134] But very soon afterwards he wanted £360 for the

purchase of prints and drawings at the Wroth sale (including a sketch by Rowlandson of 'lovely ladies drinking tea and other pleasantries'); and best of all, 250 guineas for the steelyard of the great Elizabethan City merchant, Sir Thomas Gresham, today one of the finest treasures in the Museum of London. 'I am especially delighted that we have captured it', he wrote to Harcourt, 'in as much as the Guildhall Museum were anxious to get it, but they were so dilatory in their overtures that Mr Hubbard [*the vendor*] preferred that we should have it.'[135]

There was also the ticklish business of the royal exhibits. In January Laking was employing a well-known Court dressmaker, Madame Rossiter, to supply stands and to fit on to them the dresses already lent by Queen Mary. In mid February the Coronation robes of Edward VII and Queen Alexandra were delivered from the Tower, where they had previously been stored; and Queen Victoria's robes also arrived. But Queen Alexandra forgot about her promised loan of twenty-six dresses, and had to be diffidently reminded by Laking. By this time King George and Queen Mary were back from India, and Laking was summoned to Buckingham Palace to discuss arrangements for the opening. 'The King very charming about the Museum', he reported later, 'but impressed strongly "KP" only for the time until we get our real home.'[136] Back again at 'KP', Laking was agonizing over the delicate problem of how best to display the dress which Queen Mary had worn at the Coronation of Edward VII. Might he be allowed, he asked one of the Queen's ladies-in-waiting, 'to suggest on the figure of this particular costume her hair, upon which we would place a paste copy of the diamond tiara she wore'.[137] Three weeks later, and less than a fortnight before the opening, Queen Mary paid a private visit to the museum to see for herself that all was well in this and other matters, and was 'delighted with the progress made'. She did, however, think (as she told Lord Esher) that it was 'a pity to get *too* fine things for the Museum. I mean in the way of glorious old English china and enamels. . . . The charm to me of the London Museum is seeing amusing little things connected with our city which one cannot see elsewhere, not to go in for beauty so much. . . . Am I right?'[138] And Queen Alexandra also came privately only three days before the opening.[139]

The royal tour of inspection by King George and Queen Mary took place on Thursday 21 March 1912. There had been a press reception on the previous day, and on the following day, Friday, there was a private view for a large number of invited guests. (Sir Harry Waechter, it may be noted, was certainly not present on Thursday or, so far as is known, on Friday either.) For the following Wednesday, 27 March, some 1300 tickets of admission were sent to peers and members of the House of Commons. But owing to recent disturbances by militant suffragettes demanding the vote for women,* the State Apartments at Kensington had had to be temporarily closed to the public, and the first day on which

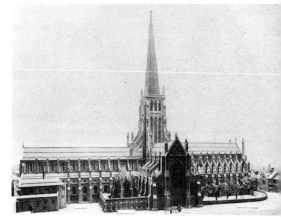

105/106 *Models of London Bridge and St Paul's Cathedral.*
These were included in the group of five models made by J B Thorp for the White City Exhibition of 1908 and subsequently purchased by the London Museum

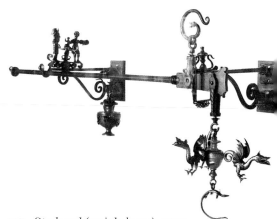

107 *Steelyard (weigh-beam), 1572. Inscribed 'Thomas Gresham London', this steelyard may well have been one of the fittings provided for the merchants using Gresham's Royal Exchange. Laking bought it in 1912*

* Lewis Harcourt himself had had one of the windows of his house in Berkeley Square smashed as recently as 4 March.[140]

108 *'Lovely ladies drinking tea' at the White Conduit House. Detail of watercolour by Thomas Rowlandson, 1787. The White Conduit House was a tea garden at Islington, converted from a tavern in the eighteenth century. This drawing was bought by Laking in 1912*

109 *Queen Alexandra in her coronation robes, 1902*

* There was a long-standing tradition within the London Museum that Mr Joicey was not originally present at the Palace on 21 March, and that a cab had to be hurriedly sent to the Junior Carlton Club to fetch him to be presented to his sovereign.

members of the public were admitted (free) was Easter Monday Bank Holiday, 8 April.[141]

Although King George, determined that the museum's stay at Kensington should only be temporary, did not want to have a formal opening ceremony, he had no objection to his visit being used to full advantage for publicity purposes.[142] Laking, accordingly, made the most of this opportunity, suggesting, for instance, to Bruce Ingram that coverage of the impending royal visit in *The Illustrated London News* might include a drawing 'of the King looking pensively at the remains of the Roman Galley'[143] – an idea duly realized two weeks later (*figure* 123). Besides numerous other letters to the press, he even found time to write to Thomas Cook and Son, the travel agents, giving them information about the museum,[144] while Harman Oates requested the District Railway Company to put up a notice at Kensington High Street Station, 'Alight here for the London Museum.'[145] And at the Palace itself a basic problem of all museums – security – was neatly solved when Earl Beauchamp (First Commissioner of Works and therefore a Trustee) was somehow beguiled into agreeing that the wages of the eight extra warders deemed necessary to patrol the State Apartments after the opening of the museum should be paid for by his department – a very important matter for an institution with such an uncertain financial future as the London Museum.[146] The wages of the constable whom the Metropolitan Police required to be on point duty at the entrance to the Palace from Kensington High Street, could not, however, 'be defrayed from Public Funds', and had therefore to be paid by the Trustees.[147]

On the great day the King and Queen, accompanied by Princess Mary and Prince George (later Duke of Kent), arrived quietly at three o'clock in a closed carriage and pair.[148] Some two hundred and fifty invited guests were awaiting them, and the royal party was greeted at the northeast entrance to the Palace by the three Trustees and Laking. In the first room at the top of the staircase – Queen Mary's Gallery – stood ten cases containing relics of everyday life from prehistoric to Tudor times – scissors, table knives, cooking utensils, swords, spurs, shoes and so on. Each case was carefully labelled, and some of them contained over a hundred objects. To relieve this visually oppressive start for visitors' tours, Laking had commissioned eight vigorous crayon drawings by Monsieur A Forestier to illustrate what life had been like for the earliest Londoners, the earliest of all, according to one newspaper, being 'an ape man up a tree threatening with a club an animal that really ought to have paid a visit to the dentist'. The second room, shown as 'the Queen's Closet, Fancy Ware' on the plan, at first contained Mr J G Joicey's porcelain and enamels. On the day before the royal visit Mr Joicey had converted all his loans into gifts, and it was probably in this room that Lewis Harcourt presented him to the King, who thanked him for his splendid generosity.[149]* Next, in 'Queen Anne's Private Dining Room', came some of the royal relics. These included such objects of purely personal interest as Edward VII's cigar-case, several pairs of his gloves, and even 'a favourite woollen muffler of his Majesty's', while King George had contributed *inter alia* a favourite blue umbrella. However peripheral to the history of London such objects subsequently seemed to later generations, the royal contributions proved, when the museum was opened to the public, to be the most popular of all the exhibits; and many of them were, of course, of great historic interest, notably the Coronation robes of Queen Victoria, King Edward VII, and Queen Alexandra, and many dresses worn on special occasions by those two queens and by Queen Mary.

All these royal objects were lent. Many other exhibits were also only on loan, and some were withdrawn after a year or two. In the Cupola Room there was a splendid array of London silver (including some borrowed from Laking's father) and several models of ships. There were also fine collections of Fulham slipware and Delft pottery (the latter supposedly made in Lambeth), some of which was later donated. The *pièce de résistance* of the museum's very own possessions was, however, the Seymour Lucas collection of costume, mostly of Georgian court dresses, which was displayed in large free-standing cases in the King's Gallery. This terminated the tour, and visitors then had to return by the same route as they had come, threading their way through the small rooms where Queen Victoria had spent her childhood and then back through the Queen's Gallery.

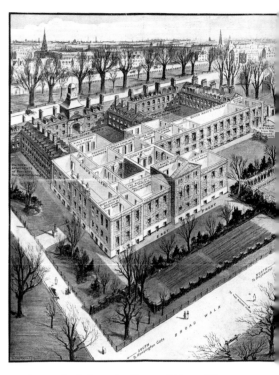

110/111 *Aerial perspective and plan of the apartments at Kensington Palace occupied by the London Museum, 1911–13*

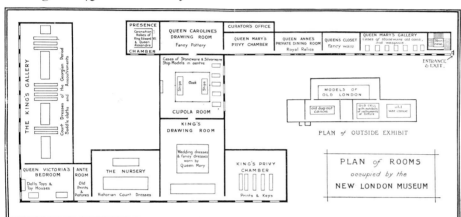

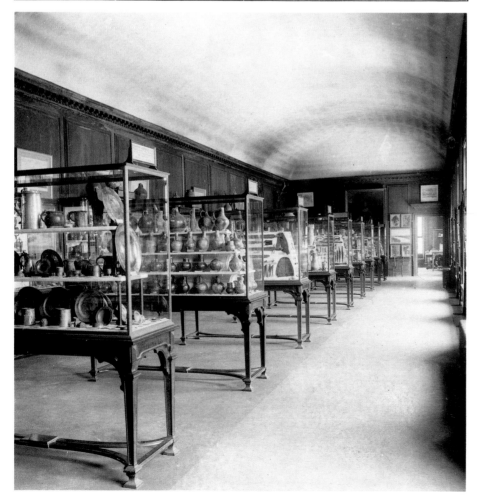

113 *Prehistoric Man. Chalk and charcoal drawing by Amédée Forestier, 1911–12. One of a group of eight drawings commissioned by Laking to illustrate the life of the earliest Londoners*

112 *Queen Mary's Gallery, 1912. The display included material which ranged in date from prehistoric times up to the seventeenth century. The serried ranks of showcases had been ordered from Felix Joubert of the King's Road, Chelsea*

115 *Queen Mary's Privy Chamber, 1912, after re-arrangement to display Mr Joicey's gifts and loans*

115

114 *Queen Anne's Private Dining Room, 1912, after re-arrangement to display Chelsea porcelain and Battersea enamel*

116 *The Presence Chamber, 1912, with the coronation robes of Edward VII and Queen Alexandra*

116

117 *Coat and waistcoat of c.1765–70, from the Seymour Lucas collection, displayed in the King's Gallery*

118 *The King's Gallery, 1912*

120 *Dress worn by the Princess of Wales (later Queen Mary) at the coronation of Edward VII, 1902*

119 *The Cupola Room, 1912. Stoneware, silver, ship-models and topographical prints were displayed within a route regulated by barrier ropes (top left)*

121 *The royal visit to the London Museum, 21 March 1912. Left to right, Lewis Harcourt talking to King George V, Prince George (later Duke of Kent), Princess Mary, Queen Mary and Guy Laking. From a drawing by Balliol Salmon*

But on the day of the royal inspection there were no such problems of circulation, and the King and Queen went on to view the Annexe. Here were the Roman Boat, the prehistoric dugout, the Wellclose Square cells (now embellished by Laking with a stuffed rat and a recumbent figure of Jack Sheppard the highwayman) and other prison relics, the architectural items (balusters, door-knockers, chimneypieces, etc.) salvaged by the LCC, five small 'peep show' models of Old London before the Great Fire,[150] and numerous prints and drawings. 'The King was in a merry mood', according to one of the more popular daily newspapers, 'and made many little jests which raised a laugh among his gentlemen'. In the more dignified language of *The Times*, 'the King expressed his satisfaction with the great progress which the Museum had made since its foundation was announced exactly a year ago'. And as he and his party drove away they were greeted by a large crowd which had waited patiently for him in Kensington Gardens, defying several drenching showers of rain.

122 *The royal party entering the Annexe. Left to right, Lewis Harcourt, Queen Mary, Lord Esher, King George V and Guy Laking*

123 *The royal party inspecting the Roman Boat in the Annexe. Left to right, Prince George, Princess Mary, Lord Esher, ?Earl Beauchamp, Guy Laking, Lewis Harcourt, King George and Queen Mary. From a drawing by Amédée Forestier*

124 *Wellclose Square prison cells, 1912, with figure of Jack Sheppard the highwayman in occupation*

When the London Museum opened to the public on Easter Monday, 8 April 1912, it proved an instant and unprecedented hit. On that day there were at least 13 000 visitors, and the queue to enter was so long that many people stood for hours 'without getting near the doors'. It was noticeable, too, that 'the working class element predominated' among the visitors, who by the end of May numbered 116 000 to the Palace and 100 000 to the Annexe.[151] 'You have doubtless read in the papers the unparalleled success your museum has been', Laking wrote at the end of the first week to Harcourt, who was on holiday. 'Its popularity with the public is nothing short of astonishing, indeed the queues waiting to get in, suggest the attractions of a musical comedy or a football match, rather than visitors calmly viewing a museum that purports to be educational? and instructive?'[152] Laking had, in fact, already placed his own lasting personal imprint upon the character of the London Museum. In putting the collection together, he said in one of numerous press interviews, 'one theme has been overwhelming, and that is to make the exhibition popular'. He had, commented the *Review of Reviews*, successfully 'combined the erudition of the historian with something of the instinct of the showman'; and this remained the aim of all Laking's successors throughout the life of the London Museum.[153]

Amidst the chorus of praise for the new museum the only immediately dissentient voices to be heard were those of the understandably disgruntled theatre people. But during the ensuing weeks and months some other criticisms were made. *The Museums Journal* thought there was too much emphasis on the 'Royal relics' and could not detect 'the guiding principle' on which the collection had been assembled.[154] In the opinion of *The Antiquary* the museum might become too heterogeneous: 'It is easy to establish a connection between London and a host of things which really have no specific claim to be included in a London Museum, properly so called.'[155] Another critic said that the costumes, for which the London Museum was to become increasingly famous, had 'no more to do with London than with any other part of England'.[156] Finally, the curator of a provincial museum, writing in *Knowledge* in January 1913, castigated the methods of display and arrangement. 'I found a number of rooms of varying sizes, each crammed with as many mid-Victorian funereal exhibition cases as it could hold, and each case similarly crammed with as many specimens as possible.' He had expected the arrangement to be chronological. 'Nothing of the sort. Any object of almost any date could be seen in almost any room – nay – in almost any case!' Case after case was 'hopelessly and unaccountably jumbled'; and the Annexe was 'arranged after the plan of the maze at Hampton Court'.[157]

There was, no doubt, much truth in these and other criticisms. Nevertheless, to have, with the very small staff and financial resources available, assembled and displayed a collection of some eighteen thousand objects within one year, and to have done so at virtually no public expense, was a very remarkable achievement indeed. Laking himself later admitted that the museum at Kensington Palace had been a 'very hotch-potch show which was all we could get together'; and it was also Laking who made the most sensible comment of all when he said in May 1912 that at Kensington Palace 'there is the nucleus of a great collection which is bound to expand with the passing of time'.[158]

A LADY WITH A PAST.

London (in her new Museum at Kensington Palace). "BLESS MY SOUL, WHAT A LIFE I HAVE LED!"

125 'Punch' cartoon published in the week after the royal tour of the London Museum. London, personified as a grand old lady, exclaims 'Bless my soul, what a life I have led!'

126 *Queen Victoria's dolls, as displayed at Kensington Palace, 1912*

127 *After the removal of the London Museum from Kensington Palace to Lancaster House in 1913, models of Old London (many of them paid for by Mr Joicey) proved 'a never-failing attraction, especially to younger visitors', as this drawing published in 'The Graphic' in 1920 demonstrates*

THE LONDON MUSEUM

1912 TO 1926

131 *Sir William Lever, later first Viscount Leverhulme, in c.1912.*
In purchasing the lease of Stafford House, Sir William's intention had been to establish a gallery of British art, but he was persuaded, probably by Lewis Harcourt, to allow it to be used for the London Museum instead

128–130 *Stafford (later Lancaster) House, St James's, before 1912.*
Stafford House was the home of the Dukes of Sutherland until acquired by Sir William Lever in 1912 and soon afterwards renamed Lancaster House. These photographs show the front entrance, the garden and the grand hall and staircase shortly before the house was occupied by the London Museum in 1913

Chapter 4
THE LONDON MUSEUM
1912 TO 1926

Now that the London Museum was open for business, the time had come to draw up a financial statement, and in May 1912 Laking set about doing this. So far as is known, all expenditure on the museum had been met out of Harcourt's private London Museum account, the only payment into which had been Sir Harry Waechter's £30000. By May 1912 £14659 of this sum (in round figures) had been advanced by Harcourt to Laking and spent by him for museum purposes, by far the largest two items being £6338 for the purchase of exhibits and £5014 for showcases and fittings. Expenditure on salaries had been extremely small, for (as previously mentioned) Laking had received nothing and had actually paid Harman Oates out of his own pocket. The balance left in Harcourt's museum account after all this expenditure must therefore have been about £15341, plus the interest accumulated since the opening of the account. At six per cent this would yield about £1000 per annum; and this was now the sole income of the museum.[1]

On 19 June Harcourt, Esher and Laking met at Harcourt's room at the House of Commons to consider the situation. They decided that the museum must live within its income, and that as salaries alone amounted (at first) to £866 per annum, all purchasing of exhibits must cease at once. Laking himself was now to be paid a nominal salary of £100, Harman Oates £200 (henceforth to be paid out of the museum Fund), Lawrence £240, Murray £156 and Read (the typist) £50. There were also the wages of the distant policeman on duty at the bottom of the road leading to Kensington Palace. Now that the first rush of visitors was over his presence was no longer needed, and in July Laking persuaded Earl Beauchamp (as First Commissioner of Works) to have his services discontinued, thereby saving the museum £120 per annum. After payment of salaries the London Museum therefore ventured into its public life with an annual income of about £250 for all other purposes.[2]

But the museum already had many friends, and as Harcourt and Laking were both masters of the arts of persuasion, many very valuable additions were made to the collections during the single year, Easter 1912 to Easter 1913, that it was open to the public at Kensington. In May 1912 Laking persuaded somebody to present a Hansom cab, which he exhibited in solitary state in the great Orangery building adjacent to the Annexe. By this time the number of Hansoms plying in the streets of London was falling rapidly and they were already far outnumbered by the new motor taxi-cabs; so the acquisition of this vehicle exemplified Laking's imaginative foresight, while his placing of it in the Orangery before he had even asked the Office of Works for permission to do so displayed his determination not to allow the London Museum to lose any opportunities through official red tape.[3] Soon afterwards the Hansom was joined by a four-wheeler cab and a knife-board 'bus of 1867, which Harman Oates bought from Thomas Tilling of Peckham, the 'bus proprietor, for £14 for the pair, a sum which the now impecunious museum was, however, unable to pay for over a year.[4]* The museum's little collection of horse-drawn vehicles in the Orangery was rounded off by the arrival in January 1913 of a post-chaise which had been used by the Duke of Wellington, lent by Lord Kenyon. And more prosaically there was also a very early domestic gas meter, dated 1869.[6]

Within the Palace itself gifts and loans poured in continuously. To mention only a few of the best, there was City Livery Companies' armorial china from Mr F A Crisp, a splendid Georgian dolls' house from Miss Blackett, and a small collection of items relating to the Royal Mail (including a fine model of a mail coach) from the General Post Office.[7] All these items were loans, and so too were the superb additions made

132 *Hansom cab exhibited in the Orangery at Kensington Palace, 1912*

* The 'bus has not survived. It could not be got into Lancaster House and therefore stood in the open air at the bottom of the garden. Eventually it became so decayed that Dr Mortimer Wheeler had it removed.[5]

by Mrs W Salting and Mr R M Walker to the museum's collection of Chelsea porcelain.[8]

These and all other benefactors were, however, quite outshone by Mr Joicey.[9] In the year following the public opening in April 1912 his contributions included more Bow and Chelsea china, snuff boxes, watches, silver, jewellery, clocks, embroidery, costumes, prints, pistols, a sedan chair and a specimen of early printing thought to be by William Caxton. In making his purchases he was easily deceived, however, some of the jewellery which he sent along on one occasion being not even English, let alone of London make; and another of his offerings which had to be returned was a large painted leather screen, sold to him as pre-1750 but which Laking at once saw was a modern reproduction.[10]

Harman Oates was now skilfully conducting most of the correspondence with Mr Joicey, and it was perhaps his idea to rename Queen Mary's Privy Chamber, to which Joicey's gifts and loans had now been removed. Gold labels inscribed 'The Joicey Room' were accordingly put up above each of the doors, Mr Steele (the artist who painted the labels) commenting that 'the little extra "fuss" will please our friend Mr. Joicey and probably influence him in deciding the ultimate fate of other objects at present only loaned by him'. It was probably with the intention of persuading him to do something like this that in October 1912 either Harcourt or Laking invited Joicey to dinner.[11] Joicey was evidently very susceptible to flattery. 'Nothing dear Mr Joicey is a trouble where you are concerned', Harman Oates wrote to him soon afterwards, adding (with unintentional ambiguity) 'I am too grateful' – so he must certainly have been much pleased by such attentions. Soon after one of his trips abroad he wrote to Laking to ask whether he might be allowed to present to the museum the whole of his collections then on loan there as a commemoration of the impending fiftieth anniversary of the arrival in England of Queen Alexandra in 1863. In due course Her Majesty graciously signified her consent – she was evidently much pleased – and on 7 March 1913 Mr Joicey's gift was announced in *The Times*. Everybody was very happy. ▣

133 *Model of a Royal Mail coach, early nineteenth century*

134 *Sedan chair, eighteenth century, given by Mr Joicey*

Not all the additions to the museum came so openly as those from Mr Joicey, and two great collections which were acquired at about this time came in somewhat covert circumstances. These were the Tangye collection of Cromwelliana and the Cheapside Hoard of Elizabethan and Jacobean jewellery.

The former consisted of books, manuscripts, pictures, miniatures, seals, medals, coins and small mementos, all relating directly or indirectly to Oliver Cromwell, and in all consisting of about a thousand items. The collection had been formed with enthusiasm rather than discernment by Sir Richard Tangye (1833–1906), knight, a Cornish engineer who founded and ultimately became chairman of the famous engineering firm of Tangye Limited of Birmingham, where he was also one of the founders of the City Art Gallery. After his death in 1906 the collection passed to his eldest son, Harold Lincoln Tangye (1866–1935), deputy chairman of Tangye Limited, who was not particularly interested in historical matters. He was, however, a fellow of the Royal Geographical Society and a great traveller, especially in the Sudan and South Africa, and it was perhaps through these interests that he first met Lewis Harcourt, who (it will be remembered) had become Secretary of State for the Colonies in November 1910. At all events Harcourt somehow persuaded

135 *Musical clock made in London by
George Pyke, c.1760.
At four-hourly intervals an organ in the
clock plays one of ten tunes, and figures on
the painted landscape are set in motion.
Given by Mr Joicey*

Tangye to present his father's collection to the London Museum, for on 6 June 1912 Harcourt's private secretary told Laking that Harcourt had 'secured' the collection, and added 'Mr Harcourt would particularly like you to say nothing about this matter until you hear further from him'.[12] On 14 June 1912 *The Times* announced among the King's Birthday Honours the conferment of a baronetcy on Harold Lincoln Tangye.[13] Harcourt was certainly involved in procuring this honour, for three weeks later Tangye was asking him to see if it could be awarded with special remainder to his brothers and/or nephews. On being told, No, he replied thanking Harcourt, and added 'I have visited the London Museum and find it highly interesting. I will seize any possible opportunity of bringing any influence to bear in the direction you desire, though naturally persons of the required type do not grow on every bush!'[14]

Although the museum remained open to the public at Kensington Palace for another nine months, none of the Tangye collection was ever exhibited there, nor was there any public announcement of the gift until the museum reopened at Lancaster House in March 1914.[15]

The circumstances in which another much more important collection was acquired and successfully retained (in large measure) for the London Museum by Harcourt show his extraordinary dexterity in a way quite different from his dealings with Tangye. When the whole business of the Cheapside Hoard had finally been concluded in 1916 Harcourt himself remarked to Laking that 'It has, I think, been a successful extrication from a rather tight place.'[16]

The story began on or about 18 June 1912, when workmen excavating on a building site at the corner of Friday Street and Cheapside discovered a bucket containing what was thought by the finders to be a collection of beads. The ubiquitous and eagle-eyed Lawrence knew better, however, and managed to buy the greater part of the find from the men for ready cash. On the very next day Harcourt and Esher, at their Trustees' meeting at the House of Commons, discussed the matter and decided that 'the entire gold treasure recently unearthed' should be brought on the following Tuesday to Laking's flat in Cleveland Row for their inspection.[17] By that time Lawrence had somehow or other got hold of a few more jewels,[18] and on 26 June Harman Oates sent him a cheque for £90.[19]* A month later he brought in four or five more pieces, 'some quite beautiful',[21] and as late as 1927 his son, Mr F L Lawrence, presented the museum with two amethysts from the by then famous Cheapside Hoard.

This hoard consisted of some 340 pieces of late sixteenth- or early seventeenth-century jewellery, some of them in unfinished condition and apparently forming the stock of a City jeweller. They included rings, pendants, chains, scent bottles, pomanders, watches and part of a Communion set in crystal and gold. Having inspected them all at Laking's flat the Trustees (or in effect Harcourt) decided with perfect propriety to consult the Treasury Solicitor as to what ought to be done. The hoard was then removed to Harcourt's house in Berkeley Square (and thence to his bank), where two eminent legal knights from the Treasury Solicitor's Department came to view it in mid-July.[22] They, acting on behalf of the Crown, decided that the hoard was treasure trove and was Crown property which could not be claimed by anyone else. Some of it was to be given to the British Museum, of which Harcourt was also a Trustee, but by far the greater part of it could and did remain in the custody of the Trustees of the London Museum; and on 18 July Laking was congratulating Harcourt on having 'settled with the Treasury with reference to the Treasure Trove'.[23] The whole affair seemed to have been concluded in a most satisfactory way. None of the jewels was, however, exhibited at

* Whether this was the full amount paid by the Trustees to Lawrence for the hoard is not clear. In August 1913 he was paid £47 for unspecified purchases for the museum.[20]

Kensington Palace, and it was not until the spring of 1914 that half a dozen items were sent to the British Museum.

In March 1914 virtually the whole hoard was suddenly exhibited, either at the British Museum or at the London Museum's new home at Lancaster House, St James's; and a paragraph in *The Times* stated that it had been found in the City of London.[24] Harcourt, of course, had not known that treasure trove found within the City was, by virtue of a royal grant of 1550, the property of the Corporation, but the Coroner did know, and very soon there ensued 'a considerable agitation in the City'.

The Corporation's chartered rights had, indeed, been infringed, but there were grave problems about how they might be vindicated. The Coroner would have great difficulty in holding a satisfactory inquest because the treasure had been removed out of his jurisdiction, and both its identity and the locality of its discovery would be hard to prove in law. The evidence as to the place of origin of the jewels had been, according to Harcourt, 'conflicting and contradictory', and in 1916 he stated that it did not at the time even convey to him 'the impression that they were found within the City'. Probably he had not wanted to know, and Lawrence had been wise enough to be vague about the matter, if only to prevent the freehold owner of the site from butting into an already delicate situation. So proof of the place of origin would certainly have been difficult. But there was another problem – the royal grant of 1550 only referred to gold and silver. The element of treasure trove was therefore relatively small, consisting only of the gold settings of the jewels and the gold base of some of the enamels, and any attempt to separate the two would have entirely destroyed the artistic and historical value of the hoard. The stones, apparently, belonged to the freeholder, whoever he or she might be.

Wisely, the City Corporation, once it had got over its initial fury, decided to seek a compromise. At a meeting held at Harcourt's house in April 1916 the City Solicitor and the Chairman of the Corporation's County Purposes Committee therefore proposed to Harcourt that 'a share of the find' (to be chosen by Harcourt) should be given to the Corporation for exhibition in the Guildhall Museum. To this Harcourt readily agreed, as also to the proposal that the display labels in both museums should state that the hoard had been 'Presented by the Corporation of the City of London and the Right Hon. L. Harcourt, M.P.' A few days later Harcourt sent over sixty-eight pieces of jewellery to Guildhall – pieces which, as Bernard Kettle, the librarian, observed, 'do not include some of the best objects found'[25] – and the matter was at last closed. Harcourt, no doubt, was much relieved, for he had been 'somewhat troubled' by it. He would certainly have been delighted that (apart from the few pieces at the British Museum) the whole hoard was later reunited at the Museum of London.

Harcourt's greatest achievement for the London Museum (apart, of course, from his founding deal with Harry Waechter) was, however, the acquisition of a semi-permanent home for it, and the permanent funding of the museum by the Government out of public money. King George was adamant that the museum's stay at Kensington Palace should only be temporary, and in any case the accommodation there was both unsuitable and much too small. In his very first letter to Harcourt after the opening of the museum in March 1912 Laking had said 'The cry of the Keeper is "Get the museum a home of its own"';[26] but no friendly

136 *Corner of Cheapside and Friday Street in 1908.*
In 1912 excavations at a building site, previously the premises of Percy Truscott & Co., revealed the cache of Elizabethan and Jacobean jewellery since known as 'The Cheapside Hoard'

The Corporation of the City of London.

TREASURE TROVE.

NOTICE is Hereby Given that the Mayor and Commonalty and Citizens of the City of London are, by ancient Charters, entitled to all Treasure Trove found within the City of London and the Town and Borough of Southwark, and that in the event of any gold or silver coins, gold or silver plate, or gold or silver in an unmanufactured state being found in any house, or in the earth, or in any private place within the aforesaid limits, **the owner of which is unknown,** such articles belong to the Corporation of the City of London, and Notice of the discovery must at once be given to me, the undersigned, Town Clerk of the said City, at the Guildhall, London, E.C.

In the event of any such articles being retained by the finder, or sold or handed over to any other person or Body, or notice of the discovery not being given to me, **the person finding the same will render himself liable to prosecution.**

JAMES BELL,
GUILDHALL, E.C., Town Clerk.
December, 1915.

5,000—D. 266—12/15.

Charles Skipper & East, Printers, 49, Great Tower Street, E.C.

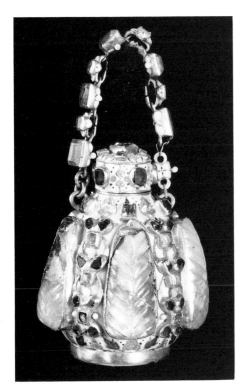

138/139 *Jewellery from the Cheapside Hoard*
(see also page X)

137 *Handbill proclaiming the City Corporation's rights to treasure trove, 1915.*
After the disputed ownership of the Cheapside Hoard had been settled the Corporation publicly re-asserted its claims to treasure trove
(left)

millionaire had turned up to buy the lease of Staple Inn, as Harcourt was still hoping might happen. And then suddenly a formidable tycoon with strong ideas of his own had appeared in the person of Sir William Lever.

Sir William Lever (1851–1925), the soap manufacturer, had been made a baronet in 1911, and in 1917 he was raised to the peerage as Viscount Leverhulme. A man of dynamic energy and well accustomed to getting his own way, he was the founder of the great commercial empire of Lever Brothers, and of the garden city of Port Sunlight on the banks of the Mersey, where his soap-works and model dwellings for his work force were built. In private life he was an enthusiastic collector of pictures, pottery and old furniture, and some years after his wife's death in 1913 he established the Lady Lever Art Gallery at Port Sunlight in her memory. Quite why he suddenly bought Stafford House, St James's, when most of his other benefactions were made in the region of Merseyside or Lancashire, is not clear; but there is no reason to suppose that there was any motive of self interest of any kind.

Stafford House was to be the home of the London Museum from 1913 to 1939, when the museum closed a few days before the outbreak of war; small parts of the building continued, however, to be used for exhibitions, as offices and for storage for some years afterwards. In 1914 its name was changed, at Sir William Lever's instigation, to Lancaster House,[27] in reference to Sir William's Lancashire connections and to the association of the reigning Sovereign with the County Palatine as Duke of Lancaster. The house stands four-square and rather dour beside the more homely St James's Palace and the more feminine Clarence House, its large but uninteresting garden extending down to the Mall and its western windows looking out over the Green Park towards Buckingham Palace. The building of it had begun in 1825 (to designs by Benjamin Dean Wyatt and Philip Wyatt) for George IV's brother, the Duke of York, who was then heir presumptive to the throne. After the Duke's death in 1827, heavily in debt, the incomplete shell was bought by the second Marquess of Stafford, who was created Duke of Sutherland in 1833. His son, who succeeded to the title in the same year, added an attic storey and completed the interior, with Sir Robert Smirke as executant architect. By 1838 the house was more or less complete, but during the ensuing years the lantern was altered and the staircase redecorated by (Sir) Charles Barry.[28] Thereafter (to quote the words of Dr Mortimer Wheeler, a later keeper of the London Museum) 'it remained for seventy years one of the great social and political centres of the metropolis. Chopin played there, Grisi sang, the triumphant Garibaldi was received there. Its great entrance-hall was the finest setting for social assembly in London', and its picture gallery contained as fine a private collection as any in England.[29]

On 13 November 1912 the London daily papers carried an announcement that Sir William Lever had bought Stafford House from the Duke of Sutherland, and that he intended to devote it 'to some public or national purpose'. *The Daily Express* went on to speculate that it might be used as either an extension of the National Gallery or as a home for the London Museum.[30] Stafford House was, however, part of the Crown estates and was administered by the Government Department then still charmingly known as the Office of Woods and Forests; so what Sir William actually bought from the Duke of Sutherland was not the freehold, but only the twenty-eight-year residue of the ninety-nine-year Crown lease commencing in 1841 and actually granted in 1842. He agreed to pay the Duke £60000 for this leasehold interest, which was also subject to the payment of an annual ground rent to the Crown of £758, and which would come to an absolute end on 5 July 1940.[31]

Sir William Lever's offer was conveyed in a letter of 12 November 1912 addressed to the Prime Minister. Sir William had just left England for a long tour of his extensive commercial interests in the Congo, and so the letter was written on his behalf by George Harley, his Liverpool solicitor, and his London agent, Howard (later Sir Howard) Frank, a founder of the well-known firm of land agents still in practice as Knight, Frank and Rutley. In this very important document they recited that Sir William had entered into a contract with the Duke of Sutherland for the purchase of the remaining twenty-eight years of the Crown lease of Stafford House, and stated that Sir William had no intention of living there himself. But, they continued, 'it appeared to him that the opportunity of securing it to the Nation as a Museum for British Works of Art, mainly of the 18th Century and earlier, for which it is so eminently suitable, ought not to be lost; and he has now authorised us to offer the lease which he has agreed to buy, as a gift to the Nation, provided arrangements can be made for the house being maintained as a Museum for British Works of Art for all time. If it is thought desirable to house what is known as "The London Museum", now temporarily in Kensington Palace, in Stafford House, Sir William will acquiesce in any wish expressed to that effect.' During Sir William's absence abroad, they went on, they had his authority 'to settle matters of detail so long as the primary object is kept in view, viz., a permanent gallery for British Works of Art, mainly of the 18th Century and earlier'.[32]

This letter shows beyond doubt that what Sir William really wanted to do was to establish some kind of gallery of British art. (He certainly had a deeply held urge to do something of this sort, for he later established the Lady Lever Art Gallery at Port Sunlight, and in 1924 he indulged this expensive hobby again when he agreed terms with the Duke of Westminster for a building lease of Grosvenor House, Park Lane, where he intended to build 'some form of public building to be devoted to the Arts' – a project brought to nothing by his death in the following year.)[33] Equally clearly, the provision of a home for 'what is known as "The London Museum"' was very much second best, an alternative perhaps suggested to Lever by someone else – probably Harcourt.

Sir William's offer was formally considered by the Cabinet, and Asquith 'handed over the matter' to Harcourt to make further inquiries. This was a rather extraordinary choice of minister to make, Harcourt then being Secretary of State for the Colonies, and it may perhaps indicate that Harcourt had already discussed Stafford House with Sir William, and that Asquith knew of this. Whether this conjecture is correct or not, however, the offer certainly presented considerable problems for the Government. First of all, there was much doubt about whether a 'Museum of British Art' was needed at all, British Art being already well catered for at the National Gallery, the Tate, the British Museum and the V&A; and from what source would come the funds needed to purchase pictures and other exhibits? But if, on the other hand, the house were to be used for the London Museum, the taxpayer would be required to pay for a purely metropolitan purpose which ought to be funded by London's rate-payers. Finally, there was the sheer magnitude of the costs involved – £20000 to buy the Crown freehold, or a rent of c.£6000 per annum if a new long lease were to be taken, plus in either case an estimated £10000 per annum for staff costs and general maintenance.[34]

For once, Harcourt's famous powers of persuasion were not entirely successful, but he did nevertheless manage to extricate at least a rented

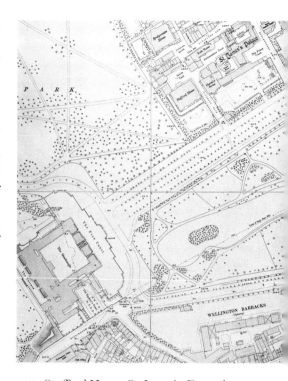

140 *Stafford House, St James's. From the Ordnance Survey of 1894*

accommodation for his London Museum. Shortly before Christmas a special committee of the Cabinet failed to reach any agreement about Sir William's offer, John Burns (President of the Local Government Board) maintaining that Stafford House was too small for the London Museum and Lloyd George (Chancellor of the Exchequer), much more importantly, objecting to the use of taxpayers' money for a London purpose. So the matter was referred back to the full Cabinet, with the suggestion that Lever might be asked to alter the conditions of his proposal.[35]

Harcourt now made the fateful decision that as he was clearly not going to get the exclusive use of Stafford House for the London Museum, this use must be shared with some other body which could claim a national as opposed to a merely metropolitan function. This body was the Government Entertainment Fund, which had been established in 1908 under Harcourt's own aegis (as First Commissioner of Works) for the purpose of providing official receptions and banquets for foreign diplomats and other miscellaneous bigwigs. In 1912 its 'vote' upon the public funds amounted to £10000, most of which was spent on entertainments for the Imperial Conference. By 1920, however, its expenditure had risen to no less than £200000;[36] and in the longer term its principal client, the Foreign Office, was to be the cuckoo which finally turned the poor harmless London Museum out of its nest.

It was therefore Harcourt himself who first suggested this shared use of Stafford House, for on 22 December, after the Cabinet meeting at which he evidently first mentioned this possiblity, he wrote to Howard Frank in the following terms: 'The Cabinet are, as at present advised, rather nervous of asking so large a sum of the taxpayers, but, as you know, I am strongly pressing the matter upon them, as I am most anxious to obtain so stately a home for the London Museum, and *I think all my colleagues agree that the contents of that Museum could be so arranged within Stafford House as to make it very suitable for the purpose of entertainments by the Government to distinguished foreigners* visiting the country for Conferences and Congresses under the provisions of the Government's Entertainment Fund....' [*author's italics*] He added that he had very little hope of inducing his colleagues in the Cabinet to agree to buy the freehold of the house, but that they might be willing to undertake the costs of maintenance; and he therefore asked Frank, on behalf of Sir William (still in the Congo), to give him a little more time to produce a satisfactory result.[37]

This was the position when Asquith, in answer to a 'planted' question, stated in the House of Commons on 31 December 1912 that the Government was still considering Sir William Lever's offer. This purely formal statement was, however, followed by an impromptu supplementary question which very nearly had dire consequences for the London Museum. This question, from a Conservative member, Mr W Moore, was 'Can the right honourable gentleman say how much the Government are giving to Sir William Lever by a concession in West Africa? . . . I want to know whether a balance will be struck on the transaction.'[38]

The exploitation of the fruit of the oil palm was then the staple industry of the coastal region of West Africa from Sierra Leone to the Cameroons, and this oil was the principal constituent in the manufacture of soap, as also of margarine. Lever Brothers had therefore obtained from the Belgian Government enormous territorial concessions in the Congo, and more recently they had turned their attention to British West Africa. At the time of Moore's insinuations, Lever's negotiations with the colonial authorities had been going on for over four years, some of them therefore before Harcourt became Colonial Secretary, and some during his period of office. The Blue Book which the Colonial Office issued immediately afterwards contained all the correspondence and showed that Harcourt had throughout the whole affair acted in a perfectly straightforward and proper manner.[39] This did not, however, prevent his being subjected on half a dozen occasions to a barrage of hostile Conservative questions in the House of Commons about 'Messrs. Lever Brothers' Concession'.[40] Then the whole matter was forgotten as suddenly as it had popped up, and a few months later Bonar Law, the Leader of the Opposition, admitted that nothing objectionable had been done.[41] Harcourt may have had no scruples about arranging for the award of baronetcies in what he considered to be the public interest, but he was not the man to use commercial favouritism to advance even such a pet project as the London Museum.

There the matter rested for three months, largely, no doubt, because Sir William Lever was still in the Congo and could not be consulted about changing the terms of his offer. On 19 March 1913, however, the Cabinet finally decided not to buy the freehold of Stafford House. This must have been a great disappointment for Harcourt, although doubtless he had long expected it; but by way of a consolation prize he was authorized by the Cabinet to ask Lever whether (in the words written by Asquith himself to the King on the next day) 'he will consent that the house should be used for the purposes of [Government] entertainment, and for the temporary accommodation of the London Museum'.[42]

The King was also very sorry to hear of the decision not to buy the freehold, as his private secretary, Lord Stamfordham, later told Harcourt. His Majesty hoped, nevertheless, that Harcourt's impending negotiations with Sir William Lever would lead to the house being used both for the accommodation of the London Museum and for Government entertainments during the remaining twenty-eight years of the lease. 'During that interval', Stamfordham incautiously added, 'many things may happen, possibly the price of the Freehold may depreciate or a good Socialist Government may bag the Crown lands!!'[43]

The first thing that happened, however, and after the lapse of less than a single week, was that Sir William Lever withdrew his offer to present the house at all. After his return from Africa his attention had been called to what he described as the 'insinuations and innuendoes' made in the House of Commons 'to the effect that I had been actuated by mercenary and improper motives in the offer I made to present to the Nation my ownership of the Lease of Stafford House'.[44] There was therefore no other course open to him than to withdraw the offer, which he did on 26 March; and three days later this was published in the newspapers.[45]

Sir William's withdrawal was in fact only intended as an emphatic protest against the unfounded 'insinuations and innuendoes' which had been made against his good name.[46] But this was not known at the time, and so there ensued a month of anxious diplomacy in which Howard Frank finally succeeded in persuading Lever to change his mind again.[47] The renewal of the offer was conveyed to the Prime Minister in a letter of 26 April from Frank and George Harley. Sir William's intention now was, they stated, to hand over the twenty-eight remaining years of the lease of Stafford House to the Government 'for the purpose of housing the London Museum collections now in Kensington Palace, and for any other similar purposes which may seem proper to the Government'. Sir William would, they added in the final paragraph, 'be very glad if hereafter it appeared possible that some of the rooms of Stafford House could be utilized for the purposes of Government entertainment to distinguished visitors given under the provisions of the Hospitality Fund'.[48]

This second offer was accepted unconditionally by the Cabinet at a meeting on 30 April, and on 1 May Asquith wrote personally to Lever to thank him. The letter of 26 April is therefore the sole authority for what Sir William finally intended and indeed actually gave; and it is hardly surprising to find that it was Harcourt who (with Lever's full knowledge) drafted much of it, including the crucial final paragraph.[49] Gone was all reference to the gallery for British Works of Art, which was the principal object of the original offer, and in its place was the London Museum, the use of taxpayers' money for which was to be justified by the suggestion that the house might also be utilized for purposes of Government entertainment. It was, indeed, a dexterous transformation, which earned for Harcourt, among other things, the pleasure of a private letter of congratulation from Sir Harry Waechter. And from up in Perthshire there came a brief note from Lord Esher which summed it all up – 'My dear Loulou, Many congratulations. You are a wonderful fighter.'[50]

There were of course one or two odds and ends still to be sorted out, notably the little matter of the ownership of the museum's collections and the terms on which they were to be handed over to the Government. If the Cabinet had bought the freehold of Stafford House Harcourt, as principal Trustee, would have handed over the collections in perpetuity;[51] but as the museum only had a leasehold interest of twenty-eight years' duration he was only going to transfer them unconditionally for that period. In order to make this absolutely clear he and his co-Trustees (Esher and Lord Beauchamp) signed a deed dated 1 July 1913 placing 'their collections' at the disposal of the Government for the term of the lease of Stafford House and, additionally, for so long afterwards as the collections should continue to be exhibited either there or in 'some other equally suitable building maintained by the Government'. The suitability of any such other building was, moreover, to be decided by the Trustees at that time in being, together with Harcourt's own legal representative if he himself were then dead. But if Stafford House ceased to be available and no alternative building were supplied, then all objects presented by particular individuals were to be returned to them or their heirs, while all objects purchased by or for the Trustees, and any unidentified objects, were to be transferred to Harcourt or his heirs 'for their own enjoyment and disposal absolutely'.[52]

In making this ingenious but entirely fair arrangement Harcourt was (as he told Sir William Lever) 'quite certain that at the end of twenty-eight years the collection, which is already a fine one, will have become so remarkable and will be so much valued by the public that there is not the least prospect of any Government being allowed to surrender it or to leave Stafford House, which as you know, is Crown property, and which will, by that time, have become intimately associated with the Collection'.[53] And over at the Treasury the chief mandarin, Sir Thomas Heath, thought much the same, though he looked at the matter from a different point of view. At the end of the lease of the house, he noted gloomily, the museum's Trustees 'will be in a position practically to compel the Government of the day to buy the freehold unless they prefer to give back the collection'.[54]

Harcourt's hope and Heath's fear both proved groundless, however, for when the lease expired in 1940 at the height of World War II the museum had been closed indefinitely; and by the time that peace had returned and people began to wonder why the London Museum, alone of all the national museums and galleries, did not reopen, it was too late. Possession is nine points of the law, and by 1945 the Foreign Office was well and truly in possession, and has remained so ever since.

What in 1913 made it all so galling to the Treasury mandarins (who never accustomed themselves to the harum-scarum ways of the London Museum) was their own apparent failure to inform the Estimates Committee of the Cabinet of the terms on which the collections were to be handed over.[54] Harcourt had made it perfectly clear to them that he was only placing the material at the Government's disposal for the term of the lease;[55] but the mandarins evidently failed (until it was too late) to see the implications of this, which were not spelt out for them by Harcourt; and so, in happy ignorance, the Estimates Committee took the vital financial decisions at a meeting on 5 June – salaries and wages, costs of removal of the museum from Kensington to Stafford House, and everything else were all to be provided for in a special Supplementary Estimate. Someone present on this fateful occasion did point out, correctly, in a note passed to Harcourt, that 'you must get Parliamentary authority for a new service on which the House of Commons has never been consulted'.[56] But nobody paid any attention, for this was certainly never done; and when the mandarins did at last realize the likely long-term effect of Harcourt's conditional transfer, it was too late. The terms of the transfer had been accepted, the three Trustees (originally nominated by King George) had been confirmed in office by the Government, the Supplementary Estimate had been voted in the Commons, and the whole new regime for the London Museum had been fossilized in a Treasury Minute of 9 July (later amended at Harcourt's instigation). In September Sir Thomas Heath set the whole situation out for the benefit of the Financial Secretary of the Treasury. This was C F G Masterman, the distinguished author and journalist, who could only reply 'I don't think anything can be done in the matter now'.[54]

The Supplementary Estimate approved by the Commons amounted to a princely sum of over £9000, most of which was for the installation of new heating and lighting and for redecoration at Stafford House; but it did also include £1800 for new showcases and furniture. The Office of Works, to whose superintendence Stafford House now passed, bought some of the Duke of Sutherland's curtains, carpets and furniture,[57] and Sir William Lever purchased (for £1750) and presented some of the Duke's finest pieces, notably some large candelabra and torchères, and two fine Georgian tables which stood in the entrance hall.[58] By virtue of the Treasury Minute Laking was appointed keeper and secretary at a nominal salary of £100 per annum, and all the other staff – Oates, Lawrence, Murray and Read – were taken on too. At Stafford House the museum in fact (though never in spirit) became a branch of the Civil Service; and on 11 August Laking told Harcourt in an appropriately official manner that 'The Administrative Department of the London Museum has taken possession of its new home, and all correspondence is being done there.'[59]

So the first stage in the story of the vagabond London Museum had come to an end. During this short period of less than three years the museum had, as far as is known, been financed exclusively by Sir Harry Waechter's £30000; and Laking's annual accounts for the year ended 31 March 1913 are therefore not without interest.[60] They showed first of all that the Trustees had entirely failed to live up to their decision, taken in May 1912, that the museum must live within its income, which was then around £1000 per annum. Some £3371 had been spent on the purchase of exhibits, which the Trustees had in May 1912 decided must cease altogether, and total expenditure for the year amounted to £6475. Secondly, they showed that since Harcourt wrote his first cheque to Laking in April 1911, £9709 had been spent on the purchase of exhibits and £5642 on cases, stands and fittings. Altogether Harcourt had paid out £19414 to Laking from his London Museum account at Child's Bank, and of Sir Harry Waechter's £30000 there therefore remained some £10586, exclusive of the interest which must have been earned. This useful sum, it is quite clear, was now to be husbanded with great care, for when Laking asked Harcourt a few months later for a cheque for £1500 'to settle up old accounts and to provide for fresh purchases', Harcourt was for once very angry. He demanded particulars of all outstanding bills and instructed Laking that 'in future no further liabilities of any kind will be incurred without my express consent'.[61]

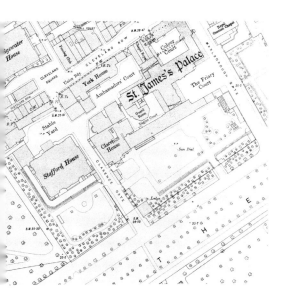

141 *Stafford House and its neighbours.
From the Ordnance Survey of 1894*

In the early autumn of 1913 the entire museum was transported from Kensington Palace to Stafford House, 'without a single breakage'. The job was done by Joubert's, whose vans were accompanied on each trip by two policemen; and by mid October the galleries of the Palace stood empty and quiet once more.[62] There was, however, no welcome for the museum from its grand neighbours who lived adjacent to Stafford House. These included the redoubtable Sir Douglas Dawson, whom we have already encountered at Kensington Palace, and Lord Knollys, joint Private Secretary with Lord Stamfordham to King George, both of whom enjoyed 'Grace and Favour' apartments in Stable Yard or St James's Palace; and only a few yards further away, at Clarence House, dwelled Queen Victoria's son, the Duke of Connaught. They were aghast at the prospect of a constant stream of members of the public passing through the hitherto unfrequented precinct of Stable Yard to visit the museum; and on the very day – 3 May – on which the news of the Government's acceptance of Sir William Lever's renewed offer of Stafford House was published in *The Times*, Sir Douglas mounted a formidable campaign of opposition. 'Residence in your house or mine', he wrote to Knollys, 'will be impossible if the narrow entrance to Stable Yard from Cleveland Row is the route taken to the Museum.' The public entrance to Stafford House must be moved to the garden side, through gates from the Mall. 'It could easily be arranged', he concluded, '*if we move at once*'.[63]

Lord Knollys quite agreed. To keep the present entrance to Stafford House would make residence in his and Dawson's houses 'intolerable'; so he asked Lord Esher (as a Trustee of the museum) to speak to Harcourt about it, and he also urged Dawson to speak to Lord Stamfordham in order to enlist the 'sympathy and assistance' of the King.[64] This was evidently very soon done, for on 9 May Stamfordham told Lionel Earle, Sir Schomberg McDonnell's successor as Permanent Secretary of the Office of Works, that His Majesty considered that it would be 'absolutely necessary to make a new approach and entrance to the House from the Mall'.[65] And soon afterwards the Office of Woods and Forests, as ground landlords of Stafford House, were also brought into the argument.[66]

Ultimately this little fracas was settled by a compromise. The idea of a permanent covered way from the Mall across the garden of Stafford House, to be used by visitors to the museum and by guests at Government entertainments, was abandoned, at any rate for the moment, because the Office of Works had no money available to pay for its construction.[67] Any proposal which entailed entering from the rear a building with such a splendid *porte cochère*, vestibule, hall and grand staircase as Stafford

House was, indeed, plainly absurd; and so it was ultimately arranged, with the King's consent, that visitors to the museum might cross Stable Yard on foot to enter the house by the front door, but that carriages and motor cars would be stopped by a policeman at the west end of Cleveland Row. Even guests to Government parties were only to be allowed to drive by special permission of the King himself, and these occasions were therefore to be kept to a minimum.[68]

When he heard this news, the Duke of Connaught was extremely cross.[69] So too was Sir Douglas Dawson, for in a chance encounter with Guy Laking at a weekend country house party at Alfred de Rothschild's, 'he laid up pretty strongly about the London Museum being at Stafford House'. Laking, always easy-going and courteous, was evidently equal to this outburst, for (as he later told Lord Esher) 'you can imagine I did my best to appease him'.[70] But Sir Douglas proved implacable, and took his revenge only a week after the museum had opened to the public in March 1914. One afternoon he saw Herbert Murray, the museum's technical assistant, drive up to Stafford House in a taxi. Hardly had Murray entered the building than Sir Douglas 'personally came across and created a considerable disturbance'. He was, he said, 'going straight to the King'. Poor Laking, who was out at the time, could only report the whole incident to Harcourt and ask for the Trustees' orders as to 'whether or no the Keeper and Staff of three are to be permitted the privilege of driving up to the Museum'. Whatever decision the Trustees might arrive at, he added, would 'be most rigidly adhered to, but the arrogance of Sir Douglas Dawson under the existing conditions, is hard to bear'.

Bear it was what he nevertheless had to do, for Harcourt evidently felt unable to reopen the vexed question of access to Lancaster House (as it had by then been renamed).[71] A few weeks later questions were asked in the House of Commons about why motor cars and carriages bound for the museum were being stopped by the police at the corner of Cleveland Row; and Harcourt, who was consulted about how this awkward inquiry might best be answered, commented that 'people will probably want to know why access to a Museum is impossible when it was admissible to a Duke'. The answers were, however, skilfully fudged – the arrangements were only provisional, and to change them would entail considerable public expense, etc.; and so the matter lapsed.[72]

After the outbreak of the war in August 1914 there were more important things to think about. In November Sir Douglas Dawson was delighted when he heard (wrongly) that 'Stafford House' (as he still insisted on calling Lancaster House) was to be used as a Red Cross hospital.[73] But when the museum was closed early in 1916 and the building soon afterwards occupied by a Government ministry, he had to acquiesce in the permission, expressly given by the King himself, for the civil servants working there, and callers on business, to drive up to the entrance. This privilege did not, however, extend to visitors to the museum, few in number as they no doubt were at this time. Soon afterwards the policeman on duty at the west end of Cleveland Row was withdrawn,[74] and it seems likely that members of the staff of the museum were thereafter tacitly allowed to drive up whenever occasion arose. Probably they felt more secure in doing so after the retirement of Sir Douglas Dawson to the peaceful seclusion of his exceedingly ugly country seat in Berkshire in 1924.

Laking took five months in which to arrange the museum in its new home. He was determined to make 'a better display than we had in our previous "hurried existence"',[75] and by mid October 1913 he was (as he told Lord Esher) 'pulling to pieces every case and re-arranging everything in strict chronological order, to leave as little room as possible for press attacks'.[76] What one journalist aptly described as 'The gentle compulsion of a fixed route through the building' was to be exercised upon visitors,[77] who after crossing the *porte cochère* and spacious vestibule passed through a series of ground-floor rooms in which the life of London from the prehistoric age to the end of the fifteenth century was presented. Monsieur Amédée Forestier's drawings enlivened the walls of some of the rooms devoted to the earlier periods, the great sun-lit dining-room on the south side of the house was used to illustrate Roman Londinium, and in the adjoining corner room was displayed the museum's collection of jewellery and gold. Thence the visitor returned to the main hall to mount the famous staircase leading to the principal reception rooms, where Tudor, Stuart and Georgian times were presented in an increasingly wide range of exhibits. The culmination of the tour was reached in the great galleries devoted to costume, which in turn found their climax in the uniforms and robes of State worn on great occasions by successive members of the royal family. These were now exhibited to much greater advantage than at Kensington, being placed in a curved recess at one end of a long gallery, protected (it was hoped) from moth and all other forms of corruption by a great sheet of floor-to-ceiling plate glass. Lastly, the visitor descended by a poky little spiral staircase to the basement, where the LCC's architectural pieces, the prison cells and other criminal relics, several horse-drawn vehicles of various sorts, and, of course, the Roman Boat, formed the main attractions.[78] The top floor of the building, which contained a series of much smaller rooms, was not yet ready to be used for display purposes.

Even so, there was vastly more floor space at Lancaster House than there had been at Kensington Palace, and the rooms themselves, being bigger, were much better suited for the easy circulation of large numbers of visitors. The museum's collections had also been much enriched, and were well worthy of their splendid new setting. First of all there was the Cheapside Hoard, now publicly exhibited for the first time, which attracted an embarrassing amount of notice in the press. 'Curiously, little has been heard about the hoard, as all the officials maintain an intense silence on the subject', said *The Manchester Guardian*. 'No one seems to know anything about it. . . . Many stories are current', etc.[79] There was also the Tangye collection of Cromwelliana, which included Cromwell's Bible and (always a most popular item) the reputed skull of Richard Brandon, the executioner of Charles I. More Chelsea porcelain had been

142 *Aerial perspective of Lancaster House as occupied by the London Museum, 1914*

143 *London in about 1400. Detail of watercolour by Amédée Forestier*

145 *Saxon London display (top)*

146 *Knitted caps and leather footwear on
display in the costume gallery
(above)*

144 *The costume gallery, Lancaster House (top)*

147 *The eighteenth-century gallery (above)*

149 *Seventeenth-century panelled room.*
A reconstruction of an early seventeenth-century room with panelling taken from a house in Wandsworth

150/151 *Oliver Cromwell's Bible and Richard Brandon's skull.*
This autographed Bible and the skull of Charles I's executioner were from the Tangye collection of Cromwelliana

148 *Eighteenth-century porcelain given by Mr Joicey, as displayed at Lancaster House*
(left)

provided by Mrs Salting,[80] and the costume display had been enhanced by the loan of the Coronation robes of George V and Queen Mary and by Mrs Abbey's gift of the costume formerly used in his historical pictures by her late husband, Edwin A Abbey, RA.[81] Sir Harry Waechter had presented a collection of over a hundred antique firearms[82] – a goodwill gesture which enabled him, as an important donor, to associate himself publicly with the museum. Other recent gifts, for display in the basement, included a very fine Georgian shopfront from High Holborn and a manual fire engine from Southwark;[83] but the offer of a bathing machine, which was at first enthusiastically acclaimed by Laking, seems finally to have been refused. 'Where on earth can I put it in Lancaster House?' he asked. The equally important question, whether bathing machines were ever used anywhere in London, seems not to have been raised.[84]

All these gifts were, however, outweighed by yet more contributions from Mr Joicey. In September 1913 there came a collection of leatherwork,[85] in October he purchased some extremely fine metropolitan slipware for the museum, and rather later there was a great clock, twelve feet high, which had been exhibited at the Exhibition of 1862 and which was most effectively displayed by Laking on the half-landing of the great staircase at Lancaster House.[86] 'Friend Joicey is still magnificent', Laking reported to Harcourt, 'and gifts arrive daily from him. . . . He is now on his way to Florence to inspect some 17th century English Costumes that he has been advised of.'[87] And, sure enough, early in the New Year there arrived from Mr Joicey three large chests which, when opened, disclosed 'such treasures' as in Laking's opinion 'I did not think existed. Costumes dating from the middle of the 16th century, also of the 17th and 18th century, not commonplace examples, but with the most magnificent embroidery and of the finest quality of material.' There were also six of 'the most remarkable hats, dating from Elizabeth to James I, I should think in existence, – The Victoria and Albert Museum possess one poor specimen only'. The whole collection must have cost Joicey thousands of pounds. 'Do please write him a letter personally', Laking asked Harcourt, 'it means so much to him, and will spur him on to fresh efforts'. And Harcourt duly obliged.[88]

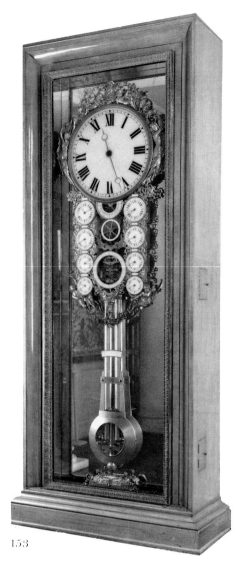

152

153

By this time Mr Joicey had branched out in another equally valuable and costly direction – models of 'Old London' (*ie* pre-Fire London). 'Your idea of the models is too splendid', Laking had told him in September 1913, 'there is no doubt the British Public prefer them to anything'. At Lancaster House there would be room for a large number of them, he was told, and so before he left for Italy Mr Joicey ordered a whole clutch of models to be made. These included a large one from J B Thorp of the Tower, and half a dozen smaller ones from J P Maginnis and W H Godfrey.[89] The latter consisted of individual models of several of the great houses which stood along the Thames between the City and Westminster, as they appeared in *c.*1650. When the whole great project was completed it was intended that all the component parts should be fitted together to form one enormous panoramic scenario. Models actually delivered by Maginnis and Godfrey included Northumberland House, the New Exchange (in the Strand), Somerset House and the Savoy, Cecil House, Winchester House and Durham House. The last of these was not delivered until early in 1916, for Maginnis and Godfrey proved very dilatory, and the plan then lapsed without either of the *pièces de résistance* – Whitehall Palace and Westminster Abbey – having been made.[90]

154

The most famous of all the London Museum's models was, however, that of the Great Fire; and the idea for this firm favourite of all the museum's exhibits undoubtedly originated with Mr Joicey himself, whilst he was in Italy.[91] It was made by Thorp and delivered to the museum, together with another one showing a Frost Fair on the Thames, in the autumn of 1914. The revolving electric lamps which created the illusion of flames were ready a week or two later,[92] and other improvements have been made to the model in later years. When the London Museum returned to Kensington Palace in 1951 the Fire model went too, and thence it was transferred to the Museum of London, where its realism has been greatly enhanced.

Joicey's last major benefaction to the museum (apart from the bequests contained in his will) was to pay for the cost of converting the rooms on the top floor of Lancaster House into exhibition galleries. In March 1914 he was offering to give the 'contents of a Map and Print Room' if a suitable room could be found there, and a few weeks later he asked Laking 'what Mr. Harcourt and you would best like me to do, on the top floor'. By this time the Office of Works had prepared plans for the necessary

152 *Flintlock pistol with bayonet by Griffin of London, c.1780, and triple- barrelled pistol by Twigg, c.1800.*
Sir Harry Waechter presented a collection of over one hundred firearms to the museum in 1913. His secret and, in this instance, public benefactions were outstanding contributions to the museum's success

153 *Regulator clock made in London by W Davis and Sons, showing the time and date in London, and simultaneously, the time in eight other cities throughout the world. Displayed at the Exhibition of 1862 and subsequently acquired for the museum by Mr Joicey*

154 *Georgian shopfront at 181 High Holborn.*
The London Museum gradually acquired a collection of shopfronts; this early acquisition was displayed in Lancaster House

conversion work,[93] but after the outbreak of war the idea was abandoned.[94] So in April 1915 Joicey agreed to pay the full cost – £1850 – which he duly did; and the work was completed in October 1915.[95]

But we must now return to the spring of 1914, when the opening of the museum was still impending. In January thirty-six 'groups' of items of costume from the Abbey collection, each male 'group' consisting of a coat, waistcoat and (where available) breeches or, in the case of a female 'group', of a dress, petticoat and bodice, were selected 'to marry one with the other' by Laking's friend Seymour Lucas, the history painter. The items in each 'group' were then tied together in a bundle and sent up to Nathan's, the Court costumiers, who were instructed to iron everything and to 'supply breeches where necessary, shoes, shirts with ruffs etc., in short make each tied-up bundle a complete costume'.[96] Soon afterwards Nathan's replied that in order to make all this material complete for exhibition it would be necessary for them to provide twenty-seven shirts and an approximately equivalent number of cravats and pairs of ruffles, breeches, shoes, shoe buckles, stockings and knee buckles, plus 'other items such as hoops and other underwear'. If real breeches were not available they would 'adapt or dye other old and suitable garments, altering their character to the desired period. . .'. For these and other services rendered early in 1914 Nathan's charged £1021 – a very substantial sum by the museum's economical standards.[97]

Models of the Tower of London (155) and of a Frost Fair on the Thames (157), made in 1914 by J B Thorp (seen at work on the Tower model, 156) and paid for by Mr Joicey

Another expensive item was the guarding of Lancaster House and its contents. At Harcourt's insistence this was done by policemen serving in the Metropolitan Police, who were supplied by New Scotland Yard. After the galleries had been opened the museum's little force consisted of an inspector, a sergeant, and sixteen constables.[98]

By the beginning of March the situation at Lancaster House was, as Laking described it to Lord Esher, 'rather like a Drury Lane production, when the day for the performance is fixed, things are a little behind hand'.[99] Ten days later, and only a week before the opening, he asked Harcourt to come for half an hour 'to walk quietly with me through the finished galleries. I do not mind telling you now, I am feeling the strain a little, and a certain amount of responsibility.'[100] On Wednesday 18 March there was a reception for the press, for whom Mr Joicey thoughtfully provided champagne. On Thursday the museum was closed for cleaning. On Friday the King and Queen, accompanied by Princess Mary, paid a private visit, at which only the Trustees, Laking and Sir William Lever were present. The tour lasted three hours, and afterwards the King sent a message of congratulation. On the following day there was a private view for benefactors, and finally, on Monday 23 March 1914, the London Museum was opened to the public.[101]

Two months later Laking's father, Sir Francis Laking, the Court physician, died, and the title passed to his only son, for whom a baronetcy somehow seems peculiarly appropriate. And in the Birthday Honours in June 1914 Sir Guy was made a Companion of the Order of the Bath. Harcourt had of course arranged this, as Laking knew perfectly well, just as he knew that Harcourt had arranged a baronetcy for Sir Harry Waechter. But this in no way diminished the value which Sir Guy placed upon his CB.[102] After all, he had not bought it, and he had not inherited it; he had been given it just for sheer personal merit.

Laking's new London Museum at Lancaster House was immediately acclaimed with enthusiasm by both the press and the public. 'We take our hats off to Mr. Guy Francis Laking', said one popular daily paper, 'A great idea has been carried out with astonishing success', said another, while *The Graphic* commented at greater length that 'Mr. Laking is not only a man of extraordinary industry and keenness, he also has imagination and rare taste, so that the arrangement of the museum is beyond all criticism'.[103] It was therefore a harsh turn of fate to Sir Guy that the days of his triumph proved to be short and soon to be overshadowed by the war and by his own illness. Only two months after its opening, when well over 82 000 visitors had already passed through the turnstiles,[104] the museum had to be closed on 22 May for fear of attacks by militant suffragettes. Then on 4 August came the outbreak of World War I, in which, despite his natural inclination, Laking's rapidly deteriorating health prevented his taking any active part. After the withdrawal of all further threats by the suffragettes the museum was, however, reopened on 17 August, and by the end of 1914 over 184 000 people had visited it.[105] It remained open until 1 February 1916, when (along with all the other national museums) it was closed for the duration of the war.[106]

By that time about half the museum's little staff had joined up. In 1914 Herbert Murray had rather unexpectedly become 'Sub Purchaser for Horses' in Eastern Command, later attaining the rank of Captain. Despite Laking's urgings to 'Join the old flock again', he did not return to the museum after the war.[107] Harry Osmond on the other hand, who had been appointed 'Porter and Cloak Room Attendant' in May 1914,

158 *Mrs Pankhurst being arrested outside Buckingham Palace in 1914 during a Suffragette demonstration. From the museum's extensive collection of Suffragette material*

IT IS FAR BETTER
TO FACE THE BULLETS
THAN TO BE KILLED
AT HOME BY A BOMB

JOIN THE ARMY AT ONCE
& HELP TO STOP AN AIR RAID

GOD SAVE THE KING

159 *Recruiting poster, World War I*

served in the Devonshire Regiment from 1915 to 1919[108] and returned to the museum's service for over thirty years, latterly as doorkeeper. And lastly there was Maurice Read, next to Laking the longest-serving member of the staff, who had been the museum's typist since March 1911. He joined up in March 1916 and was killed on the Somme on 16 September, aged twenty-two.[109]

Laking seems for reasons of health to have spent much of the war years in the country. His museum correspondence shows that between 1911 and 1914 he had frequently been ill (or 'seedy' as he called it),[110] severe bronchitis being the main trouble. Soon after the opening of the museum at Kensington Palace in March 1912 he had had 'a severe illness, which necessitated his laying up for some weeks'.[111] In November 1914 he was living at his 'country' house, York Gate, Broadstairs,[112] and later he was for a while at Wargrave, near Henley.[113] In the summer of 1915 he stayed with Lewis Harcourt at Nuneham Park, where he proved to be 'a dreadful duffer at cards',[114] and in the autumn he was at Barton Manor in the Isle of Wight, where he rearranged the royal museum at Osborne.[115] In the spring of 1918 his doctors ordered him to 'lie up' for at least three months with heart trouble, and he took 'quite a small place' at Esher.[116] For a while there was some improvement,[117] but in November he was 'seriously ill with pneumonia, following influenza and heart trouble', and was going to be away for 'some considerable time'.[118]

All these afflictions did not, however, prevent his actively looking after the museum. He was particularly anxious to acquire exhibits illustrating London in wartime, and he even got Harcourt to ask the Home Secretary (Sir John Simon) at a Cabinet meeting for permission to photograph damage done during the zeppelin air raids.[119] Other acquisitions included two bombs, a set of war posters from the Stationery Office, an air-raid siren, menus from the Savoy Hotel, women's uniforms, and a map of London found in a German aeroplane shot down after a raid on the capital.[120] And as late as August 1919 he was wanting to get hold of a twenty-hundredweight anti-aircraft gun (of which more later).[121]

The museum remained shut for three and a half years. Immediately after its closure on 1 February 1916 Lancaster House was taken over by the Foreign Trade Department, which remained in occupation until May 1918, when it was replaced by no less than 180 members of the staff of the Shipping Controller.[122] By that time fifty-three cases containing the most valuable of the museum's exhibits had as a precaution against air raids been removed (in April 1918) to a tunnel being constructed for the Post Office tube railway in the City.[123] But only four days after the signature of the armistice on 11 November 1918 Harcourt was having them brought back, and requested the Office of Works 'to eject' the Shipping Controller and 'reconstitute' the galleries on the top floor, for which Mr Joicey had paid but which had never yet been used by the museum.[124] In February 1919 the Shipping Controller was still in occupation of Lancaster House, and Harcourt (who had been created a Viscount in 1916) raised the matter in the House of Lords.[125] Eventually the occupation came to an end in July 1919,[126] the Office of Works did some rapid remedial work on the building, and after three months of strenuous exertion by Laking and his little band of helpers, the museum reopened on 22 October 1919. The display included several of the galleries provided by Mr Joicey on the top floor, where there were prints and drawings and three rooms devoted to London during the war years.[127]

Sadly, Mr Joicey did not live to see this happy day, for he had died at Broadstairs on 8 July 1919, aged fifty-six, leaving effects valued at nearly £250000. Subject to life interests to his brother and sister, he bequeathed

£50000 for the founding of a museum in Newcastle upon Tyne to be called the John George Joicey Museum, and the residue to the Trustees of the London Museum for the purchase of exhibits.[128] After the termination of the life interests in 1942, Mr Joicey's Trustees used his bequest to Newcastle in 1969-71 to restore the derelict Holy Jesus Hospital (the only remaining Jacobean brick building in that city) and convert it into a very fine and flourishing museum of local history, named, as he had stipulated, after its founder. The residue of the estate, amounting to over £25000, has since 1944 been successively used by the Trustees of the London Museum and latterly by the Governors of the Museum of London for the purpose prescribed by Mr Joicey, to the lasting enrichment of the collections. He had indeed been a great benefactor, who from first to last had in all his dealings with the London Museum behaved, in Laking's words, 'in a most princely manner'.[129]

Some four months later the museum suffered an even greater loss in the death of Sir Guy Laking. He had written his last letter on behalf of the museum on the day after its reopening – very characteristically, a letter of thanks to the Office of Works for 'the excellent way in which the work of redecoration has been carried out'.[130] But he had over-taxed his strength, and soon afterwards became seriously ill again. By mid-November, when Queen Alexandra sent a telegram of inquiry, he was slipping away, and he died on 22 November 1919 at his London home at Meyrick Lodge, Avenue Road, aged only forty-four.[131]

It is almost impossible to conceive of the London Museum without Sir Guy Laking. He, far more than any of the other three founder-figures – Harcourt, Esher and Waechter – put the indelible stamp of his own personality and outlook upon the museum. He had been the professional man in day-to-day charge, who had decided such fundamental matters as the arrangement of the galleries in chronological order, and who had laid it down from the very beginning that 'dullness in a museum is the deadliest of all sins'. 'If you set out to teach you are apt to fail in your object because you run the risk of becoming dull', he thought. 'On the other hand, if you seek to interest and amuse, you may be able to achieve something incidentally in the way of teaching.'[132] So it was he who had welcomed or even sought out such 'popular' exhibits as the prison cells or the Roman Boat or the model of the Great Fire; and it was he who had infused his little band of devoted colleagues with his own tremendous energy and enthusiasm. He had, moreover, a deep feeling for London itself, where almost all his life had been passed. He actively concerned himself with the defence from demolition of its ancient buildings, which he regarded as 'of daily increasing value to London, both as examples of architecture and as links of association with a byegone age'; and he even publicly castigated the City Corporation for its 'scandalous' destruction of a large number of old houses in Cloth Fair.[133] But he remained to the very end hopeful and full of *joie de vivre*. 'London can never be exhausted', he wrote shortly before his death. 'Let us then get its history and associations more and more into our thoughts, into our very blood, till we rightly recognise that of a surety are we citizens of no mean city.'[134]

The funeral service took place at the Chapel Royal at St James's Palace, both the King and Queen Alexandra being represented, and the burial was at Highgate Cemetery. Sir Guy left a widow and a young son and daughter, but all three died within a few years, and the baronetcy became extinct. His collection of arms and armour and *objets d'art* was sold by auction at Christie's in 1920 and yielded over £34000.[135]

After Laking's death the immediate problem for the Trustees was the appointment of a successor. If there were not exactly any skeletons in

160 *Cloth Fair looking west, 1904: watercolour by Philip Norman*

161 *G F Harman Oates, 1922.*
Sir Guy Laking died in November 1919
and was succeeded as keeper of the London
Museum by his assistant, Harman Oates

* By this time Sir Harry had suffered
severe lung damage from gas poisoning
during the war, and (accompanied by his
mistress, his marriage having broken up)
he had gone to live in Rhodesia, where he
bought land near Salisbury and died in
1929. He seems to have had no contact
with the London Museum after 1915.[136]

the London Museum's cupboards, there were nevertheless one or two little matters, notably the Waechter baronetcy and 'the Fund' arising therefrom, which had still (in the interests of propriety) to be kept quiet for some while. Although Sir Harry Waechter might well not have minded much if the whole transaction had been made public,* Lords Harcourt and Esher would certainly have been a little embarrassed thereby. The principal qualification for Laking's successor therefore had to be discretion – someone upon whom the Trustees could rely implicitly to keep his mouth shut. So of course they appointed Harman Oates; or rather they recommended Oates's appointment as keeper and secretary at a salary of £500 to the Prime Minister (Lloyd George), who agreed. They also recommended that Lord Esher's younger son, Lieutenant-Colonel the Hon Maurice Brett, should be appointed part-time assistant keeper and librarian at a salary of £250 per annum; and the Treasury agreed to that too.[137]

Harman Oates's service as Keeper lasted until his retirement in 1926. He was very much the creature of the Trustees, and at times the almost sycophantic tone of his letters to Harcourt or Esher echoes that of the relationship of servant and master – 'I think you know you can count on my absolute support and fidelity. . . .' etc.; and he usually signed himself 'Always yours loyally.'[138] But it would nevertheless be a mistake to belittle Harman Oates. He was in charge (albeit under the Trustees' thumbs) at a very difficult period in the museum's history; and he undoubtedly possessed the personal confidence of the King and Queen – an essential virtue for the keeper at that time. In December 1920 the King appointed him keeper of the King's Armoury, much to the satisfaction of Queen Mary, who commented to Lord Esher that 'I am glad to feel we shall have a good friend in him'.[139] In 1922 he was made a Member of the Victorian Order, a distinction granted for important or personal services to the Sovereign, and he was also given apartments at Windsor Castle, perhaps at Lord Esher's instigation. On his return to his office at Lancaster House after his fairly frequent visits to Buckingham Palace he always had a rose in his buttonhole, for which Walter Henderson, then a young messenger at the museum, had to provide water and a suitable vase.[140]

Harman Oates's difficulties were compounded by his own want of expertise in matters antiquarian – relative, at any rate, to that of his predecessor, Laking, or to that of any of his successors – and by the almost total lack of it in his sole curatorial assistant (apart from Lawrence, who was seldom at the museum). Colonel Brett's appointment as assistant keeper and librarian prompted a correspondent of the *Pall Mall Gazette* to comment that 'He seems to know a good deal about horses, but I never knew he was an authority on antiques or books before.'[141] He is remembered by one of his colleagues at the museum as an agreeable gentleman who asked for nothing more than a good book to read at the fireside of his beautiful office at Lancaster House, where he was 'very nicely, thank you'.[142]

By far the most important event in Harman Oates's years as keeper was the death of Lord Harcourt, on 24 February 1922, at the age of fifty-nine. He was the true author and begetter of the London Museum. It had, in his own words, been 'the dream of my life to establish a London (Carnavalet) Museum',[143] and by his own ability and sheer force of character he had made his dream come true. He had fashioned the museum out of nothing, and in so doing had taken considerable risks with his own public career and reputation. Today he is largely forgotten – much more so than is Lord Esher, his lifelong friend and coadjutor at the museum – but the Museum of London provides an enduring and fitting monument to him as well as to his son, who was to be its more immediate creator.

Lord Harcourt died in bed at his house at No 69 Brook Street, Mayfair, to which he had in 1920 removed from Berkeley Square. He had been in ill-health for over two years, and at the subsequent inquest it was said that death was due to heart failure, accelerated by an overdose of sleeping draughts. The Coroner's verdict was 'death by misadventure'.[144] A memorial service was held at St Margaret's, Westminster, and burial was in the family vault at the old parish church at Nuneham Courtenay.[145] He was deeply mourned by his widow, who wrote a number of touching letters to Lord Esher about her bereavement; and also by his son William, second Viscount Harcourt, who had just started school at Eton and who in later life was to become chairman of the Governors of the Museum of London. 'It will change everything, even Nuneham if he is not there', he wrote to Lord Esher, 'he used to make everything there go'....[146]   ◨

Only a few months before Lord Harcourt's death Lord Esher had written him a most affectionate letter reviewing their long and close friendship. 'I feel that no one else is quite like you or can fill your place', he had concluded.[147] And this very soon turned out to be the case, for on 28 February, within a week of his death, Lord Harcourt's solicitors and executors, Walker, Martineau and Company, wrote to 'the Curator' of the London Museum (*ie* Oates) to inform him that there was over £40000 on deposit in Harcourt's London Museum account at Messrs Child and Company's Bank, and asking for information about Harcourt's co-Trustees.[148]

The London Museum's 'Fund' had originated in the £30000 paid in 1910–11 by Harry Waechter for his baronetcy. We have already seen that by 31 March 1913 some two thirds of this sum had been spent and that there remained some £10586, exclusive of interest earned. In the ensuing sixteen months before the outbreak of war Harcourt provided cheques for over £4360 for purchases and/or unspecified purposes.[149] During the war years little more than £500 was spent out of the Fund,[150] but between Laking's death in 1919 and Harcourt's in 1922 it was used for payments amounting to about £1000.[151] Harcourt was certainly careful to invest the Fund to the best advantage – in 1917, for instance, he asked Child and Company what rate of interest would be available 'if I were to discount the whole of the Treasury Bills on my London Museum Account and deposit the money with you at long notice'[152] – but the scale of the payments made out of the Fund between 1913 and 1922 does nevertheless indicate that as there was over £40000 in it when Harcourt died, there may have been another contributor or contributors to it besides Sir Harry Waechter.

A letter which Harcourt wrote to Esher in 1919, and which will be mentioned again later, certainly indicates that there were several such donors, for in reference to the Fund he mentioned 'the receipt of our last big donation' as having been made shortly before August 1913.[153] From the earliest days of the museum both Harcourt and Laking had frequently persuaded generous men of substance into paying for the acquisition of particular items – Joicey, of course, on numerous occasions, Sir Harry Waechter in 1915 for casts to be made of the medieval effigies in Great St Helen's and the Temple Church,[154] a Mr Warre who paid £80 for a picture of Greenwich Park,[155] Alan Hooke for two pictures by Paul Sandby, and so on.[156] Cecil Harmsworth, MP and later chairman of

Associated Newspapers Limited, spent £500 on behalf of the museum at an auction sale in June 1913,[157] and it was probably he who subsequently provided six hundred guineas to buy one hundred topographical drawings of London (mostly previously on loan) by Dr Philip Norman.[158] All these sums are, however, small in relation to the £40000 in the Fund at the time of Harcourt's death. Within the museum there was, on the other hand, a long tradition that the founding benefactors were (in addition to Sir Harry Waechter) Pierpont Morgan, Alfred de Rothschild and Joseph Duveen (latterly Baron Duveen).[159] All three of these exceedingly rich gentlemen were either friends or associates of either Harcourt or Esher or Laking – Harcourt's wife, indeed, was Pierpont Morgan's niece – and all three of them gave or lent one or two items to the museum in its early days. But no evidence has been found in support of this tradition, and their names did not appear on the Benefactors' Board which Harcourt caused to)be erected in the hall at Lancaster House, though that of Sir Harry Waechter did appear on it.[160]* So if there were any other large contributors to the Fund, their identity remains a mystery.

When Oates received the letter of 28 February from Walker, Martineau and Company, he immediately got in touch with Lord Esher, who was in Paris on public business. Esher on 2 March sent a letter to Oates which has not survived. He also enclosed a letter to Walker, Martineau, in which he informed them that in Lord Harcourt's safe they would find a document signed by both Harcourt and by Esher, the purpose of which was to prevent the Fund being calculated for probate purposes among Harcourt's personal assets. This document had evidently been drawn up by Harcourt in 1919 as a precaution against such an undesirable contingency, and at his request it had been signed also by Esher – hence the letter previously referred to in connection with donations to the Fund. In this letter of 1919 Harcourt had stated that 'these monies are the sole property of the Trustees of the London Museum and on my death should be transferred to the survivors'. . . .[162]

In his letter of 2 March Lord Esher also informed Walker, Martineau that 'As the Fund was privately administered by *him* [*Harcourt*] on behalf of himself and myself as Trustees of the *contents* of the London Museum I am the person who in due course must give a receipt to the Executors or Messrs. Child and Co.'

On 3 March Oates reported to Lord Esher that, as instructed, he had forwarded the letter to Walker, Martineau, and he also sent Esher the deed of loan of 1 July 1913 kept in the museum's safe whereby the Trustees had laid down the terms on which the contents of the museum had been placed at the disposal of the Government at Lancaster House. 'Whatever, my dear Lord, you decide to do', Oates had concluded, 'I think you know you can count on my absolute support and fidelity and I deeply appreciate the confidence you have so generously expressed to me with reference to the transference of the fund'.

There is no doubt that the Fund was in fact transferred to Lord Esher.[163] Nor is there any doubt that during Harcourt's lifetime both he and Harcourt had regarded themselves as Trustees of the Fund, which was to be used for the benefit of the London Museum.[164]

After Lord Harcourt's death in 1922 Lord Esher had, of course, become chairman of the Trustees, and remained so until his own death in 1930. He had at first been much concerned about whom Lloyd George might appoint to fill the vacancy on the Board – 'It is most important to see that the PM does not push some one in that I do not like . . .', he told Maurice Brett.[165] Lloyd George did not, however, make any appointment, and went out of office in October 1922. In fact no Trustees' meeting took

162 *Camelford House, Park Lane, 1913: detail of watercolour by Philip Norman (top)*

163 *Holywell Street looking east, 1901: watercolour by Philip Norman (above)*

* The full list of benefactors named on the board in 1920 was: the King and Queen, Queen Alexandra, Joicey, Lord Leverhulme, H J Mankiewicz (who presented some fine views of London), and Sir Harry Waechter. The names of Charles Edward Jerningham and Sir Robert Nevison, Bart, were probably added in 1921.[161]

[92] place for a year after Harcourt's death, until February 1923, when Lord Esher took the chair for the first time, Bonar Law's new First Commissioner of Works, Sir John Baird, who was indeed at that time the only other member of the Board, being also present.[166] Later in the year, however, Viscount Lascelles was nominated by Bonar Law as a Trustee. His wife was Princess Mary, daughter of King George and Queen Mary, and he was therefore the King's son-in-law. In 1929 he succeeded to the Earldom of Harewood, and after Lord Esher's death in the following year he served as chairman of the Trustees until his own death in 1947. And in 1925 Viscount Burnham, proprietor of *The Daily Telegraph*, also joined the Board.

Meetings of this tiny aristocratic council were infrequent – except during 1926 there was hardly ever more than one a year – and the existence of the Fund is not mentioned at all in the minutes. Purchases of specimens did, however, continue, most of them being of an archaeological nature and therefore presumably bought from Lawrence for quite small sums; and in 1922 Lord Esher contemplated buying a more expensive item (a panelled room from a house in Highgate), but did not actually do so.[167] In 1926, however, Dr Mortimer Wheeler was appointed keeper in succession to Harman Oates, to the chagrin of Lord Esher, who had wanted and indeed some time before actually promised the job to his son.[168] Dr Wheeler's arrival brought into the curatorial staff for the first time an outsider who did not know about the history of the Fund.[169] Lawrence retired in the same year, 1926;[170] and whether for these or other reasons purchases of all kinds virtually ceased in 1927.

What is known thereafter about the Fund is best related here, though it falls outside the chronological scope of the present chapter. In 1927 a Royal Commission was established to inquire into the National Museums and Galleries. Dr Wheeler submitted a memorandum on behalf of the Trustees and subsequently, in October 1928, he gave evidence to the Commission orally. In answer to the question 'How much do you spend on purchases at the London Museum?' he replied 'Not a penny. We have no purchase-fund at all at the London Museum. . . . We have to rely entirely on private benefaction, which is sometimes obtainable in the case of large and valuable specimens but is difficult to ask for in the case of small things which are of equal historical importance in themselves.'[171] In an appendix published by the Commission in 1929, and based, it cannot be doubted, upon information supplied to it by Wheeler on behalf of the Trustees, the London Museum is listed as having no 'permanent benefactions, endowments, trust funds and other non-official donations' from which it was 'at present benefiting';[172] and in its final report, dated January 1930, the Commission stated categorically – again, based, it cannot be doubted, upon information from the same source – that the London Museum did not 'enjoy any permanent private endowment fund for the acquisition of specimens'.[173]

One of the recommendations made by the Royal Commission was that the number of Trustees of the London Museum should be increased. After Lord Esher's death in 1930 this proposal was quickly implemented, one of the new members of the greatly enlarged Board being Lord Esher's son, Oliver, third Viscount Esher (1881–1963), who by his marriage had become a man of wealth and leisure. His name had first been proposed by Wheeler, who in February 1930 had made various suggestions to Lord Harewood, then the heir apparent to the chairmanship. Lord Harewood had been slightly doubtful about the new Lord Esher, but his name had nevertheless gone forward to the Prime Minister (Ramsay MacDonald) and in due course been approved.[174]

The first meeting of the new Board, attended by no fewer than nine members, including Oliver Esher, took place on 5 June 1930. By that time, however, the new Lord Esher had received a letter from his brother Maurice, the assistant keeper. For this impending meeting, Colonel Brett had written,[175] 'I want you to consider the following: – At the meeting Wheeler will tell the Trustees of his great ambition, which is to have a Scholarship in Archaeology founded by the Museum and devoted to *London* archaeology. No other Museum has a scholarship and it is an innovation and a badly needed one. My idea is that when he explains it you should jump in and say that you think it a wonderful idea and will give the necessary £300 pa for ten years. You might say that you give it in [*Reginald Esher's*] memory as it would look well in the Press and it would, of course, be called the "Esher Scholarship".' And all this duly came to pass, more or less. At the meeting on 5 June Dr Wheeler presented his customary report, in the course of which (so the minutes record) he 'expressed the hope that in the future the Museum might be placed in a position to do for higher education and research what it was already attempting to do for elementary and secondary education'. Whereupon Oliver Esher immediately 'expressed his willingness to place the sum of £300 annually at the disposal of the Trustees for ten years for the purpose of promoting original research into the history or archaeology of Greater London'.[176] This offer was accepted, and for seven years he financed the Esher Research Studentship in memory of his father.* But in December 1937 he informed the Trustees that 'he was compelled reluctantly to discontinue' the studentship. It was, however, continued by the Leverhulme Trustees, who were persuaded to renew the association between the first Lord Leverhulme (died 1925), as donor of the lease of Lancaster House, and the London Museum; and they accordingly agreed to maintain a Leverhulme Research Studentship for five years, under conditions similar to those of the former Esher Studentship.[177] ◨

The early 1920s were not amongst the most distinguished in the history of the London Museum. It was Harcourt, in happy partnership with Sir Guy Laking, who had made 'everything go' there as well as at Nuneham Park; and now they were both dead. Lord Esher had never been so actively interested in the museum, essential as his contribution to its foundation had been; and now he was getting old, and spending much of his time at his house in distant Perthshire. The Treasury exercised an almost unbelievably tight grip over the museum's tiny ration of public money, which in 1926 amounted to only £4462 net, compared, for instance, with almost double that amount for the Wallace Collection four years earlier.[178] At Whitehall's instigation an admission charge of six pence on Wednesdays and Thursdays was introduced in 1921, in addition to the existing charge of one shilling on Tuesdays (reduced to six pence in 1935);[179] and even the keeper's wife was required to pay this levy if she visited her husband at his office on a paying day.[180]

So Harman Oates did not have an easy time of it. When the chairman of the Board is the doting father of the second-in-command, the man at least nominally in day-to-day charge has to tread warily. The voluminous correspondence between Lord Esher and Maurice Brett contains numerous references, often contemptuous in tone, to the keeper – Titus, as they called him, in allusion to Titus Oates, the perjurer notorious during the Popish Plot. Nevertheless his plebeian origins as a commercial traveller had their uses when it came to disposing of unwanted possessions,

* The three Esher Research students, and the subjects of their work, were: Mr G C Dunning, 'The dating and development of mediaeval pottery in London'; Miss M E Gibbs, 'Early charters of the cathedral church of St. Paul, London' (published in 1939 by the Royal Historical Society as volume lviii of Camden Miscellany Third Series); and T F Reddaway, 'The Rebuilding of London after the Great Fire of 1666' (published in 1940 by Jonathan Cape).

for he was 'a damned good seller'; and shortly before his retirement in 1926 they did their best, but without success, to get him an honour.[181]

The guarding, or patrolling, of the galleries was now done by police pensioners, many of them ex-servicemen, who were recruited by the Police Pensioners' Employment Association.[182] There was also the 'handy-man porter', David Sagar, a little man with a cloth cap who had been a galloper (*ie* messenger) in the 12/17th Lancers and who for many years presided in the workshop in the basement, latterly as head craftsman.[183] Above all there was Walter Henderson, one of half a dozen members of the staff who at various times gave almost all their working lives, and a great deal more of themselves as well, to the London Museum. In the early days of the war, and at a very early age, he had enlisted in the army and had served in France, where his left hand had been shot away. He had joined the museum in October 1915 as successor to Harry Osmond, who had just left for four years' military service. For some time Mr Henderson served as the museum's messenger, but on one occasion he had been ordered by an exasperated Harman Oates to lock himself in the Board Room and balance the monthly accounts, Oates himself having been unable to do so. After his successful elucidation of this problem Oates had encouraged him to take the examination for entry into the Civil Service, and by the early 1920s he had transferred to the administrative side of the museum. He remained there, except during the years 1939 to 1944, when he was again in the army, until his retirement in 1958, having served five successive keepers and directors.[184]

Despite his problems and limitations, Harman Oates's keepership certainly did have some useful achievements. Royal accessions, in the acquisition of which he almost certainly had a hand, included the loan, by King George, of the cradle used by Queen Victoria for all her children,[185] by Queen Mary of her own dolls' house,* and by Princess Alice of the Broadwood grand piano formerly belonging to Princess Charlotte, daughter of George IV. Mr P A S Phillips, a notable donor in these years, presented a fine collection of watercolours of London; the rector and churchwardens of St Martin in the Fields placed twenty-two magnificent pieces of ecclesiastical silver plate, mostly gilt, on permanent loan, and Mr and Mrs Ernest Makower gave the blue silk vest worn by Charles I on the scaffold – a portent of other benefactions from the Makowers in later years.[186] In 1923 there were even two valuable purchases, made presumably with money from the Fund, of a pair of Victorian oil paintings by Phoebus Levin of Covent Garden Market and Cremorne Gardens.[187]

The arrangement of the galleries on the top floor of Lancaster House was also largely Harman Oates's work. He devised the Children's Room, where both Royal and more 'common or garden' toys were displayed. In 1921 he used two small rooms and a corridor in the basement to exhibit a series of maps showing the growth of London.[188] Two years later he opened two or three new rooms upstairs for the first time, using them mostly for the display of pictures, and at about the same time the space devoted to the Great War was reduced, public interest in it having declined considerably.[189] Four little 'guide books', selling at three pence each and describing respectively the Pre-Historic Room, the Roman Room, the Anglo-Saxon Corridor and the Medieval Room, were produced, and there was also a selection of twenty-four postcards for sale at the turnstiles.[190] By 1925, shortly before Oates's retirement, Queen Mary felt able to say, after one of her periodic visits to Lancaster House, that 'she was extremely pleased with the whole museum, and expressed the opinion that it showed marked progress'.[191]

164 *Walter Henderson with his wife and daughter after receiving the* MBE *in 1958*

165 *Queen Mary's dolls' house*

* Not to be confused with the dolls' house designed by Sir Edwin Lutyens and presented to Queen Mary in 1923, and permanently exhibited at Windsor Castle.

166 *The Palace of Westminster and Westminster Abbey, 1872: oil on canvas by John Anderson. Given by P A S Phillips*

167 *Covent Garden Market, 1864: oil on canvas by Phoebus Levin*

168 *The Dancing Platform at Cremorne Gardens, 1864: oil on canvas by Phoebus Levin*

The most important development of the early 1920s was, however, the establishment of regular lectures for schools – the foundation, in fact, of the educational service provided nowadays by the Museum of London. This was a matter particularly dear to Lewis Harcourt, if only because his father, Sir William Harcourt, had as early as 1874 unsuccessfully urged the employment of guide lecturers at the British Museum.[192] By 1912, when the London Museum opened at Kensington Palace, 'guide demonstrators' (as they were then called) had recently been appointed at both the Bloomsbury and South Kensington sections of the BM,[193] but at the London Museum there was as yet no money available for such a purpose; and even after the Treasury had assumed financial responsibility for the museum there were still no funds from which to pay for the 'Classes for Teachers' desired in 1914 by the metropolitan educational authority, the London County Council.[194]

Many schools did, nevertheless, send groups to the museum, in the Kensington days as well as to Lancaster House,[195] and when the Treasury agreed in 1920 to pay for a guide lecturer at the Wallace Collection, Lord Harcourt went to Whitehall to see what could be done for the London Museum.[196] Harman Oates told him that Colonel Brett, habitually short of money and as yet only working at the museum part-time, 'would take this work on';[197] and so it came about – for of course Lord Harcourt got what he wanted – that guide lecturing began at Lancaster House in April 1921.[198]

During the first finanical year, 1921–2, the project seems to have been conducted on an experimental basis, lectures being given to the public on Monday and Thursday afternoons at three o'clock.[199] School parties continued to pour in (some two hundred during the year), and by November 1921 Oates was arranging with the LCC for Colonel Brett to give special lectures to parties of elementary school children in 1922–3.[200] Sadly, however, Lord Harcourt had died (in February 1922) before this permanent system of lectures for schools began in April 1922. At least twelve lectures, each lasting half an hour, were given every week, mostly by Colonel Brett, and in the first year alone over eight thousand children received instruction in this way.[201]

Harcourt himself was personally responsible for the inauguration of this vital part of the work of the London Museum. At a much lower, day-to-day, level it was, however, Harman Oates who proved extremely good in the ticklish business of sharing the museum's nest with the Government's official guests. At first, in 1914, King George had objected to the use of Lancaster House for more than two or three small dinners a year;[202] but after the war there was a great proliferation of diplomatic and other quasi-official to-ings and fro-ings, and by the early 1920s about a dozen dinners, or large receptions for up to eighteen hundred people, were held there annually, the permission of the Trustees being requested for each event. The arrangements for these expensive occasions were made by the secretary of the Government Entertainment Fund (which was a part of the Office of Works) and caused much inconvenience for the museum, which had to be closed to the public for at least one day every time. Display cases had to be moved, and as guests were usually free to wander through the ground- and first-floor galleries, security had to be provided. At first all went well, and relations between Harman Oates and Mr J Conway Davies, the official in charge of Government hospitality, were extremely cordial – so cordial, in fact, that the Treasury even appointed Oates to take the requisite half-yearly stock of the Government's wines and spirits stored in the cellars of Lancaster House.[203] Unfortunately, however, this happy state of affairs came to an end soon after Conway Davies had been succeeded by Mr E E Beare in 1922. 'Keep Beare in order!', Lord Esher had thought it necessary to instruct Harman Oates in April 1924.[204]

In 1926, the year of Harman Oates's retirement, visitors to the London Museum numbered just over 240000; and this figure in itself provides favourable testimony to the quality of his keepership.[205] Yet for whatever reasons, the London Museum did in his years lose the vivacity and *brio* which it had had under Sir Guy Laking and was to have again (in a different style) under Dr Mortimer Wheeler; and this lack of drive is encapsulated in the droll incident of The Gun.

It was Sir Guy who had originally wanted it – a three-inch, twenty-hundred-weight anti-aircraft gun, 'if possible, one used in the London area', he had told the War Office in July 1919, adding with characteristic insouciance, 'if not troubling you too much, would you have the weapon forwarded to Lancaster House, at any time convenient'. Colonel Brett had gone to see somebody at the War Office about it,[206] and after a week or two the museum was informed that the matter was receiving attention.[207] After Laking's death in November Colonel Brett, being a military man, had taken the matter over, but he had not pressed it, and in May 1920 he may well have been surprised to receive a letter from Mr J C W Reith of the Ministry of Munitions (and later of the BBC) informing him that 'Gun Q.F. 3″ – 20cwt MKIII No. 1450 and Mounting H.A. No. 3376', which had been used near London, and was now in store at Chilwell in Nottinghamshire, could be made available for the museum. There was, however, a snag – the War Office had no funds to cover the expenses of transportation, 'but it is presumed that this matter had already been considered by the Museum Authorities'. Accordingly, he was 'making the necessary arrangements for the Gun to be moved from Chilwell to London by rail, but after that I am rather at a loss to know how this gun and mounting is to be conveyed from the Midland Railway Goods Station to Lancaster House'.[208]

Colonel Brett was evidently rather at a loss too, for it was Harman Oates who hastily replied. 'We find that the Public Interest in the War Rooms has somewhat abated', he wrote to Mr Reith, 'in fact, we have already closed one room, and filled it with water colour drawings of London !! In the circumstances, we think we cannot allow the War Office to incur the very considerable expenses there would be in removing the Gun, and fixing the same at Lancaster House. We therefore think, with your permission, that the matter should be dropped, and we will not trouble you to take any further steps to forward the Gun.'[209]

But it was too late – the Gun had already been dispatched from Chilwell. 'Under these circumstances', wrote another man from the Ministry, 'it would create a great deal of confusion if this Gun had to be returned after having to be written off charge, etc., [*so*] I must ask you to be good enough to accept the Gun and Mounting'. And he concluded helpfully that 'As the Gun is a free gift to you from Mr. Churchill [*then Secretary of State for War*] and the Army Council, it is immaterial to this Department what is done with it so long as the Advice Notes are signed and returned to Chilwell'.[210]

The arrival of the Gun at Lancaster House was, nevertheless, somehow averted. Perhaps it never got further than the Midland Railway's Goods Station, where it may conceivably still repose. However that may be, it is certainly impossible to imagine a gun, or any other museum specimen, being handled in such maladroit fashion under either Sir Guy Laking or Dr Mortimer Wheeler.

169 *George V, Queen Alexandra, the Dowager Empress of Russia and Queen Mary attending the wedding of Lady Mary Cambridge, 1923. The royal collections of the London Museum were dependent upon the generosity of British royal patrons in the pre- and post-World War I periods*

170 *St Pancras Hotel and Station from Pentonville Road, 1884: detail from oil on canvas by John O'Connor. Bought in 1952 for £220 with money from the Joicey Trust Fund.*
The London Museum gradually acquired a fine collection of paintings, prints and drawings illustrating the evolution of the capital

LATER YEARS OF THE LONDON MUSEUM
1926 to 1975

Chapter 5
LATER YEARS OF THE LONDON MUSEUM
1926 TO 1975

175 *Sir Mortimer Wheeler: pastel by J A Grant, 1960*

Photographs of London and its inhabitants provide a vivid record of the changes which have taken place over the last 150 years.

171 *The Strand and Nelson's Column, Trafalgar Square, c.1930. Note J Lyons and Co's Strand Corner House*

172 *Blackfriars Underground Station, c.1935*

173 *Prefabricated temporary houses on a bombed site in Clerkenwell, 1945*

174 *The Festival of Britain site, 1951, showing the Royal Festival Hall, the Dome of Discovery and the Skylon*

There are many different opinions about Dr R E M Wheeler (1890–1976), latterly Sir Mortimer Wheeler. For some of his contemporaries he was the greatest archaeologist of his day, a man of affairs of outstanding ability who could have made his mark in any walk of life. Others thought that his scholarship was flawed, or that he was a great machinator with an evil mind. For yet others, he was an inspiring leader to be loved and obeyed despite all his faults. Fortunately, a fine biographical portrait of this complex man has already been painted by Jacquetta Hawkes, and the historian of the London Museum needs only to concern himself with Wheeler's work as keeper of the museum from 1926 to 1944. There the record is plain and straightforward – he saved the museum from sinking into oblivion and even, perhaps, into extinction; he earned for it a recognized place in both the learned and the more popular fields of metropolitan cultural life; and he also used the museum as a base from which to further his own ends, archaeological and otherwise.

First and foremost, Dr Wheeler was a soldier. As a young man he had served in France with great distinction and been awarded the Military Cross; and much of what he did in later life was done in the military style. After a brief spell on the staff of the Royal Commission on Historical Monuments he had moved to Cardiff in 1920 as keeper of archaeology at the National Museum of Wales, of which he became director four years later. But it was only in London that his great ambition could be achieved – the establishment of an Institute of Archaeology for the systematic training of students in that infant but already rapidly growing science. And so by the summer of 1926 he had left what he had come to regard as the comfortable provincial security of Cardiff and was back in the metropolis as keeper of the London Museum.

Lord Esher had intended that the job should go to his son, Colonel Maurice Brett, the assistant keeper. Ever since he had become chairman of the Trustees after the death of Lord Harcourt in 1922, Lord Esher had irritated the Treasury with his demands for an increase in the salaries of both Harman Oates and Colonel Brett. 'Considerable expenditure of pathos from Lord Esher, mainly on behalf of the Assistant' was how a senior gentleman in Whitehall summarized the resulting correspondence. Finally he did get an extra £100 per annum for Oates, but when the Treasury mandarins realized that Colonel Brett's lectures to the school parties were only of half an hour's duration, they actually reduced his salary in July 1925.[1] At about the same time Lord Esher was also in hot water with the Treasury over another matter – the contract which he personally had made with a firm of printers for the production of picture postcards of museum exhibits, for sale at the entrance to Lancaster House; and early in 1926 he was having to eat humble pie – he would 'take care *no* further contracts shall be made . . . without full Treasury Sanction'.[2]

Lord Esher seems, however, to have been unaware of the displeasure with which he was evidently now regarded in Whitehall, at any rate so far as the London Museum was concerned. In October 1925 (when Harman Oates was approaching the compulsory retirement age of sixty-five) Esher wrote to Colonel Brett about 'trying to get the succession considered *now*. The atmosphere seems favourable.'[3] No meeting of the Trustees was, however, held until 15 January 1926, when the three members of the Board present – Esher, Viscount Lascelles and Viscount Burnham – unanimously decided that Lord Esher 'should see the Prime Minister [*Baldwin*] and ascertain whether in the event of the Assistant Keeper's name being proposed by the Trustees as Mr Harman Oates' successor, it would receive favourable consideration'.[4] This Lord Esher duly did, and was told, noncommittally, that he should 'set in motion the usual notification'.[5]

At this time Colonel Brett was aged only forty-three, and so this amiable but undistinguished man might well have held the keepership for over twenty years. It is painful even to contemplate what the fate of the London Museum might have been had this happened. Both Lord Burnham and Lord Lascelles nevertheless supported Brett's candidature, and the former even thought that the Trustees' recommendation to this effect should be sent to the Treasury forthwith, without another meeting of the Board. Lord Lascelles, however, thought that another meeting was 'essential', and this took place on 3 February.

By that time Lord Burnham had received three disturbing letters, two of them recommending the appointment of Dr Wheeler.[6] The first of these was from Lord Kenyon, President of the National Museum of Wales. 'Dr Mortimer Wheeler tells me that he is an applicant for the Directorship of the London Museum', he began. 'He is an excellent Director, full of resource and energy. . . . His subject being archaeology he seems peculiarly well fitted for the London Museum, especially when so much of underground London is being exposed as is the case now.' The author of the second letter was Walter Godfrey, architect to Crosby Hall, Chelsea, author-editor of several volumes of the *Survey of London* and an active Fellow of the Society of Antiquaries, on whose writing paper he now wrote.

'. . . my excuse for writing to you is the anxiety felt by London antiquaries in a decision which I believe the Trustees of the London Museum are about to make. It is common knowledge that since the Guildhall was unfortunate enough to lose the services of Mr [*Frank*] Lambert [*Museum Clerk at the Guildhall Museum 1907–24*], whose researches into Roman London are well known, no reliable expert has been available to watch the excavations which proceed daily in the City in the various building reconstructions. In nearly all these cases the whole strata recording Roman and Medieval London are removed and destroyed, and the absence of detailed observation is a calamity.

'It has been hoped in many quarters that on the retirement of Mr Harman Oates of the London Museum the services of an archaeologist of proved reputation might be obtained. . . . There is one candidate who stands out as pre-eminently fitted for this work, and this is Dr R E Mortimer Wheeler. . . . [*He*] has proved himself a brilliant exponent of just those things which touch most on the antiquities of London. If he could be prevailed upon to exchange Cardiff for London, it would be an event of very great archaeological moment.

'I am sure all prominent antiquaries will endorse my view, and feel that the London Museum has a great opportunity for performing a vital service towards the elucidation of the history of London.'

The third letter, from the Council of the London Society (an influential body which included the Earl of Crawford and Sir Aston Webb), also drew attention to 'the way in which evidences of Roman and Medieval London are being carted away daily as a result of excavations for the great buildings now being erected in the City', and emphasized the need for the new keeper to be 'a keen and experienced archaeologist'.

Despite these three powerful letters (which had clearly been concerted, probably at the Society of Antiquaries), the three Trustees stuck to their support of Colonel Brett – an astonishing testimony to Lord Esher's powers of persuasion. At their meeting on 3 February Lord Burnham 'put in' the letters from Lord Kenyon and Walter Godfrey, but the Board's recommendation to the Treasury was still for the chairman's son.[7]

Over in Whitehall, however, the general view was summarized by one mandarin's note that 'an appointment of new blood is highly necessary, I should say, for the London Museum'; and after Wheeler had been privately asked whether he would accept the Prime Minister's nomination for the vacancy, a Treasury Minute of 5 March finally settled the matter.[8]

The appointment of Dr Wheeler to the keepership was a turning point in the history of the museum, if only because Lord Esher could no longer treat the place as his own personal fief, as he had done ever since the death of Lord Harcourt. Shortly after his arrival on 1 July 1926 Wheeler was, as Colonel Brett informed his father, 'rearranging the cases, collecting all the scattered examples of different things and putting them together. He is also busy on the general guide',[9] which was actually published by the end of the year. For his part Lord Esher seems to have accepted the new situation with a good grace, and in August he wrote to Wheeler 'Thank goodness we have your motive power behind our old machine.'[10] He did not, apparently, react unreasonably when Wheeler had to inform him of the theft of Oliver Cromwell's watch from its showcase on 30 August[11] (it was never recovered). And, at first, the purchase of London 'finds' offered for sale by Lawrence was continued, as for instance on 3 December 1926, when the Trustees' minutes (written by Wheeler) record euphemistically that after Lawrence's offerings had been examined by the Board, 'As on previous occasions, the Chairman found a benefactor who readily acquired an important selection of the finds for the Museum.'[12] But thereafter (as previously stated) purchases of all kinds virtually ceased for a number of years.

In his autobiography, *Still Digging*, Wheeler contrasted the vigorous men of commerce upon whom he had relied for support down in Cardiff with 'the pedantries of an ancient courtier' up in London. The museum itself, he found, was 'derelict'. It 'had to be cleaned, expurgated, and catalogued; in general, turned from a junkshop into a tolerably rational institution'. This was certainly a harsh description for the institution so painstakingly created by Harcourt, Esher and Laking; but new and higher standards were now to be applied, and certainly much to the benefit of the museum.[13]

In the bracing process of expurgation which now began, Wheeler was much helped by the timely establishment, in July 1927, of the Royal Commission (briefly mentioned in the previous chapter) to inquire into the National Museums and Galleries. In the memorandum which he submitted in October 1928 on behalf of the Board he stated that the Trustees were 'in particular impressed with the urgent necessity of amplifying the Staff of the London Museum';[14] and in the oral evidence which he subsequently gave he expounded his ideas in his most persuasive manner on such matters as admission fees, relations with the Guildhall Museum and with the Treasury, and the feasibility of setting up a Folk Museum in Regent's Park. His main thrust was, however, directed towards enlarging the museum's educational work, not only amongst the elementary school children (already catered for) but also amongst the universities, the learned societies and the general public – or, to use his own term – 'the citizens of Balham, Hampstead and the like'; and this 'educative influence' should also be made 'to extend even to members of His Britannic Majesty's Government who are brought here [*to Lancaster House*] periodically in connection with the Government hospitality which is dispensed from time to time within this building'.[15]

The Royal Commissioners were evidently impressed, for in their Final Report, presented to Parliament in January 1930, they stated that as a national museum devoted to illustrating the history of the capital, it might justly be expected that the London Museum 'should set a national standard for other Museums of its kind'. But it was impossible for it to play its part, either 'as a model local museum' or 'as an educational centre, until its staffing arrangements have been placed on a more satisfactory basis'.[16]

The Commissioners also recommended that the Board of Trustees should be enlarged. It had, in fact, been reduced, by the death of Lord Esher on 22 January 1930, to only three – the Earl of Harewood (previously Viscount Lascelles), who succeeded Esher as chairman, Viscount Burnham and the First Commissioner of Works, who was then George Lansbury. After some private consultations, in which Wheeler took part, Lord Burnham wrote to the Prime Minister with a number of suggestions, most of which were accepted. As finally decided by Ramsay MacDonald, the new Board consisted of the Lord Mayor of London, the chairman of the LCC Education Committee and the president of the Society of Antiquaries, all ex officio; Mr Robert Holland Martin, a leading City banker who had already interested himself in the museum; Mr J J Mallon, Warden of Toynbee Hall (of which Lord Burnham was chairman); Mr J W Samuel, a retired schoolmaster; Miss Ishbel MacDonald, the Prime Minister's daughter; and Oliver Esher, the third Viscount, whom Lord Burnham described in his letter to MacDonald as 'a man of wealth and leisure [who] would be in many ways a useful member of our Body'. And at the last minute the name of Mr Ernest Makower, a rich silk merchant and generous benefactor of the museum, was added to the list. With the three existing members, the Board's total complement was now twelve (or, to be accurate, thirteen, for successive Lord Mayors served for two years – for their year of office, and for that of their immediate successor).[17]

Confronted by the recommendations of the Royal Commissioners and the representations of the enlarged Board of Trustees, the Treasury had to give ground, and by the end of 1930 had agreed to the part-time post of assistant keeper (still held by Colonel Brett) being made a full-time one, and to the creation of a new full-time post of assistant, the duties of both these positions to include lecturing. There was also to be a shorthand-typist, and Wheeler's own hitherto minute salary was increased substantially.[18] By the end of 1931 Miss Thalassa Cruso had been appointed to the new assistantship, and Mr Martin Holmes, who after leaving Oxford had taken a secretarial course and also done some voluntary unpaid work at the museum, had become the temporary shorthand typist, *ie* Dr Wheeler's secretary. The foundation of a professional staff structure had been laid.

The Royal Commission also made one other important recommendation – that the museum should be provided out of public funds with a small annual sum for the purchase of specimens. We have already seen in the previous chapter that the Commissioners had been informed that the museum had no 'permanent benefaction, endowments, trust funds and other non-official donations' from which it was then benefiting; and it is the years 1927–8, when the Commissioners were making their inquiries, rather than the year 1926, when Wheeler was appointed keeper, that seem to mark the virtual cessation of all purchases. By 1931, however, the Treasury was providing a purchase fund of £200 per annum, reduced in 1932, as 'an economy measure', to £50 and by 1936 restored only to £150.[19]

By that time Dr Wheeler had found another source of money for the museum, for he had been successfully encouraging a new private benefactor, comparable (almost) in munificence with the late Mr Joicey.

176 *Vest worn by Charles I at his execution, 1649.*
The pedigree of this remarkable object, knitted in pale blue silk, comes through the family of Dr Hobbs, the physician who attended King Charles. The stains which it bears were in recent years analysed at Scotland Yard and pronounced to have been made by human tissue, either tears, sweat, vomit or blood[21]

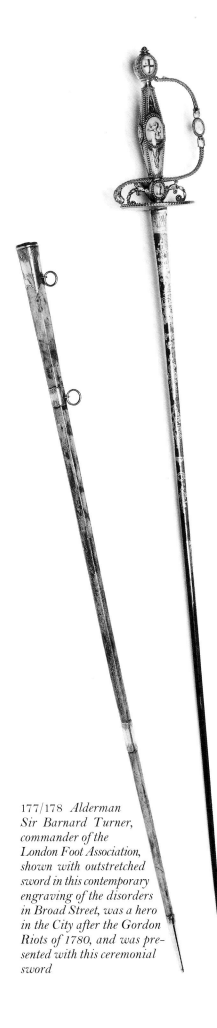

177/178 *Alderman Sir Barnard Turner, commander of the London Foot Association, shown with outstretched sword in this contemporary engraving of the disorders in Broad Street, was a hero in the City after the Gordon Riots of 1780, and was presented with this ceremonial sword*

This was Ernest Makower (1876–1946), the silk merchant who joined the enlarged Board of Trustees in 1930. He had first appeared at Lancaster House in 1924, unannounced and unknown, and bearing under his arm a parcel containing the vest which King Charles I had worn at his execution, and which he (Mr Makower) had recently bought at Sotheby's.[20] He followed this up in 1925 with the gift of the Court sword presented to Alderman Sir Barnard Turner, commander of the London Foot Association during the Gordon Riots in 1780;[22] and in 1927–8 there came quite a shower of gifts, chiefly Stuart or Georgian personal relics. So in June 1928, when to all intents and purposes the museum had no money at all for the purchase of specimens, Dr Wheeler suggested to Lord Esher (in the best tradition of the London Museum) that in return for a substantial down-payment, Mr Makower might be given an honour.[23] 'Mr Makower is a very good friend to the London Museum', the keeper's confidential note began. 'He has already spent over £1500 upon it, and is continually adding to the collections. He proposes to continue his benefactions, but is anxious at the same time to bestow a permanent endowment upon the Museum for any purpose which may seem good to the Trustees.

'The present lack of any endowment of this kind very seriously limits the effectiveness of the Museum, and means that objects which would add materially to the interest and value of the collections are frequently lost through the absence of any purchase-fund. This specially applies to objects of comparatively *small* cost, for which it is scarcely advisable or possible to approach a private benefactor.

'I now know Mr Makower pretty well, and am convinced that the mainspring of his benefactions is a sincere and enthusiastic interest in the Museum. I therefore have no compunction in suggesting that, if he endows the Museum to the extent of £10,000 – £20,000, a good case might be made out for obtaining an honour for him. He would, I know, very greatly appreciate an honour, but his interest in the Museum is undoubtedly independent of the possibility of reward. I feel that if, instead of spreading his gifts at his own discretion over a number of years, he is prepared to place a very considerable sum unreservedly at the service of the Trustees, he will be doing a real service to the Nation and will genuinely deserve acknowledgment . . . . May I ask you to consider this suggestion?'

Whatever Lord Esher may have done about this idea, Mr Makower never got an honour, nor did he ever provide the museum with a capital endowment. But he did nevertheless provide numerous benefactions of various kinds, amounting in all to well over £20000 in monetary value, and Wheeler was always careful to retain his interest and confidence. The issue of detailed and scholarly catalogues, for instance, as he told Makower, would 'bring the really scientific or historical importance of the Collection to the notice of the interested public'. So in 1927 there appeared the first of the seven catalogues, each dealing with a particular period or aspect of the museum's collections, which were prepared during Wheeler's reign. This harbinger of the series, *London and the Vikings*, was written by Wheeler himself in his evening hours – 'I rarely went home till midnight', he later recalled – and was followed by *The Cheapside Hoard of Elizabethan and Jacobean Jewellery* (1928), *London in Roman Times* (1930), a handbook still of interest despite all the more recent archaeological discoveries, and *Parliament and the Premiership* (1931). In later years he regarded the whole series as 'a satisfactory intermingling of *vulgarisation* and scholarship' – well attuned, some may think, to the general philosophy of the London Museum.[24]

179 *Speaker's Chair from the House of Commons, c.1769–82.*
This chair, used by Fletcher Norton, first Lord Grantley, when Speaker of the House, was given to the museum by Viscount Burnham in 1930

Parliament and the Premiership (1931) was a revised version of the catalogue of a temporary exhibition held in the winter of 1928–9. This was the third such exhibition organized by Dr Wheeler, the first two having been displays of drawings of London by Hanslip Fletcher (1927) and Herbert J Finn (1928). *Parliament and the Premiership* was, however, a much more elaborate affair, and was only made possible by Makower's backing. The idea of forming a permanent 'Prime Ministers' Gallery' at the museum, the nucleus of which was to be a complete series of engraved portraits of all forty or so Prime Ministers since Sir Robert Walpole, had first been mooted before Wheeler's arrival,[25] the originator being, perhaps, Lord Burnham. But when Wheeler turned his attention to the matter in the autumn of 1927 this idea was soon improved. The subject was to be the more recent history of Parliament with special reference to the Premiership, and first of all there was to be a temporary loan exhibition. When this display closed, many of the lenders would, with any luck, convert their loans into gifts, leaving the museum with a permanent display of this important subject. And so it came to pass. Mr Makower, whom Wheeler had persuaded to pay for a reception for the National Art-Collections Fund at Lancaster House in March 1928, undertook to foot such bills as there might be, and soon he and his equally active wife were busy buying or borrowing exhibits. Besides the portraits these included such varied items as William Pitt the Younger's posset pot, the silver-mounted hoof of Lord Derby's horse Dauntless, Mr Gladstone's axe and Mr Baldwin's pipe; and at a more serious level, the Speaker's chair from the old House of Commons and the Woolsack from the old House of Lords. When everything was nearly ready Mr Makower wanted to have a grand opening ceremony to which, *inter multos alios*, the whole of the Cabinet should be invited. 'I don't know if you think I have gone too far', he wrote to Wheeler, 'but it seems to me that the more distinguished men we can get there on the opening day the better'. In the event, the King's illness and the absence of the Prime Minister (Baldwin) meant that he had to be satisfied with much less; but there were long and enthusiastic notices in *The Times*, which commented that 'by far the greater part of the collection has been brought together by means of the generosity and the unremitting energy of two habitual benefactors of the London Museum, Mr and Mrs Ernest S Makower'. So it was all very gratifying.[26]

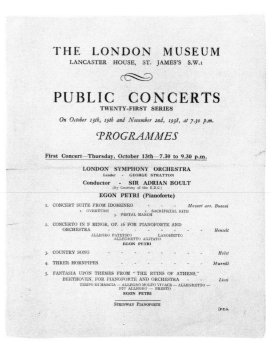

This was far from being the end of Mr Makower's benefactions. In 1929, when the museum had no purchase fund of any kind, he began to provide an annual sum of £100 to buy inexpensive objects.[27] In 1931–2 he helped with a temporary loan exhibition of London-made musical instruments. In 1932 he bought and presented the splendid horse-trappings used by the first Duke of Marlborough on the occasion of his ceremonial visit to the City after the Battle of Blenheim in 1704, and later he helped Wheeler stage a loan exhibition of Marlborough relics.[28] After Lord Esher (the third Viscount, Oliver Esher) had in 1937 discontinued the Esher Studentship, Mr Makower undertook to have the matter laid before Lord Leverhulme, whose father had presented the lease of Lancaster House to the nation in 1913, with the result that the Leverhulme Trustees agreed to maintain a similar studentship for five years. And it was due to Mr Makower that in 1938 a tablet inscribed 'In memory of William Lever, First Viscount Leverhulme 1851–1925 who by his generous gift of the lease of this building provided the London Museum with its present home' was unveiled in the great hall of Lancaster House.[29]

180 *The Entrance Hall, Lancaster House, showing the tablet commemorating Viscount Leverhulme*

181/182 *Programmes for concerts at Lancaster House organized by Ernest Makower*

More important than any of these, however, was the series of evening concerts which Mr Makower organized and financed and which were held in the great hall at the museum. The first of these was held on 6 June 1929, and during the next ten years such great musicians as Harriet Cohen, Artur Schnabel, Sir Thomas Beecham, Sir Henry Wood and Dr Malcolm Sargent all performed there. Wheeler himself had little knowledge of music, but he nonetheless greatly welcomed the concerts. As he later recalled,[30] they were 'a great success. The audience consisted of an astonishing medley of critics, music students, tradesmen, guardsmen with their girls, passers-by and pilgrims of all sorts. They stood or sat about on the stairs or balconies or vacant patches of floor, without any special provision; indeed the slight discomfort contributed to the sense of informality and adventure. No stage separated listener from performer, and the resultant sense of intimacy gave an unusual quality to the scene.'

Mr Makower was, indeed, ahead of his time in his views about what museums ought to be doing; and this was also shown in the field of education by his provision of silver cups for an Essay Competition to be held each year for all children who had visited the London Museum. Wheeler, too, was equally keen to extend the museum's educational work. In 1928 he was able to tell the Royal Commissioners that some nine thousand children from LCC elementary and secondary schools were in the course of a year conducted round the galleries by the museum's exiguous staff. 'On school holidays', he added, 'it is only fair to say that the building is infested with children, who in some cases drag reluctant parents with them'. School teachers themselves, he found, 'more often than not need a good deal of instruction', and so he arranged special courses of lectures for them on winter evenings. As the holder of an honorary lectureship in British Archaeology at University College, London, he himself gave his twice-weekly lectures at Lancaster House; and if funds were available, he felt that the prestige of the museum could be greatly enhanced by short series of public lectures to be given in winter by 'scholars or public men of distinction'.[31]

183 *Henry Irving as Mathias in 'The Bells', c.1871–2: oil on canvas by James Archer. Lent to the Irving exhibition in 1938 and later presented to the museum*

Although no such funds were available, there was nevertheless plenty of space at Lancaster House, and this was ingeniously used by Dr Wheeler to generate a little extra income. Somehow he managed to persuade the Treasury not only to allow the London Society (the 'civic society' of the entire metropolis) to occupy three small rooms on the top floor in return for a small rent, but also (an amazing concession!) to permit this money to be used for the benefit of the museum. It amounted to £190 per annum, which Wheeler used to pay for the salary of a part-time assistant and lecturer.[32] With one learned body thus installed at Lancaster House, it was easier to insinuate others, and in later years both the Royal Archae-ological Institute and the London Survey Committee had *pieds-à-terre* there.[33] With the establishment under the auspices of the Trustees of the Esher Studentship in 1930 (described in the previous chapter) the London Museum was, indeed, becoming – as Wheeler had always in-tended that it should – the recognized centre of metropolitan archae-ological and historical studies.

Throughout the 1930s the strength of the creative urge with which Dr Wheeler animated the museum hardly slackened. There were more catalogues – *Costume* (1933) by Thalassa Cruso, *London and the Saxons* (1935) by Wheeler himself, and lastly the *Medieval Catalogue* (1940) by J B Ward Perkins, Miss Cruso's successor as assistant. And there were more temporary exhibitions too, notably on Victorian wedding dresses and on recent archaeological fieldwork in Britain, both in 1932;[34] and in 1938 an important theatrical display commemorating the centenary of the birth of Sir Henry Irving. Useful anniversaries were, indeed, never missed in Dr Wheeler's day, and it was a particularly happy idea to celebrate *Twenty-Five Years of the London Museum* by the publication in May 1937, under that title, of 'an album of photographs illustrating the range of the collections'. Mr Makower threw a tremendous party for some eight hundred guests, and shortly afterwards a number of the museum's exhibits were displayed for the first time on the BBC's infant television service.[35]

184 *One of Henry Irving's costumes for Macbeth, presented at the Lyceum Theatre 1888–9*

At a more mundane day-to-day level, the museum was regularly cleansed and frequently (but often unexpectedly) scrutinized by its formidable keeper, who after one of his frequent absences might suddenly reappear and be found striding round the galleries like the commanding officer of a battalion on inspection parade. A new and much better system for the numeration of accessions was introduced, and is still in use at

the Museum of London. A second children's room and a nineteenth-century gallery were opened, and some efforts – perhaps not as systematic or determined as they might have been – were made to acquire such currently obsolescent everyday objects as a gas-lamplighter's stick and a muffin man's bell. But the old horse 'bus which Sir Guy Laking had exhibited in the Orangery at Kensington Palace had had to stand in the garden at Lancaster House, and was now so decrepit that Dr Wheeler had it broken up. The list of accessions acquired in one way or another by the museum during the Wheeler years is nevertheless a formidable one, and particularly so as there was so very little money available for purchases. It includes such items as the Garraway Rice collection of palaeolithic implements from Yiewsley, the medieval carved oak doorframe from the church of St Ethelburga's, Bishopsgate, the Dymoke suit of armour made in *c.*1625 in the Royal Armoury at Greenwich, the splendid oil painting of the frozen Thames near London Bridge in 1677, the chessboard reputed to have been given by James II to Samuel Pepys, the Garton collection of glass, a fire-engine from Woolwich Arsenal, several State Crowns and additions to the costume collection.

185 Flints from the Garraway Rice collection

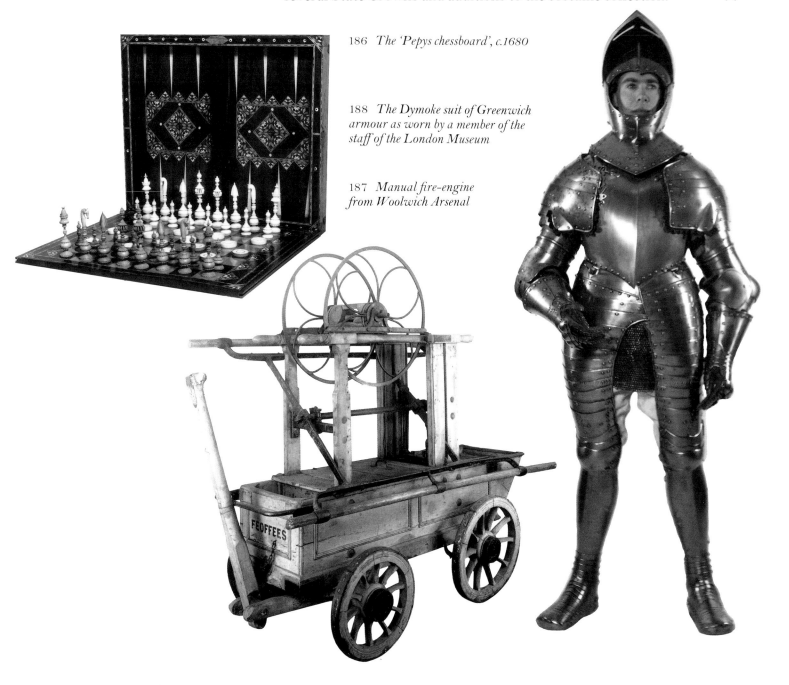

186 The 'Pepys chessboard', c.1680

188 The Dymoke suit of Greenwich armour as worn by a member of the staff of the London Museum

187 Manual fire-engine from Woolwich Arsenal

About half way through his reign Dr Wheeler received a letter from the young curator of a provincial museum asking for his views on 'publicity', to which he succinctly replied as follows:[36] 'If a Museum keeps itself clean, changes its exhibits, issues intelligent catalogues, and lectures to the local young; and if its Curator is a man of standing in some department or other of Science or Art; his Museum will obtain all the notoriety that it wants without the aid of a big drum and flood-lighting.' Dr Wheeler certainly practised what he preached, but in his recipe for the ideal museum he might perhaps have referred to the contribution of the supporting staff.

First and foremost, there was his wife – his first wife – Tessa, herself an archaeologist of distinction who had been her husband's partner in excavations at Caerleon (1926), Verulamium (1930–3), Maiden Castle (1934–7) and elsewhere. She had accepted the large fall in salary which Dr Wheeler's exchange of the National Museum of Wales for the London Museum had entailed, the depressing basement flat off Victoria Street which the keeper's late working hours at the museum prevented from ever being a real home, and even his ill-concealed philanderings with some of the young ladies who formed an increasingly important part of Wheeler's entourage, both at Lancaster House and on safari at the current 'dig'. Within the museum itself Colonel Brett had in 1928 been 'anxious to find a substitute who could relieve him of his lecturing duties', and in consultation with his father, Lord Esher, chairman of the Board, he had accordingly delegated them to the long-suffering Mrs Wheeler.[37] For the next three years she gave most of the museum lectures, at what if any salary is not known, and from 1931 she received an honorarium provided by the London Society's rent.[38] She died suddenly, in April 1936.

Next in point of time was Thalassa Cruso, who (as we have already seen) came to the museum as the assistant in 1931. She combined a sound scientific training in archaeology and anthropology with a considerable knowledge of the history of costume.[39] She was immediately put to work upon the museum's now large collection of costume, and within two years she had produced an excellent catalogue (twice reprinted in later years) which also contained a survey of London fashion from the sixteenth century to 1914. In 1935 she resigned shortly before her marriage to an American archaeologist, Hugh Hencken, but continued to do part-time lecturing for a while.[40] Her successor was John Ward Perkins, later director of the British School at Rome, who in the short space of his three-year stay at the museum compiled the *Medieval Catalogue*, published in 1940 and still regarded many years later by Wheeler himself as 'a unique study of a neglected subject'.[41]

Dr Wheeler certainly had a very good eye for promising young recruits to his staff, and two other appointments were of immense and lasting value to the museum. The first of these was Martin Holmes, whose first paid job at Lancaster House had been as the keeper's secretary, but who after Colonel Brett's unexpected death in 1934 had become an assistant. Holmes was one of that select band of people who devoted the whole of their working lives (except the war years) to the London Museum, of which at the time of his retirement in 1965 he had for many years been the senior assistant keeper. Unlike many of his colleagues whom he saw come and (often) go, he never used the museum to further his own career. He became a recognized authority on a wide variety of subjects, all connected in some way or other with some aspect of the museum's collections. It was he who in 1933, while still only a 'shorthand typist', induced Dr Wheeler to ask for the loan from Lord Amherst of

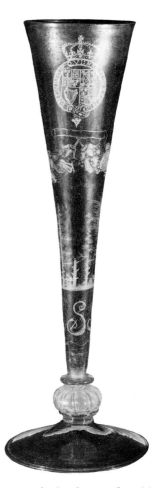

189 *The Scudamore flute (cider glass), c.1640–60. From the Garton collection*

190 *Martin Holmes*

191 *Arthur Trotman in the conservation laboratory at the Museum of London*

Hackney of the three empty crown-frames connected with the coronations of Charles II, Queen Charlotte and George IV; and soon afterwards he read a paper on the subject – the first of his many papers – to the Society of Antiquaries of London. In 1937 he was actively involved, through the museum's own collection of royal robes of state, in the preparations for the coronation service of George VI. Arms and armour, bellarmines, or the topography of Tudor and Stuart London all commanded his interest and extraordinary knowledge, which he constantly purveyed to wondering junior colleagues without ever a hint of superiority and with an endearing blend of enthusiastic delight and sometimes Rabelaisian wit. But the theatre was perhaps his greatest love; and as he became over the years the author of half a dozen books (written in his spare time), chiefly about Shakespeare or the Elizabethan stage, as well as of a dozen plays of his own, it was to Martin Holmes that Dr Wheeler entrusted the preparation of the Irving centenary exhibition and the general enhancement of the museum's theatre collection. He became, in fact, a very considerable scholar indeed, and one of the great servants of the London Museum.

Another of these was Arthur Trotman, chosen by Dr Wheeler straight from school out of twenty applicants. He came in April 1936 as a 'boy learner', aged fourteen, to assist David Sagar, the 'handyman porter', in the workshop in the basement of Lancaster House; and he stayed until his retirement in July 1986 as chief conservation officer of the Museum of London. At first he had performed such humble duties as removing the traces deposited nightly by the museum's resident cat on the sand with which Sir Guy Laking had adorned the Roman Boat. But very soon Dr Wheeler had observed Arthur's weird and wonderful gifts, and was showing him how to make drawings of Roman potsherds, done in his lunch-hour or at home and paid for by the keeper at the rate of 9d each, or 1s 3d for a whole pot. After war-service in the RAF as an electrician he returned in 1946, declining better pay elsewhere, and over the years by diligent study mastered the arts of carpentry, joinery, photography, horology, picture restoration and, indeed, all the varied and increasingly scientific skills of conservation, many of which have now developed into separate disciplines in their own right. His unrepeatable career at the museum is now over, but the immaculate condition of thousands of objects in it provides a lasting monument to his fifty years of service.

Compared with the length of service of either Martin Holmes or Arthur Trotman, Dr Wheeler's eighteen-year sojourn, as keeper from 1926 to 1944, was relatively short; and during the last five years of it the museum was partially shut and Wheeler himself away in the army. He had, indeed, often been away in the years before the war, busy on one of his great excavations at Verulamium and Maiden Castle or on exploratory tours in the Middle East (1936) or in northern France (1938–9); or even just elsewhere in London, working indefatigably for the establishment of his Institute of Archaeology, which was eventually opened in 1936. The museum's out-letter files abound with explanations for his frequent absences, written on his behalf by various members of his staff. 'Dr Wheeler's movements are at the moment extremely uncertain', wrote Thalassa Cruso, for instance, in 1933, 'he comes here only when the weather makes work at St Albans impossible, and we cannot therefore make any appointments for him.' Or, a little later, 'Dr Wheeler's visits to town have been patchy and very busy and concerned mostly with immediate work'.[42] But despite his being out so much of the time, he cannot (at any rate until the last few years) be fairly accused of neglecting the museum. The record of his activities there, already described, speaks for itself; and with Martin Holmes always on hand to 'mind the shop', or in perhaps more appropriate military parlance, to act as Wheeler's adjutant, supported by the ever-faithful Walter Henderson as the station warrant officer, the London Museum was, to quote a characteristically half-mocking phrase of Wheeler himself, 'an honest, hard-working and occasionally useful institution'.[43] So, at all events, thought the general public, for whereas between 1927 and 1937 attendances at such great national institutions as the V&A, the National Gallery and the Tate Gallery all fell heavily, at Wheeler's little upstart London Museum they rose by no less than 31 per cent from 276 525 in 1927 to 364 097 in 1937.[44]

The smallness of the London Museum did, indeed, present a problem about how the keeper should best use his time. Now that the museum had an expert and efficient though still very small assistant staff, there was not enough for a man of at any rate Wheeler's prodigious energy to do within its immediate orbit, and it was therefore natural and even desirable that he should take on extra-mural work, as the Trustees acknowledged soon after his arrival.[45] It was also natural, in Wheeler's case, that such work should be of an archaeological nature, and that if it was to have any connection with the history of the metropolis, it should be principally concerned with excavation and recording within the square mile of the City. Wheeler's work in this field, and the question of whether he did all that he might have done in it, will be discussed in the next chapter.

Far more important than this, however, and indeed far more important than everything that went on at Lancaster House, was the future – even the continued existence – of the London Museum. In 1940 the twenty-eight-year lease of Lancaster House presented by Sir William Lever in 1913 would expire; and what then? When Sir Harry Waechter wrote privately to Lewis Harcourt to congratulate him on the acquisition of Stafford House he had remarked that 'the nation can now never consent to [*the London Museum*] ever becoming homeless in the future'.[46] When Harcourt wrote to Lever to convey his thanks he was, he had said (in a letter already quoted in the previous chapter), 'quite certain that at the end of 28 years, the collection, which is already a fine one, will have become so remarkable and will be so much valued by the public that there is not the least prospect of any Government being allowed to surrender it or to leave Stafford House which, as you know, is Crown property and which will, by that time, have become intimately associated with the Collection'.[47] The Treasury, too, thought that as the Trustees had only handed over the collection for the duration of the lease, they would be able 'practically to compel' the Government of the day to buy the freehold of the house.[48] And Lord Esher, chairman of the Trustees, had said as recently as 1927 that he had 'no fear' that Lancaster House would ever 'be put to any other use'.[49]

These hopes were evidently still held in the 1930s. With the King's brother-in-law (Lord Harewood) as chairman of the Trustees, and a member of the Government (the First Commissioner of Works) also on the Board it seems to have been tacitly assumed that there would be no problem about either transferring the freehold of Lancaster House from, in effect, one Government department to another, or at any rate renewing the lease. In Dr Wheeler's time relations between the museum and the Government Entertainment Fund were in general good, and although the dozen or so dinners and receptions which were held at Lancaster House each year did cause considerable disturbance, there was no reason why the shared use of the building should not have continued. Nobody could have foreseen that the combination of the expiry of the lease, the partial closure of the museum during the war, and the vast increase in Government entertainments and official conferences which ensued from the war, would create a fatal threat to the museum's continued occupation of Lancaster House.

The war itself had, however, been foreseen, and measures for the protection of the collection had been taken by Dr Wheeler with his usual efficiency. In 1937 he had divided the principal objects in the museum into three categories – those of primary importance which in the event of war would be transferred by means of hand-carts to a disused corridor of the former Dover Street Tube Station, accessible from the present Green Park Station; secondly, those which would be stored in a specially strengthened section of the basement of Lancaster House; and thirdly, those (chiefly costumes) to be evacuated to one of the Rothschild family's houses in Buckinghamshire.[50] In August 1939 Wheeler was abroad, exploring archaeological possibilities in northern France, whence, towards the end of the month, war being then almost certain, he sent back concise orders to Martin Holmes for the execution of his carefully prepared plans. By 26 August he was back, not at Lancaster House but at Enfield, where, as Major Wheeler, he was forming a Light Anti-Aircraft Battery, which had been commissioned to guard the powder and small arms factories in that locality.[51] By 2 September, the day before war was declared, all the most important objects had been removed from Lancaster House, and all the rest of the material to be evacuated had gone less than two weeks afterwards.[52] The Wheeler era was virtually over.

Major, later Colonel, and eventually Brigadier Wheeler, did, however, remain keeper in name until February 1944, but from the summer of 1941 until the end of 1943 he was far away, serving successively in North Africa and Italy. With Private (later Major) Holmes and Sergeant Henderson also in the army, and Arthur Trotman in the RAF as soon as he was old enough, the management of the museum devolved upon the two Assistants, Beatrice de Cardi, who had joined the staff early in 1936 as Wheeler's secretary,[53] and Margot Eates, who came in 1937 as a part-time lecturer.[54] In November 1940 a bomb which fell nearby destroyed most of the windows on the south front of Lancaster House, as well as all the glass in the lantern above the main hall: and in 1941 another bomb did severe damage to the north-west corner of the building. In March 1941 all the material stored in the corridor at Dover Street Tube Station was removed to a passage in Piccadilly Circus Station, where later in the year it was joined by the nineteen crates hitherto stored in Buckinghamshire.[55] After the relaxation of enemy air attacks some of the galleries were reopened to the public on 17 March 1942, and attendance figures returned almost to their pre-war level. Several successful exhibitions (consisting chiefly of photographs), on such subjects as London's Heritage, and the Growth and Amenities of London, were organized by Beatrice de Cardi and Margot Eates and held in 1942–3; and the museum remained continuously open until 22 November 1943.[56]

On that day the Minister of Works requisitioned the first and second floors and part of the ground floor of Lancaster House for use for the conferences and secretariat of the European Advisory Commission – a tripartite body established by Churchill, Roosevelt and Stalin at their recent conference in Moscow. The museum was, however, to be allowed to retain its offices on the ground floor, plus all of the basement for storage purposes; and when he reported this untoward event to his fellow Trustees, the chairman, Lord Harewood, was moreover able to tell them that he had been 'assured that the building would be returned to its normal use on the close of hostilities'.

At that same meeting, held on 13 January 1944, Lord Harewood also reported the appointment of Brigadier Wheeler, recently released from the army and for a brief while back in London, to the post of Director General of Archaeology in India for a period of four years. Wheeler had already tendered his resignation from the keepership, but he had also suggested that the Trustees might prefer him to be seconded to the Indian Government for the four-year term of his new appointment. In the event they decided to accept his resignation; and so the London Museum suddenly found itself deprived of both the use of its exhibition galleries and of the services of its keeper.[57]

For several years repeated efforts were made to get Lancaster House back for the London Museum, but all were in vain, and the Foreign Office remains to this day in possession of the building, which it only uses very intermittently.

The legality of this occupation was widely regarded as extremely dubious. When the lease presented by Sir William Lever had expired on 5 July 1940 the new one, for forty-two years and negotiated between the Commissioners of Crown Lands as landlords and the Board of Works as tenants, contained a clause that 'The messuage hereby demised shall be used and kept only as the Head quarters of the London Museum or other similar Museum . . . or as an Art Gallery and for Government and other Official receptions and entertainments.' Expert legal opinion was never sought on whether these last nine words could be interpreted to justify the diplomatic conferences for which Lancaster House was now chiefly to be used, but the mandarins at the Ministry of Works thought privately that they did *not* cover such activities; and in 1948 the (Socialist) Government was still being accused by a Conservative Member of Parliament of having 'pinched' Lancaster House from the museum. Whatever the rights and wrongs of this may be, there is no doubt, however, that the Government had the statutory right to requisition the building under its emergency wartime powers; nor can there be any doubt that the Government did need a properly equipped and suitably impressive building in which to hold international conferences. On the other hand, the Trustees and staff and many members of the public felt with good reason that the London Museum had been very shabbily treated; but in the longer term the retention of Lancaster House might well have proved a formidable obstacle to the fusion of the London Museum with the Guildhall Museum.[58]

The campaign to evict the Foreign Office started as early as August 1944, when Lord Harewood told the Minister of Works that on a recent tour of the building he had found only half a dozen clerks and secretaries in occupation;[59] and in June 1945 Margot Eates (now in sole charge of the museum, Beatrice de Cardi having left for arduous service with the Foreign Office in China) heard that the Foreign Office was contemplating releasing Lancaster House and removing the European Advisory Commission to the former German Embassy in Carlton House Terrace.[60] But at the Potsdam conference, held in July, the Allied leaders set up a Council of Foreign Ministers, whose first meeting was to be in London in September; and so the Minister of Works in Mr Attlee's newly installed Labour Government, George Tomlinson, decided that there was 'no alternative' to using Lancaster House, which, he added, would be needed for about twelve months.[61]

Lord Harewood was unfortunately ill at this time, and no new keeper had yet been appointed; but Lord Esher, deputizing for Lord Harewood, did his best, demanding from Tomlinson undertakings that the occupation of Lancaster House in peace-time (the war having ended on 14 August) should be for three months only, or if this was impossible, that temporary exhibition galleries should immediately be provided elsewhere. But it was no use arguing, for the decision to hold the Foreign Ministers' conference at Lancaster House had actually been taken by the Cabinet itself. And worse was to come, for when the Russian delegates began to arrive in September for the conference they immediately demanded 'bigger, better and brighter accommodation'; and so at only two days' notice the entire museum staff was bundled unceremoniously out of even its offices at Lancaster House.[62]

At this nadir in the fortunes of the London Museum its staff at least had the pleasure of being able to observe from their temporary offices in Lord Rothermere's Warwick House, facing Lancaster House, the comings and goings of the captains and the kings of the *corps diplomatique*; and no doubt they took a certain gloomy satisfaction in the unexpectedly quick end to the conference, which enabled them to return in October, by kind permission of the Foreign Office, to their own offices, records and library, but not to their exhibition galleries.[63]

This was the unpromising situation which confronted the new keeper, W F ('Peter') Grimes, who took up his duties on 1 December 1945. In the previous March the Trustees had unanimously recommended his name from a strong field to the Prime Minister (then Mr Churchill), but there was some confusion at the Treasury about whether the term of office of two members of the Board had not expired, and until this had been sorted out Mr Churchill refused to act about the keepership. During the summer and autumn two new Trustees were recruited – Professor (Sir) John Neale and Professor David Douglas, both historians, who were probably chosen in deference to the Board's view that the later historical periods should receive more emphasis in the museum than hitherto. In October, however, the enlarged Board reiterated its recommendation of Grimes, and in November the Prime Minister (by now Mr Attlee) appointed him keeper.[64]

192 *W F Grimes*

Grimes was then forty years of age, and he served as keeper, or from 1947 as director, of the London Museum until 1956. From 1926 to 1938 he had been assistant keeper of archaeology at the National Museum of Wales, and thereafter assistant archaeology officer at the Ordnance Survey at Southampton. During the war he had been seconded to the Ministry of Works to excavate and record historic monuments on defence sites. He was, therefore, first and foremost an archaeologist; but at the first Trustees' meeting held after his appointment he said, in reply to Lord Esher's welcome, that 'it would be his aim to try to give museum expression to the history of London in all its periods and aspects'.[65] And so he certainly did. In 1945 he found the museum closed, dejected and forlorn, but he left it open, in a new home thronged by over a quarter of a million visitors a year and served by a greatly enhanced staff. By working long and unconventional hours he somehow combined his museum duties with the arduous and time-consuming excavations which year in year out from 1946 he conducted in the City (to be described in Chapter 6). There (besides much else) he discovered the Cripplegate Fort, which transformed knowledge of Roman London, and the Temple of Mithras, which earned him the honour of a CBE in 1955. He was a great encourager of junior colleagues, always easily accessible (at least when not busy in the City), considerate and kind. And although perhaps he did not find the social ambience of St James's, much frequented by tall gentlemen with bowler hats and neatly furled umbrellas, particularly to his own taste, the check trousers, green waistcoat and flower in his buttonhole which he often favoured gave him his own personal and more original brand of distinction as he paced briskly past the guardsmen on sentry – go outside the Palace and up St James's Street to a meeting of the Society of Antiquaries at Burlington House or to a late breakfast at Jo Lyons. He was a man of great integrity, much beloved and respected by many of his staff and archaeological colleagues.

His principal task was, of course, to obtain suitable accommodation for the museum and then get it open to the public there. On his arrival in December 1945 he had found that in 1938, when negotiations for the renewal of the lease of Lancaster House were first discussed, Wheeler had told the Board of Works that 'the house will be required indefinitely for the London Museum . . .'.[66] But early in 1944, shortly before his departure to India, Wheeler had suggested in a memorandum to the Trustees that a new specially designed building, maybe in the museums area of South Kensington, would be needed.[67] For some time thereafter the Trustees were uncertain whether to try to get Lancaster House back or whether to press for a new building somewhere else. In October 1945, however, (Sir) Eric de Normann, Deputy Secretary at the Ministry of Works, stated that there was no hope of their recovering Lancaster House 'for a long time to come, if at all', and that it was useless to invoke the terms of the new lease for that purpose.[68] In May 1947 Grimes told them that Lancaster House was too small for the museum's needs – the exhibition space amounted to about 60000 square feet[69] – and that a move to larger permanent premises would sooner or later be necessary.[70] Thereafter efforts to dislodge the Foreign Office virtually ceased.

But, either way, the museum was going to need a temporary home, for museum-building commanded only a very low priority in the post-war era of shortages of labour, materials and money. So during 1946 and 1947 Grimes examined several possibilities tentatively offered by the Ministry of Works. These included Bridgewater House (just round the corner from Lancaster House), No 143 Piccadilly, Bath House (also in Piccadilly), and No 12 Belgrave Square. All of these were, however, too small, and the great estimated cost of refurbishing several of them, particularly Bridgewater House, could not be justified for merely temporary quarters.[71] In May 1947, however, the Trustees did actually agree, reluctantly, to go temporarily to No 12 Belgrave Square, which provided a mere 5000 square feet of exhibition space; but, fortunately, the owners withdrew the property shortly afterwards.[72]

It was at about this time, when the museum's departure from Lancaster House had become a certainty (though not its destination), that Grimes went to see William, second Viscount Harcourt, to ask for his consent to the impending removal of the collections from Lancaster House. This was needed, it will be recalled, under the terms of the deed of loan by which his father, Lewis Harcourt, and his co-trustees had handed over the museum's collections to the Government in 1913. William Harcourt was in 1947 managing director of the family firm of City merchant bankers, Morgan Grenfell and Company, and was later, as chairman of its Board of Governors, to play almost as important a role in the foundation of the Museum of London as his father had in that of the London Museum. He proved to be entirely unaware of his responsibilities under the deed of loan, but stated that he would accept the judgement of the Trustees as to the suitability of any accommodation which might be offered for the museum.[73]

This ultimately proved to be Kensington Palace, the museum's first home long ago in 1911–13. Parts of the old building had been severely damaged by incendiary bombs in 1940, and were in urgent need of repair; but with the post-war shortages already alluded to it would have been impossible to justify the expenditure of public money on a royal palace without some corresponding direct public advantage.[74] The idea that the museum should return there was being discussed in November 1945; Grimes thought that the rooms offered – formerly the apartments of the late Princess Beatrice, daughter of Queen Victoria – 'would be suitable for the time being';[75] and early in 1946 a Government spokesman announced in the House of Commons that King George VI had 'indicated his willingness' to permit part of the Palace to be used by the museum.[76] By June, however, there had been a change of plan, and Kensington Palace was (in Lord Harewood's words) 'quite off'. Grimes began to wonder again about Lancaster House, the greater part of which had then been empty for many weeks,[77] and scratching about at Bridgewater House and Bath House was also resumed. But by February 1948 Kensington Palace was 'on' once more, the King having consented that the museum should be accommodated there for a period definitely limited to fifteen years; and the Trustees gratefully accepted this offer.[78]

Meanwhile, discussions had also been going on about a permanent home for the museum. The fundamental problem was – to quote the words of Mr W G Hall, Financial Secretary to the Treasury, in the House of Commons in January 1946 – that the position of the London Museum was 'rather peculiar', for although it did not belong to the State, its upkeep was mainly paid for out of State funds. The remedy for this was, in the eyes of the Treasury, quite clear. 'It has always seemed to me wrong', the Financial Secretary opined, 'that a museum dedicated to the history and greatness of London should not be in the hands of the appropriate authority which rules and governs London'; and he therefore hoped that a site might be found for the museum on the South Bank, an area between County Hall and Waterloo Bridge which the London County Council was then planning to redevelop.[79]

The idea that the museum might be handed over to the LCC greatly annoyed Lord Harewood, who put down a question in the House of Lords about it.[80] But he nevertheless went to see Lord Latham, Leader of the Labour Party Group which then controlled the LCC;[81] and rather desultory discussions between the Trustees and the Council, and occasionally the Treasury, about a site on the South Bank continued for a number of years. Several sites were offered by the Council, but there was always something wrong – one was too small, another was outside what was then referred to as the LCC's 'cultural centre' and was not even in the Council's possession; and in 1947 Lord Harewood died and Lord Latham left the Council. The Trustees were determined that the museum should remain a National Museum, but they were, of course, entirely dependent on the Treasury for money. The LCC, on the other hand, might well have provided a site and even a building free if it had been able to take control of the museum; but as this was impossible, it expected the Trustees to provide the necessary capital. The Treasury would (privately) have been happy to see the LCC take over, but in this scenario there was always the risk that the Trustees might invoke the deed of loan of 1913 and demand the return of the collections to the heirs of the original donors. So Treasury policy was to temporize, the excuse for doing nothing being that as building the museum would not start for some ten to fifteen years, it was still premature to give any definite assurance about money being made available. In 1950–2 an altogether different site was mooted – Holland House, Lord Ilchester's then derelict mansion in Kensington, which the LCC was in course of buying; but this, too, came to nothing. Nor was any real progress likely until the Treasury gave a lead.[82] In all these conversations it may be noted that the City Corporation was never involved at all. ◉

After the Trustees had in February 1948 accepted King George's offer of part of Kensington Palace as a temporary home, over three years elapsed before the museum opened to the public. For the first nine months the officials of the Ministry of Works (which in conjunction with the Lord Chamberlain's Department was responsible for the maintenance of royal palaces) were involved in endless discussions about how best to meet the wishes of the formidable resident housekeeper whose apartment at the Palace was affected by the plans for the museum. As finally executed, the scheme of refurbishment included the installation of a heating system capable of heating the whole Palace, a handsome new boiler-house being built upon the site of Sir Guy Laking's now decrepit Annexe, which was demolished. Work finally began in October 1949, and the total cost amounted to over £225000, plus some £50000 extra incurred in respect of the museum only.[83]

The accommodation provided at Kensington contained some 20000 square feet, of which about 15000 square feet were exhibition space.[84] The display area was therefore about one quarter of that provided at Lancaster House, and so the museum's second sojourn at Kensington Palace, like the first one, was never regarded by anyone, from the King downwards, as anything but temporary. The museum's rooms were on two floors, most of them being immediately below the State Apartments occupied by the museum in 1911–13. The main entrance – indeed the only entrance permitted – was again from the north side, via Kensington Gardens, and all the old problems of access were again experienced, for members of the public had, of course, to walk from either Bayswater Road or Kensington High Street, visitors' cars or taxis being absolutely *verboten*. The rooms themselves varied greatly in size, ranging from the handsome entrance hall (where Queen Victoria had held her first Privy Council meeting in 1837) and stone staircase compartment down to quite small ones little more than passages. Nor did they readily lend themselves to the chronological sequence of displays which Grimes was determined to have. Unlike at the Museum of London, where visitors pass through the foyer and at once find themselves in the prehistoric and Roman galleries, at Kensington they had to wend their way downstairs by devious routes to find the historical starting point. The concentration of those comparatively few visitors who managed to do this was moreover soon distracted, for to get from the medieval to the Tudor galleries, they had to pass the Royal room, where the Coronation robes, dresses and other relics were displayed, and mount the main double staircase, where toys, dolls' houses and some fine oil paintings all diverted attention. Those models of Old London for which space could be found were firmly placed by Grimes in the room of the period to which each one related (unlike at Lancaster House, where they had all been either in the basement or in one of the small top-floor rooms); and the Great Fire model, refurbished by Thorp's, found its correct place (as it still does at the Museum of London) in the historical sequence. Beginning in the Tudor gallery, costume was also exhibited in context, there was a not very satisfactory Georgian 'period' room, and some of the smaller rooms and passages displayed a Georgian shop window, theatrical material and a few relics of Parliament and the Premiership. The museum's offices,

193 *The London Museum's front entrance at Kensington Palace, 1951–75*

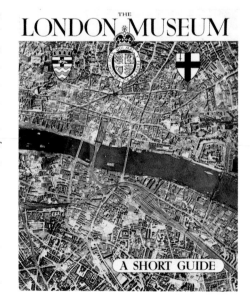

194 *The cover of 'A Short Guide' to the London Museum, published in 1951*

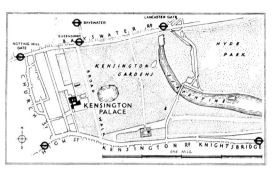

196 *Location plan of Kensington Palace showing the nearest Underground stations*

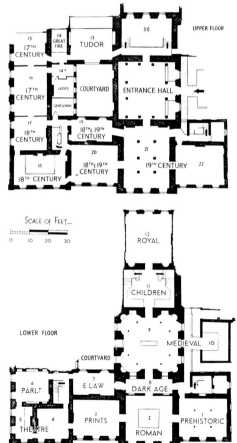

197 *Floor plans of the public areas at the London Museum, Kensington Palace*

198 *The entrance hall in the 1950s. Familiar treasures from Lancaster House, such as the 1862 Exhibition clock and royal wedding dresses, welcomed visitors to the museum*

199 *The Tudor room*

198

200 201 202 203

library, workshops and costume store were all situated in the north range of the Palace, directly beneath the State Apartments.

The removal of some of the more portable parts of the museum's collections from the basement of Lancaster House to Kensington had started in December 1950, and countless exhibits which had been stored in packing cases since 1939 were seen by younger members of the staff for the first time. 1951 was the year of the great post-war Festival of Britain, and the reopening of the London Museum was to form a small part of this national celebration. The Trustees hoped that King George might be able to perform the opening ceremony, but this proved impossible, which was perhaps just as well, for the Treasury refused to allow more than £25 to be spent on the occasion.[85] On hearing of this Sir James Mann, one of the Trustees, remarked that on such a limited budget it would be impossible even to have the invitation cards engraved, and he personally never accepted invitations on unengraved cards.[86] So the chairman of the Trustees, Lord Esher, did the honours very quietly on 11 July, and on the following day members of the public were at last

A mainly chronological sequence was followed at Kensington Palace, with the earlier periods at the lower level and the later at the entrance level. Displays drawing upon thematic topics or on special collections were interspersed throughout the rooms

200 *Georgian costume*

201 *The shopfront from High Holborn*

202 *Reconstruction of a mid-Victorian parlour*

203 *Part of the nineteenth-century room*

204 *Oliver Brett, third Viscount Esher, chairman of the Trustees of the London Museum 1947–61*

205 *Francis Sheppard, general editor of the 'Survey of London' and Arthur Trotman, head of conservation at the London Museum, in conversation at the opening of the Nonsuch Palace exhibition in 1968*

able to visit the museum again – the London Museum being, by a considerable margin, the last of the national museums to be reopened after the war.

The reopening of the museum at Kensington Palace was very much Grimes's own personal achievement, which was well rewarded in 1953, when the museum's existence had become more widely known than it had been at first, by visits from over 236000 members of the public.[87] His staff had helped too, of course, but several valuable members dating from Wheeler's day had left – notably Beatrice de Cardi and Margot Eates, who between them had kept the museum together during the war. On the other hand Grimes still had the support of three highly experienced men who had returned after doing military service. These were Walter Henderson, who made the office wheels run smoothly and finally retired in 1958 with an MBE, Arthur Trotman, now a widely experienced craftsman in charge (amongst other things) of all conservation, and Martin Holmes, who had been promoted to assistant keeper in 1946. They had been joined by another stalwart of the London Museum, Jean Macdonald, who came in 1946 as Grimes's secretary. After studying in her spare time for a degree at London University she was promoted first to senior museum assistant and then to senior assistant keeper in the Prehistoric and Roman Department of the Museum of London, where she remained until her retirement in 1985, a fine scholar with an encyclopaedic knowledge of the London Museum's collections. Amongst the uniformed staff there were still in 1951 Charles Burgin, the senior messenger, Walter Henderson's brother-in-law, who from 1923 until 1961 combined (with unfailing cheerfulness) service to the museum with the enthusiastic pursuit of his own avocations, mostly associated with the racecourse. And over at Lancaster House old Mr O'Connor, an ex-policeman and holder of the Croix de Guerre from the First World War, still (until his retirement in 1962) guarded the museum's numerous possessions which had been left behind there.

After prolonged negotiation with the Treasury, Grimes had also been able to strengthen the curatorial staff. It was he who re-established the departmental structure which still exists in enlarged form at the Museum of London, namely the division of curatorial responsibility on the basis of historical periods rather than of type or group of objects in the collection. In his day there were four 'departments' – Prehistoric, Roman and Dark Age, with Grimes himself in charge, actively assisted by Jean Macdonald; Medieval; Tudor and Stuart, presided over by Martin Holmes; and the Modern Department (*ie* 1714 to the present day), of which Francis Sheppard was the first assistant keeper, from 1948 to 1953, and John Hayes his successor in 1954. From 1947 to 1952 the Medieval Department was looked after by George Dugdale, temporary part-time assistant, who was later for many years to be librarian to the Royal Geographical Society. After his departure responsibility for the Middle Ages passed, by one of the best appointments ever made for the museum, to Brian Spencer, then a young man fresh from the University of Leeds, who was to give his whole working life to the London Museum and the Museum of London. And the museum struck gold again in 1954 when Davina Fennemore arrived as a clerk, and stayed to become personal assistant to successive directors of the London Museum and the Museum of London.

During Grimes's time the museum's collections were greatly enriched by a number of purchases. In 1942 the life interest to which the bequest made by J G Joicey as long ago as 1919 was subject at last expired, and the Trustees found themselves possessed of a capital sum of some

[122] £25000.[88] A few years later the executor of the late Mrs Mackenzie Bell of No 8 Orme Square, Bayswater, requested the Trustees to make themselves responsible for a projected museum to commemorate her late husband, Mr H T Mackenzie Bell, a writer and literary critic, who had died in 1930 leaving his estate, subject to his wife's life interest, for this purpose. The idea was totally impracticable, but Grimes was able to make alternative suggestions which in 1956, after prolonged legal processes, resulted in the museum acquiring a trust fund of over £38000 for the purchase of exhibits.[89] So, after several decades of virtual penury, the Trustees found themselves possessed once more of funds. Items which Grimes was now able to buy included a silver-gilt salt made in London in 1562, the London cup bearing the arms of James, Duke of York as Lord High Admiral, and made to commemorate the launching of HMS *London* (purchased with the help of the National Art-Collections Fund), and the gilt crown provided in 1727 for the coronation of Queen Caroline (re-set with paste). Most of this new wealth was, however, used to buy a number of fine oil paintings, of which the best were the superb view of the Great Fire, by an unknown artist, William Marlow's North End of Old London Bridge, and John O'Connor's St Pancras Hotel and Station from Pentonville Road, which has since become the most famous of all the museum's pictures, and for which the princely sum of £220 was paid in 1952.[90] And in 1949 came the Lloyd collection of prehistoric antiquities, mainly from the Richmond area, which was placed on permanent loan at the museum by Richmond Borough Council.

There were also two other notable accessions. In 1948 came the large collection of material relating to the women's suffrage movement, presented in 1948 by the Suffragette Fellowship, and of which historians have in more recent years made extensive use. And two years later Grimes saved the great *batterie de cuisine* from Apsley House, Hyde Park Corner. This had been the town house of the first and subsequent Dukes of Wellington, but in 1949 most of the house was acquired by the Victoria & Albert Museum. The officers of that institution had no interest in the complete set of kitchen equipment, never used since 1914 and still wrapped in copies of *The Morning Post* of that date, which occupied the basement, now to be converted into a boiler-room. So Grimes, with rather more wisdom, had it all recorded and removed, but because it was not possible to display it at Kensington Palace it was lent to the Brighton Pavilion, where the Prince Regent's great kitchen provides it with an ideal setting, and where it still remains.

206 *Silver-gilt salt with London hall-mark for 1562*
(left)

207 *Gilt-brass crown frame set with paste jewels in openwork silver overlay.*
This was worn by Mary of Modena, consort of James II at their coronation in 1685 and by the Prince of Wales at the coronation of George I in 1715, before being remodelled for Caroline of Anspach, consort of George II, for their coronation in 1727
(centre left)

208 *The Great Fire, 1666: oil on canvas by an unknown Dutch artist who was probably an eye-witness, from a boat near Tower Wharf*
(far left)

211–215 *The collections of material relating to the Women's Suffrage Movement began to enter the museum in 1948. They include photographs, banners, badges, sashes, newspapers and both personal and group memorabilia*
(right)

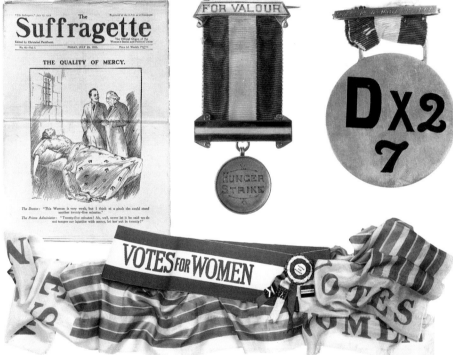

209/210 *Kitchen and 'batterie de cuisine' at Apsley House in 1949*
(below)

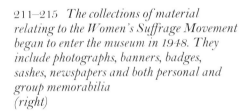

In the immediate post-war years there were a number of small gifts from Queen Mary, whose interest in the museum was revived by its return to Kensington Palace, where she herself had spent much of her childhood. In 1949 Lord Esher and Grimes had been summoned to her home at Marlborough House to show her the plans for the galleries at Kensington, and early in 1951 she paid more than one private visit to the Palace to inspect progress, including one on the day before the opening. On informal occasions such as these Martin Holmes was expert in the niceties of courtly conduct, and in her later years he enjoyed a high degree of Her Majesty's personal confidence and esteem. In June 1952, with her own coronation impending, Queen Elizabeth II, accompanied by Queen Mary, visited the museum to examine the Coronation robes.[91]

Soon after Queen Mary's death in 1953 Queen Elizabeth suggested that a room at the museum should be devoted to the display of some of Her late Majesty's possessions, to illustrate her personality and interests as a collector. This would have involved a grave interruption of the historical sequence of the museum's galleries, to which Grimes attached such importance. So ultimately it was agreed that the proposed display should be in the State Apartments, responsibility for which was vested in the Trustees of the museum in 1955. Some structural modifications were needed, and the Apartments were opened under the museum's auspices in 1956, after a visit from Her Majesty the Queen on 28 November.[92] They remained under the museum's administrative control for the rest of the museum's existence. The pictures and works of art were displayed under the direction of the Surveyor of the Queen's Pictures. There was also a selection from Queen Mary's own collections, and a number of royal costumes were exhibited. Entrance to the State Apartments was quite separate from the entrance to the museum – it was, in fact by the same door at the north-east corner of the Palace as had been used by the museum in 1912. The average number of visitors was about 140000 a year.[93]

In 1956 Grimes left the museum to become director of the Institute of Archaeology and professor of archaeology at London University. He was succeeded by Dr D B Harden, who took over on 1 December of that year. In his earlier days Dr Harden had travelled in Italy and Tunisia and accompanied an archaeological expedition to Egypt sent by the University of Michigan, where he had been awarded his doctorate. Since 1929 he had been on the curatorial staff of the Department of Antiquities of the Ashmolean Museum at Oxford, latterly as keeper. He had already served both as Vice-President of the Society of Antiquaries and as President of the Council for British Archaeology. His particular speciality was Roman glass, but he also had a wide knowledge of many other subjects, including Dark Age Britain.

Donald Harden was director until his retirement in 1970, aged sixty-nine. His two main aims were to find a new, permanent home for the London Museum – with six years of the museum's allocated period of fifteen at Kensington Palace already over, this was urgent – and to join forces with the Guildhall Museum. Like his friend and contemporary Norman Cook, keeper and latterly director of the Guildhall Museum, he proved to be in happy degree the right man for the job at this time. He was very receptive to the new ideas often put forward by the younger members of his staff, and he was a great committee-man (most important at this juncture of the museum's history) of infinite patience, never discouraged by the numerous setbacks encountered on the long road towards amalgamation. In 1965 he became the first acting director of the new Museum of London, and by the time of his retirement in 1970 building work was at long last to begin within a few months.

This, the most important side of Dr Harden's work, will be described in Chapter 7. But he also continued Grimes's policies in the fields of exhibitions and publications, and he did so to such good effect that annual attendances (which had fallen from some 236000 in 1953 to only 158000 in 1959) began to mount steadily, and by 1970 had exceeded 290000 – an increase of over 80 per cent since 1959.

Most of the exhibitions were held in a not very large room on the lower ground floor, and sometimes they overflowed into adjoining rooms and passages and odd corners. It was hardly an ideal setting, but it was all that was available. The first one of all was in 1954, on 'The London of Dickens'. It was followed by the Anna Pavlova Commemorative

216 *H M the Queen with Mr Grimes and Lord Esher at the State Apartments in 1956*

217 *H M the Queen and Mr Grimes viewing the Anna Pavlova commemorative exhibition in 1956*
(top right)

218 *One of Anna Pavlova's most memorable roles was that of the 'Dying Swan'. The museum's collection of Pavlovian costumes, photographs and personalia was displayed again in 1981, the fiftieth anniversary of her death. This photograph was used for the cover of the accompanying booklet and poster (right)*

219 *Dr D B Harden*

Exhibition (1956–7), which occupied five rooms and for which an admission charge was for the first time made. Then came 'The London of Queen Elizabeth I' (1958), 'The London of the Restoration' and 'Thomas Rowlandson Drawings' (both 1960). In 1962 the museum celebrated its Golden Jubilee with a special display entitled 'London 1912–1962' and a large reception was held upstairs in the State Apartments. The exhibition was opened by Lord Esher (Oliver Esher) in what proved to be the last public act of his life trusteeship of the London Museum, which he held from 1930 until his death in 1963. For fourteen of those years he had been chairman, but in 1961 he had resigned the chair to Lord Harcourt, whom he had himself proposed as his successor. This was William, second Viscount Harcourt, son of Lewis, the first Viscount (d. 1922) and founder of the London Museum. His work in the formation of the Museum of London will be described in Chapter 7.

In Dr Harden's later years exhibitions included 'Elizabethan Maps of London' (1963), 'Shakespeare in London from Alleyn to Gielgud' (1964) and 'Two Hundred Years of Jigsaw Puzzles' (1968). And there were also several temporary displays concerned solely with items chosen from the museum's own permanent collection, one of the most notable being that of 1964 showing the great collection of English glass acquired by the museum many years before from Sir Richard Garton.

The 'Garton Glass' exhibition was followed in 1965 by the production of a detailed catalogue of the collection, one of several of the publications produced by the museum in the 1960s and early 1970s which were related to the exhibitions of the day. John Hayes's *London Since 1912*, his *Catalogue of Rowlandson Drawings* and Martin Holmes's *Moorfields in 1559* are cases in point. Other publications in what amounted to a veritable stream included *Arms and Armour in Tudor and Stuart London* (1957), *Dated Post-Medieval Pottery* (1966), *Stage Costume and Accessories* (1967), and *Catalogue of Women's Costume 1600–1750* (1969). There were also guides to the museum and to the State Apartments, and in 1962 a picture book, *Roman London*, mainly for children.

In acquiring accessions the 1960s were one of the most fertile periods in the museum's history. Gifts or loans included fragments (later reassembled in the museum by Arthur Trotman) of the Imperial State Crown made for Queen Victoria in 1838, given by Her Majesty the Queen, a fine early Tudor wall painting from Brooke House, Hackney (from the London County Council), and the Layton collection of London antiquities, particularly important for its prehistoric material. As in the latter part of Grimes's time, the museum also continued to benefit from the Joicey and Mackenzie Bell funds, and of course from the Treasury's grant for purchases, which in 1970 was raised from £3000 to £8000 per annum. With these resources, which in comparison with the pre-war days amounted to 'wealth beyond the dreams of avarice', the museum bought some splendid things – the virginal made in London by James White in 1656 (£360, 1959); the copperplate engraved with the Moorfields portion of a map of London of c.1560, with (on the reverse) an oil painting of the Tower of Babel (£1250, 1962); and the Sudeley Castle Jug or 'Parr pot', a Venetian glass jug with silver-gilt mounts bearing the London hallmark of 1546–7, and decorated in enamel with the arms of the uncle of Queen Katharine Parr. This in 1967 cost £18000 and its importance was recognized by grants from the National Art-Collections Fund, the Pilgrim Trust and the Goldsmiths' Company, and by a special grant from the Government.

The 1960s were, indeed, active years for the London Museum, and the busy atmosphere which Donald Harden engendered there enabled

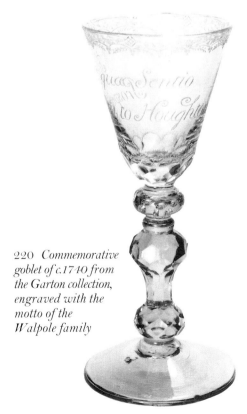

220 *Commemorative goblet of c.1740 from the Garton collection, engraved with the motto of the Walpole family*

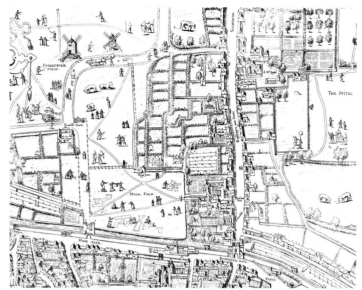

him to extract from the Treasury an increase of no less than one third in the total staff (from 54, including warders, in 1959 to 72 in 1970). Some of these new posts were used to revive two old activities of the London Museum – educational and archaeological. In 1957 a schools officer (Helen Young) was appointed, the small 'Parliamentary' room was taken over for the use of school parties, and by 1962 the museum's schools service had proved so popular that an assistant, Mary Speaight, was appointed, the post being funded by a special grant from the London County Council. In 1965 Mrs Speaight succeeded Helen Young as the schools officer, and under her auspices the museum was latterly receiving over twelve hundred school parties a year. Meanwhile in the world of archaeology a field officer (Francis Celoria) was appointed to collect and record items of archaeological interest on sites where commercial excavation and demolition were taking place, and to encourage local amateur fieldworkers such as the Thames Basin Archaeological Observers' Group – a sort of latter day G F Lawrence, in fact. By 1964 he had established a valuable network of local contacts, was conducting excavations himself, particularly in the West Middlesex area, and was branching out into 'industrial archaeology'. He was even provided with a Land Rover in which to get about – a luxury undreamed of (as we shall see in Chapter 6) by his contemporaries at the Guildhall Museum.

In addition to the revival of the museum's old educational and archaeological roles, there was also an entirely new one – press and public relations. This was masterminded by Sally Kington, who set herself (with great success) to improve the 'public face' of the museum, and who in the early 1970s, in the planning of the Museum of London, was to be an influential advocate of the public's needs and desires.

At the curatorial level Martin Holmes was still 'minding the shop', always at hand and busy in his office, surrounded by his own collections of books and arms and armour. After the war he had continued his studies of the royal Crowns and of the coronation robes and regalia, and with Major-General H D W Sitwell, keeper of the Jewel House at the Tower of London, he was the joint author of a work on *The English Regalia*. When a large seventeenth-century manuscript map of London and the Thames Estuary was lent to the museum by the Ministry of Works he was able to demonstrate that it was probably the one which Samuel Pepys had in 1664 hung in his office in Mincing Lane. And it was he who first recognized the engraved copperplate (previously mentioned)

221/222 In 1962 the London Museum bought a copperplate engraved with the Moorfields portion of a map of London c.1558 with, on the reverse, an oil painting of c.1595 of the Tower of Babel by Martin van Valckenborgh

223

224

225 *The 'Parr Pot', a Venetian glass jug with silver-gilt mounts, and decorated with the arms of Queen Katharine Parr's uncle, was purchased in 1967*

226 *The lead coffin and remains of Anne Mowbray, the infant wife of the younger of the two sons of Edward IV, were discovered in 1964–5. Brian Spencer, who with Francis Celoria was much involved in the ensuing stir, is at the centre back of this photograph, behind Arthur Trotman, with Alfred Rooke (centre left) and Dr Harden (centre right)*

223/224 *The Layton collection of antiquities was acquired in 1963. Fine pieces include a horn cap from a chariot and a handled tankard made of oak staves cased in bronze sheet, both Iron Age*

as being the work of Franciscus Hogenberg, and who by putting on the exhibition of 'Elizabethan Maps of London' discovered the existence of another of the original plates (bought by the Museum of London in 1985) of this the first large-scale map of the capital.

Martin Holmes retired in 1965. Responsibility for the Tudor and Stuart periods was taken over in the following year by Philippa Glanville, a young Cambridge graduate who had taken the post-graduate course in archive administration at University College, London. During her fourteen years' stay she brought flair, imagination and youthful zest to first the London Museum and then to the Museum of London in its formative years. She was quickly given exhibition work to do, and 'Nonsuch. A Lost Tudor Palace', presented at Kensington Palace in 1968 and containing finds from recent excavations at Nonsuch, supplemented by numerous borrowed items, was her first big job.

After Martin Holmes's departure Brian Spencer became the museum's curatorial anchor man. He had come to the museum in 1952 (as previously mentioned) to look after the medieval period, but his field of activity soon spread far beyond the confines of the Middle Ages. It was he who in 1954 had organized the first temporary exhibition at Kensington Palace, on 'The London of Dickens'. He did most of the preparatory work before the opening of the State Apartments in 1956, he arranged for the transfer of the Layton collection of antiquities to the museum, and for years he spent much time on such basic routine matters as the improvement of the museum's own records. He soon made the medieval room one of the best galleries in the museum, and after Martin Holmes's retirement he revised the Tudor room. It was he who in 1967 did most of the donkey work for the loan of Coronation robes and other royal material for an exhibition in Tokyo, and again on a similar occasion in 1969. Outside the museum, he was always willing to give lectures, and with Francis Celoria he assiduously fostered amateur archaeological enthusiasts. Also with Celoria he was during the winter of 1964–5 much involved after the discovery of the lead coffin and remains of Anne Mowbray (*d.*1481, aged eight years, infant wife of the younger of the 'two little Princes in the Tower') on the site of the Abbey of the Minoresses in Stepney. This event made a great archaeological stir, in which the police, the Home Office, the Dean of Westminster, the Duke of Norfolk and even the Queen (not to mention the press) were all involved. His work on various classes of objects, and particularly on medieval pilgrim souvenirs, was to help make the London Museum, and subsequently the Museum of London, one of the country's principal centres for the study of medieval small-finds.

In 1969, when his retirement was impending, Donald Harden was awarded the CBE, and soon afterwards applications for the post of director were invited by the Civil Service Commission. Five applicants, including both Brian Spencer and John Hayes, were interviewed, and John Hayes was appointed. He took over the directorship on 1 July 1970. By that time he had been an assistant keeper for sixteen years, most of his work having been concentrated upon the large and rapidly growing collection of prints, drawings, watercolours and oil paintings in the museum. In 1958 he had been elected to a Commonwealth Fund Fellowship for study in the United States, and was granted unpaid leave by the Trustees; in 1969 he had been for a semester a visiting professor at Yale University. His doctoral degree, awarded by London University in 1962 for a study of the landscape paintings of Thomas Gainsborough, made him an acknowledged authority on that artist. Within the museum he had been primarily responsible for the Golden Jubilee exhibition of

1962, for the exhibition on Rowlandson's drawings and on the Garton Glass collection, and he had written the publications which accompanied those events; he had also arranged twice yearly exhibitions of prints and drawings. In 1970 his *Catalogue of the Oil Paintings in the London Museum* was published, and with Batsford's he was also the author of *London. A Pictorial History.* There were numerous articles, too, in such periodicals as *The Burlington Magazine* and *Apollo*; he had in fact got a very fine record of publication.

John Hayes was director for only three and a half years. It was an uncomfortable time in which to be in charge, for each member of the staff had half an eye on what future the Museum of London (whose impending birth was now almost certain) might hold for him or her, and all activity at Kensington had now to be viewed in the context of the new institution. His short and almost necessarily somewhat hectic reign was nevertheless not undistinguished; and, indeed, if attendance figures are any guide, they suggest a remarkable degree of success – a rise of nearly 30 per cent, from 290 924 in 1970 to 375 518 in 1973. He continued to strengthen the staff, which by the end of 1973 had risen to about ninety. He was particularly concerned that the museum should come right up to the present day, and the weakest section of the museum, the modern department, was greatly enlarged, principally by the recruitment of Colin Sorensen, a man not only of extraordinary width of knowledge but of great dedication and insight, who at once got down to the daunting problems of collecting and presenting material; and Kay Staniland, who came from the famous gallery at Platt Hall, Manchester, took charge of the costume. A separate Publications Department was established, which was in time expected to become a profit-making organization and under Philippa Glanville's auspices the museum shop in the entrance hall was revived, and the range of its stock greatly enlarged.

There was also a series of ambitious exhibitions. 'Time Off in 1870', opened in November 1970, was the first of the London Museum's exhibitions to be presented by a professional outside designer, Christopher Firmstone, and was visited by nearly 60 000 people. It was followed by 'Elizabeth R', a display of the costumes worn by Miss Glenda Jackson in the recent television series of that name. And then came Brian Spencer's 'Chaucer's London', the best and most important exhibition ever mounted by the London Museum, which ran for five months in the summer of 1972, attracted over 75 000 visitors and (an admission charge having been made) even earned a profit against the cost of mounting it. It was also a landmark in the museum's history because it was designed by Higgins, Ney and Partners (and by Jasper Jacob in particular), the designers of the displays then in course of preparation for the Museum of London, and 'Chaucer' provided their first experience of museum work. It attracted much favourable public comment, and, as Dr Hayes told the Trustees, 'The praise for Mr Spencer's splendid achievement has been universal'.

'Chaucer' was followed by 'London in the Thirties', a complex subject organized by Mrs Alice Prochaska (a valuable member of the Modern Department during her short period of service in the museum), which during its five-month run in the summer of 1973 attracted nearly 70 000 visitors. 'The Dutch in London' (1974) was organized in conjunction with the Government's celebration of Britain's entry into the European Economic Community, and was selected as an appropriate theme in view of William III's association with Kensington Palace; this was co-ordinated by Philippa Glanville, but, in view of the impending amalgamation with

227 *Brian Spencer at the 'Chaucer's London' exhibition in 1972 with members of the cast of the stage version of 'The Canterbury Tales' which was then running at the Phoenix Theatre. The medieval stall was lent from Much Hadham, Hertfordshire*

228 *Colin Sorensen with the doors of Astley's Circus, formerly in Lambeth, which he found in a derelict synagogue in Whitechapel. He joined the London Museum as keeper of the Modern Department in 1971 and quickly began to collect material for the proposed Museum of London (right)*

the Guildhall Museum, was organized by outside scholars and administrators. Lastly, as part of the policy of showing that the museum could and should be as much about contemporary London as the London of Roman or Tudor times, there was 'Mary Quant's London', designed by Michael Haynes and organized by the director himself. This was criticized as having little to do with London, and attendances proved disappointing – a sad end to an otherwise impressive series of exhibitions. A final one on 'Regency London' was cancelled at the request of the new director of the Museum of London, Tom Hume.

229 *Dr John Hayes (left) with Mary Quant, Lord Harcourt and Alexander Plunket Greene at the opening of 'Mary Quant's London', 1973*

230 *Kay Staniland, who joined the London Museum in 1971 to curate its fine collection of costume and textiles, preparing a display of royal wedding dresses in 1972*

231 *Crown frames as exhibited in a display of coronation costume in 1973.*

STORES

During these years Dr Hayes was also responsible for co-ordinating the redecoration of the State Apartments carried out by the Department of the Environment and the Lord Chamberlain's Department, and he wrote the new History and Guide. Pictures and furniture were transferred from other royal palaces, and the King's Gallery was restored to something of its original glory. The State Apartments remain today almost exactly as they were left in 1974, but, beneath them, on the two floors soon afterwards vacated by the museum, some of the rooms have been restored to suggest their appearance when Queen Victoria's parents lived there, and others incorporate a fine display of Court Dress.

At the end of 1973 John Hayes left the London Museum to become director of the National Portrait Gallery, and on 1 January 1974 Brian Spencer became the acting director of the London Museum for the remaining seventeen months of its life. These were thankless times. Compulsory admission charges, which Mr Heath's Conservative Government had been talking about for all the national museums and galleries, had finally to be introduced on 2 January 1974. After only three months Mr Wilson's Labour Government announced that they were to be discontinued, but not before attendances had fallen by about a quarter. Almost all work was now concerned with preparation for the Museum of London, but the future seemed uncertain. So the acting director had to exercise constant vigilance, tact and genial optimism to hold together a hard-pressed and partially inexperienced staff, depressed by feelings of insecurity and by the resignation, early in 1974, of a dozen long-serving colleagues. New recruits added to the already considerable number of the staff engaged on a period, temporary or casual basis and lacking, as yet, a developed sense of loyalty to the museum. An abnormal amount of consultation became the order of the day, and the adoption of all sorts of expedients to keep essential work moving smoothly. When warding staff showed signs of restlessness, Spencer even found the time to talk at length to each warder in turn. In its last days the museum was, indeed, fortunate to have been in the charge of such a man.

The London Museum closed its doors for the last time on 31 May 1975, and its formal amalgamation with the Guildhall Museum to form the Museum of London took place on the following day, 1 June 1975.

232 *Educational work was an important element of the London Museum's activities. It provided for the close involvement of children with the exhibits on display and in the study collections*

233 *Excavations in 1968 at an Iron Age site at Heathrow, West London, being conducted by Roy Canham, the museum's archaeology officer, prior to runway extensions*

234 *W F Grimes (left) on the site of the excavations on the west side of Walbrook which revealed the remains of the Roman Temple of Mithras in 1954. In this photograph Mr Grimes is setting out an explanatory notice which reads 'Head [of Mithras] found here'*

LATER YEARS OF THE GUILDHALL MUSEUM
1911 TO 1975

235   236

Chapter 6
LATER YEARS OF THE GUILDHALL MUSEUM
1911 TO 1975

The Museum of London has a large collection of photographs, many of them taken in Victorian and Edwardian times

235 Farringdon Road and Holborn Viaduct in c.1890. Photograph by George Washington Wilson

236 Ludgate Hill and St Paul's, c.1910. One of a series of impressionistic 'pictorial' views by the American artist-photographer Alvin Langdon Coburn

237 Bank Underground Station, looking toward the Royal Exchange, after a direct hit by a German bomb, 11 January 1941. Photograph by Arthur Cross and Fred Tibbs for the City of London Police

'In many respects the history of archaeology in the City of London recalls the story of the Sibylline Books. Knowledge is offered to each generation at a price – and is destroyed when the price is not paid. The price rises for each generation – in terms of actual cost and also of difficulties to be overcome – and the remaining store of information diminishes. None has yet been prepared to pay in full – and only a very small part of the exceptional bargain offer made by the Sibyl in 1946 was accepted. If ever a generation arises that is prepared to pay the full price of a total scientific excavation over whatever area is then available, complete pages of the Book will be won. But by that time very few pages indeed will remain.'[1]

So wrote Ralph Merrifield, for twenty-eight years a senior member of the staff of, successively, the Guildhall Museum and the Museum of London, and the author of three distinguished books on Roman London. In that passage, written in 1965, he summarized the tragedy of the unique opportunities presented in the mid twentieth century for the study of London's early history, and now lost for ever. In more recent years, however, a generation has arisen that is prepared to pay if not the full price, at any rate a very high one for the surviving remnants of the Sibylline Books. Already the loss of archaeological desposits within the City of London has been very substantial, and within the next century the bulldozers and the mechanical diggers will have largely destroyed most of what remains so that there will be little more left to be disclosed.

The history of the later years of the Guildhall Museum is inextricably bound up with that of archaeology within the City of London. Ever since the days of Roach Smith things dug up in the course of excavation for building redevelopment have provided a large proportion of the museum's collections. There were, of course, notable collections of other material, such as tradesmen's tokens, civic badges, medals and miscellaneous insignia, inn and shop signs, church plate and so on; but no systematic attempt was ever made to illustrate the more recent centuries of the City's past, and the museum's main attention was always fixed upon matters archaeological. By the early years of the twentieth century (where we left it at the end of Chapter 2), the City Corporation had acknowledged that its museum needed a full-time qualified curator, or museum clerk, as the post was inelegantly denominated; and in 1907 Frank Lambert (1884–1973) had started work. One of his duties was, specifically, to 'watch all excavations within the City'.

'Excavations' at that time, and for many years thereafter, meant excavations made for building or engineering purposes, and had none of the archaeological connotations which the word has acquired in more recent years. Ever since Roach Smith's day the watching of such 'excavations' in the City had been intermittently performed by enthusiastic private individuals; and in the early years of the twentieth century the influence of General Pitt-Rivers' scientific methods was beginning to make itself felt there. Dr Philip Norman, many of whose accomplished topographical drawings of London were (as we have already seen) later bought by the London Museum, and Francis W Reader kept a careful eye on building sites, and in the exemplary reports of their observations, published in *Archaeologia*, they used pottery seen on site as evidence for dating.[2] Early in 1914 Dr Norman even persuaded the Corporation to spend up to £50 on the excavation (in the archaeological sense) of a number of Roman rubbish pits which the rebuilding of the General Post Office in St Martin's-le-Grand had uncovered.[3] This work was directed by Frank Lambert, who by collecting and analysing layer-groups of pottery was able to construct a chronological sequence for much of the coarse Roman pottery already in the museum's collections; and this led

him on to study 'the distribution throughout the City of various closely detailed types of pottery, in an attempt to throw light on the development of Londinium'.[4] He was, in fact, deploying some of the new techniques and modes of inquiry of modern archaeology, as his reports, published in *Archaeologia* in 1915 and again, after the interruption of the war, in 1921, make amply clear.

As the Corporation's salaried museum clerk Lambert has good claim to be regarded as the first professional archaeologist ever to work in the City. He was also ahead of his time in seeing the need for photographic records to be made of old buildings about to be demolished. In May 1912 the Corporation's Library Committee 'permitted' him to undertake this duty and supplied him with 'a photographic outfit' at a cost of £27. Soon afterwards the City engineer was persuaded to notify the librarian (Lambert's master) of all impending demolitions, and by the time of the outbreak of war in 1914 over a hundred photographs had been taken, including some of Cloth Fair, large parts of which were being demolished by the Corporation at about that time.[5]

Most of Lambert's time must, however, have been spent on the improvement of the museum itself. In 1910 the crypt of the Guildhall was opened to the public for the first time. It was connected to the museum by an oak-panelled passageway, and was mainly used for the display of such large objects as the Roman sculptures dug up at the Camomile Street bastion in 1876, and several large stone coffins. Hundreds of exhibit labels were printed by hand within the museum, and several large general labels – 'much appreciated by the public' – were added to various sections of the display. Numerous parties of school children were escorted round the gallery, and in 1911 the Library Committee decided 'to endeavour to add to the popularity of the Museum by introducing the system of picture postcards', over five thousand of which were sold in the following year. After his return from the army in 1919 Lambert began to compile 'a card catalogue on scientific principles of the contents of the Museum', and he also inaugurated a 'clearance of objects not relating to London'.[6]

But the post of museum clerk must always have been a dispiriting one, the museum being only an unloved adjunct of the library, and its

238/239 These two watercolours by Philip Norman were included in one of the articles written by him and F W Reader and published in 'Archaeologia' in 1912. Site of Christ's Hospital, looking east, in 1907, with Christ Church, Newgate Street, in background (above left)

Christ's Hospital site, looking west, in 1907, showing Bastion 19 of the Roman city wall under excavation (above)

STATUE OF A ROMAN WARRIOR
FOUND IN A BASTION OF THE LONDON WALL
CAMOMILE ST. BISHOPSGATE
ROMANO BRITISH PERIOD

241 *Statue of a Roman soldier from a funerary monument found at Bastion 10 of the Roman city wall in Camomile Street, as displayed in the Guildhall Museum*

242/243 *Photographs of Cloth Fair, taken by Frank Lambert in 1913 before large parts of it were demolished by the City Corporation*

244 *Picture postcard sold in the Guildhall Museum*

245 *The Guildhall Museum in 1927*

240 *Bastion 19 under excavation, photograph. Christ's Hospital was the first site for which there was a planned series of investigations, specifically to locate and record the city wall and its bastions. Norman persuaded the Government to agree to the preservation of Bastion 19 beneath the yard of the General Post Office* *(left)*

badly paid clerk, perpetually at the beck and call of the librarian, having no prospects of promotion. It was surely symptomatic of Guildhall's general indifference towards it that the museum was closed for over four years (6 April 1915 to 8 September 1919) during and after the war, and again from 2 January to 4 October 1921 'on account of the unsettled state caused by the Irish disturbances', although the library remained open as usual throughout all of these untoward events.[7] So in 1924 Frank Lambert resigned from the Corporation's service, moving to the provinces where the value which was placed upon his worth led him ultimately to the directorship of the Walker Art Gallery at Liverpool and to the honour of a CBE.

GUILDHALL MUSEUM, LONDON
SIGN OF THE BOAR'S HEAD, EASTCHEAP, 1668

Printed at the Oxford University Press

It was at about the time of Lambert's departure that the Sibyl made one of her more important offers of knowledge. In the early 1920s a boom in the building of banks and offices within the City had begun, which continued until about 1935. During these years excavations for rebuilding the Bank of England, for new headquarters of both the Midland and the National Provincial Banks in Princes Street, and for numerous other works in such areas as Leadenhall Street, Gracechurch Street, Upper Thames Street, Fish Street Hill and Cornhill (to mention only a few) had at one time or other presented unique opportunities for the scientific investigation of London's distant past. The new post-war generation of young and vigorous professional archaeologists was at hand, eager for an opportunity to practise their skills. All that was needed was a lead, and a little money – even a very little money.

The Sibyl's offer was not, however, taken up by the Corporation. Lambert's successor as museum clerk, at a salary of four pounds a week, was Quintin Waddington, who in 1924 was fifty-six years of age, and who held the post until his retirement at the end of 1945, aged seventy-seven.[8] Dr Mortimer Wheeler thought of him as 'a good fellow and anxious to learn but . . . in no sense a qualified archaeologist'.[9] Nevertheless it was upon him that the Corporation relied for the surveillance of builders' excavations during these important years. The mere acquisition of finds became, indeed, almost the be-all and end-all of the museum. The year 1930, for instance, had in the words of the new librarian, J L Douthwaite, 'furnished an unusually large supply of archaeological material';[10] and nobody at Guildhall – least of all Douthwaite – seems to have had much understanding of the wider opportunities presented by the rebuildings.

The Sibyl's offer was, however, taken up with some vigour by three other bodies, the Royal Commission on Historical Monuments, the London Museum and the Society of Antiquaries, whose combined achievements between the mid 1920s and the onset of war in 1939 were very considerable. The driving force behind all their efforts was largely supplied by one man, Dr Mortimer Wheeler, who in 1926 was the newly appointed keeper of the London Museum. It seems to have been he who suggested to the Royal Commission that Roman London should form a separate volume in the Commission's London series, and that an *ad hoc* committee of specialist scholars was needed to prepare an authoritative report.[11] It was certainly he who from its establishment in 1925 until the publication of the Roman London volume in 1928 acted as the committee's honorary secretary, and who wrote the Introduction, a brilliant survey of the whole subject as it was then known. The Royal Commission's Roman London volume remained, indeed, the standard work of reference until the publication of Ralph Merrifield's *The Roman City of London* in 1965; and even thereafter, much of its overall picture has not been superseded.[12] And for good measure Dr Wheeler was also the author of the London Museum's catalogue, *London in Roman Times*, published in 1930.

246/247 *Excavations in 1933–4 for the rebuilding of the Bank of England revealed two fine Roman tesselated pavements. This one has been restored for display in the Bank*

Dr Wheeler was, furthermore, actively involved in the efforts made by the Society of Antiquaries. The Society had for some time been anxious about the prevailing threat to Roman antiquities in the City, and when Walter Godfrey, a prominent fellow, wrote on the Society's writing paper in January 1926 to Lord Burnham, one of the Trustees of the London Museum, in support of Wheeler's candidature for the keepership he had said (as already quoted in the previous chapter) that ever since Frank Lambert's departure in 1924 'no reliable expert has been available to watch the excavations which proceed daily in the City in the various

building reconstructions'. And, he had continued, 'In nearly all these cases the whole strata recording Roman and Medieval London are removed and destroyed, and the absence of detailed observation is a calamity.'[13]

Wheeler's solution to the problem was clear and straightforward – the creation of 'a trained archaeological inspectorate . . . responsible for visiting all City excavations not less than three times a week and preferably every day'. It was to note 'the occurrence of finds in relation to structural and stratigraphical evidence', and be able to call upon an architectural draughtsman for the making of plans, as required. And in order to gain the interest of as many City men as possible there was also to be 'a large committee or congress thoroughly representative of the City Administration, the City Livery Companies, prominent City land-owners, leading contractors and others', which was to meet annually to receive reports.[14]

These and other ideas were discussed in July 1926 at a conference convened by the Society of Antiquaries, to which Douthwaite, as librarian in charge of the museum, Waddington and Sydney Perks, the City surveyor, were invited, as well as representatives of the RCHM, the British Museum, the Bank of England and some City livery companies. The chief problem, as Wheeler foresaw, was that the City Corporation would claim that in the person of librarian Douthwaite it already possessed the fully qualified archaeologist who was so urgently needed; and it would certainly resent as interference any notion of a 'congress' (which was therefore promptly dropped). Ultimately, and after the most careful consideration, Lord Crawford and Balcarres, as president of the Society of Antiquaries (he was also chairman of the RCHM), wrote to Perks, in a letter of masterly tact, to suggest that an 'archaeological surveyor' might be appointed as a permanent official under Perks's direction (thus circumventing the problem of Douthwaite). With such an officer in charge, he added, he was sure that 'a number of well-qualified scholars would . . . be prepared to place themselves at your disposal whenever something of interest or consequence turns up'.[15]

In due course (after an interval of nearly three months) the Library Committee invited Lord Crawford to attend its next meeting to 'express his views and explain the importance of the proposed work'. This he did on 1 November 1926, after which the matter was referred to a Special Sub-Committee.

Ultimately, towards the end of April 1927, some nine months after the Antiquaries' first approach to the Corporation, Lord Crawford received a letter from the town clerk. This stated that architects and building contractors working on sites within the City had been requested to cooperate with the Corporation in the discovery and preservation of antiquities; that publicity had been given to this request; and finally, that a part-time amateur gentleman was to be experimentally engaged, unpaid, for a few months to assist the museum clerk in the inspection of archaeological sites.[16]

The main point at issue – the need for a salaried whole-time trained archaeologist – had thus been shelved, the temporary appointment of Mr Anthony Lowther, a young architect in practice in Bloomsbury, being only a sop. He had, to quote Dr Wheeler, 'done a little amateur digging on the site of a Roman villa in Surrey', but he had had 'no archaeological training whatever', and indeed did not even claim any special knowledge of the subject. Again according to Wheeler, writing in May 1927, 'The persistent inactivity and even obstructiveness on the part of the City officials' was 'at last really beginning to stir up feeling in the Society of Antiquaries'. And Lord Crawford, who was a very distinguished and cultured man and not used to being treated in such an offhand manner, was said to be 'very much up in arms' about it all.[17]

So he went to Guildhall to see the chairman of the Library Committee, Major Champness, and no doubt the interview took place in the stately Gothic office of the librarian, who was also present, though he said very little. Lord Crawford was particularly annoyed that a paragraph evidently inspired from Guildhall had appeared in *The Times* claiming that the Society of Antiquaries approved of such little action as the Corporation had seen fit to take. He pointed out that outsiders often got to know of archaeological opportunities in the City before the Library Committee or the librarian was aware of them, and reiterated the need for frequent regular inspections of building sites by a salaried and qualified archaeological officer. Major Champness replied that while members of his Library Committee would probably be willing to have such a person, they were 'well aware that the Common Council would permit no such thing'; and they would deprecate action likely to produce a snub from that body. So the interview achieved nothing and Lord Crawford departed, convinced that archaeological investigation in the City would continue to be 'conducted in a very amateur and haphazard fashion'.[18]

Dr Wheeler at first wanted to continue the struggle 'through the Common Council direct',[19] but by August he was contemplating an attempt to persuade the leading City livery companies, and particularly the Goldsmiths', to pay the annual £350 needed for an adequate Inspector of Excavations. 'If the City Corporation of London', he wrote to a friend, 'which is already streets behind other cities in the country in the care of its antiquities cannot manage to produce this comparatively small sum, I feel sure that the City Companies and other similar bodies interested would show the way'. In the end, however, the Antiquaries decided against making any further approaches in the City; and no doubt the Sybil sadly tore out another page from her Book of Knowledge.

This episode in the Corporation's history was summarized by Dr Wheeler as follows: 'I know of no city or large town anywhere in Great Britain which leaves its museum to fend for itself under the supervision of a solitary clerk who has no independent status at all but is merely an adjunct of the Library. And when in addition to this we remember that *everyday* in several parts of the city historical evidence is being dug up and irreparably destroyed without record or observation, one can scarcely believe the obtuseness of a City Corporation which is so blind to its own obvious responsibilities!'[20]

This was written in a private letter in 1927. Three years later, in the preface to his London Museum catalogue, *London in Roman Times*, he said the same thing in more lapidary style. 'The opportunity has been lost, and the best friends of the city must lament the apathy of recent generations of City Fathers who, like Gallio, have "cared for none of these things".'

Urban archaeology needs the active interest and support of the local municipal council and local property owners; and it also needs money. In Wheeler's time these conditions did not exist in the City of London; so it is hardly surprising that after 1930 the foremost archaeologist of the day turned his prodigious energy elsewhere, notably to Verulamium and Maiden Castle; and their gain was London's loss.

It was, however, almost certainly due to Dr Wheeler's influence that the Society of Antiquaries proved willing to pay the ever-mounting price for knowledge. The Society's interests were world-wide and its means very limited – as recently as 1926 it had had to curtail its excavations at both Stonehenge and Richborough through lack of funds. But from 1928 to 1937 it nevertheless found the money to pay for a professional investigator of excavations in the City. This money was raised privately by Robert Holland Martin, a fellow of the Society who was also a Trustee of the London Museum and a banker in Lombard Street, and whose other activities included the preservation of the precincts of Tewkesbury Abbey in Gloucestershire. By February 1928 he had secured promises which (if kept) would produce the sum of £250 per annum for five years,[21] and the first investigator, Eric Birley, later professor of Romano-British History in the University of Durham, was appointed shortly afterwards.

In his brief tenure Birley was concerned with only one site – the very important one at the Midland Bank in Princes Street, on which he produced a report published in *The Antiquaries' Journal* in 1929. In that year he was succeeded by Gerald Dunning, later to become an inspector of Ancient Monuments and an authority on medieval pottery – the subject which he had studied as the London Museum's Esher Student from 1931 to 1933. During his five years in the City he obtained and published

250 *Roman donkey mill found by Eric Birley in 1928 during the rebuilding of the Midland Bank, Princes Street, as reconstructed in the Museum of London*

important evidence relating to the Roman basilica, investigated the evidence for the two great fires in Roman London, and recorded many other Roman structures in other parts of the City. But the provision of funds for his salary proved very difficult, and the Council of the Society of Antiquaries twice decided, very reluctantly, to terminate his appointment. On both occasions, however, Holland Martin was able to get hold of more money at the last moment, though Dunning's salary had to be slightly reduced.

The last of this distinguished trio was Frank Cottrill, later curator of the Winchester Museum. Because money was so short he was only paid an annual retaining fee of £25, supplemented by other fees payable whenever builders' excavations were actually being made – the system then known in the archaeological world as 'ten bob a hole'. During his three years he too recorded much material unearthed during rebuilding works, and published a valuable account of the Roman city wall. Ralph Merrifield has stated that Cottrill also made 'a major contribution towards our scanty knowledge of the street-plan of Roman London'.[22]

After Cottrill's departure in 1937 no successor was appointed, and such recording as continued was done by Quintin Waddington, the museum clerk. Perhaps because of his age (he was now nearly seventy) and the often dirty and physically demanding nature of the work required, the Corporation did, however, decide in 1939 to provide him with a younger colleague. This was Adrian Oswald, an experienced archaeologist who also knew about the inside routine of museums. Before he left for the army in 1940 he just had time to observe an excavation for a subway in Aldersgate Street which revealed the existence of a late Roman gate in the city wall, and also to conduct an investigation on the site of All Hallows, Lombard Street. This Wren church had been closed in 1937 and the site sold to Barclays Bank for their head office. The cost of Oswald's work here, it may be noted, was borne by the Society of Antiquaries.[23]

251/252 *Building works in the City continued to reveal evidence about the Roman city walls and street plan (above).*

Bastion 2 at Trinity Place, Tower Hill, was visited by the Duchess of York (later H M Queen Elizabeth) shortly before its demolition in 1935.
In 1852 part of a funerary inscription had been discovered here, and Charles Roach Smith had suggested that it referred to the Roman Procurator Julius Classicianus, who featured prominently in Tacitus' account of the Boudiccan revolt of AD 60. Some scholars had doubted this hypothesis, but the discovery in 1935 on the same site of another piece of this inscription posthumously proved Roach Smith to have been right

253 *Works on the site of All Hallows, Lombard Street, 1939: one of a number of sites redeveloped during the inter-war years which provided opportunities for observations leading to the elucidation of the Roman basilica-forum*

Within the Guildhall Museum itself there is little to relate for the years between Frank Lambert's departure in 1924 and the outbreak of war in 1939. Additions to the collections, chiefly archaeological, continued in fair number, and property owners redeveloping their sites were even encouraged to deposit their finds at the Guildhall. But the bland tone of Douthwaite's annual reports reveals the underlying indifference for the museum which prevailed at Guildhall. In 1930, so the Library Committee was informed, 'The introduction of the use of a vacuum cleaner has proved most labour-saving and effective.' And the scheme for the presentation of duplicate specimens to what Douthwaite described as 'colonial museums' but which were actually in the Dominions of Canada or Australia had the great advantage of reducing the stocks stored at Guildhall. No special exhibitions were ever held in these years, and no more catalogues were published – in marked contrast with the feverish activity engendered by Dr Wheeler at this same time at the London Museum. It is therefore hardly surprising to find that attendances fell from some 124 000 in

1925, the inter-war peak year, to below 60000 in 1932. And it was wholly characteristic of this depressing era in the Guildhall Museum's history that 'As a precautionary measure' the collections were closed to the public in February 1939, some six months before the war actually began.[24]

During the period of the 'phoney war' in the autumn and winter of 1939–40 (when hardly any hostilities took place) 'certain of the Museum's treasures' were sent to the safety of a country house in Berkshire, and the objects exhibited in the showcases were packed away in boxes. The value of these precautions was shown on the terrible night of Sunday–Monday 29–30 December 1940, when the roof of Guildhall itself and all of the apartments to the north of the hall were devastated by fire. In the library the north-west corner was also gutted, and when the staff arrived at about 9.30am they found two bays there 'open to the sky' and the roof timbers ablaze. Two large holes had been burnt in the floor, and the red hot debris which had fallen through had set some of the museum's wooden showcases alight. The fire brigade was so heavily engaged elsewhere that it was not able to come until three o'clock in the afternoon, but in the meantime the staff fought the flames with stirrup pumps, water being obtained from the wash basin in the Librarian's lavatory. There was smoke everywhere, and the weather was bitterly cold. Downstairs in the museum there was no light, and the floor was in several places inches deep in water.[25]

The library lost some twenty-five thousand books, and many more were damaged by water. In another raid a few months later the art gallery was totally destroyed. By contrast, the museum's losses were relatively light. But the devastation wrought during the war, both in much of the Guildhall precinct itself, and throughout many other parts of the City, nevertheless had a profound influence upon the future of the museum. It confronted the Corporation with two inter-related questions – how to provide for its unloved but increasingly important museum, and how to cope with the archaeological challenge presented by the bombed areas. The last thirty years of the museum's life, from the end of the war in 1945 until the establishment of the Museum of London in 1975, are the story of the Corporation's responses to these problems.

Even before the war the museum had in fact been under some degree of threat. Plans drawn up in 1935 for the rearrangement of the whole Guildhall precinct by the Corporation's consultant architect, Sir Giles Gilbert Scott, had proposed converting the museum into a bookstore for the library; and in 1944 this idea was taken up by the new librarian, Raymond Smith, who was not always a friend to the museum. 'To a visitor', so he told the Library Committee, 'the interior is gloomy and unattractive', and the existing accommodation 'could be better used as a storeroom for the Library'. He was, of course, hoping to see 'a new Museum worthy of the treasures it houses and of the great Corporation whose property it is', but in the meantime he was putting up steel shelves in the museum, and books were being 'regrouped' there. By 1946 it had become Corporation policy that this use should be permanent.[26]

This was the discouraging situation to which Adrian Oswald returned in December 1945, when Waddington retired. Two-thirds of the museum collections were still down in Berkshire, but by March 1946 Oswald had managed to put on the first of a series of small temporary displays in the Basinghall Street entrance lobby and on the main staircase leading up to the library. It dealt with 'the story of the Jug', and was followed by others on such subjects as 'Fires of London' and 'Religious Life in London'. In 1947, however, this exiguous accommodation was enlarged

254/255 *Guildhall and the Guildhall Art Gallery were badly damaged by incendiary bombs and fire in separate bombing raids in 1940 and 1941.*
In 1988 Roman London's amphitheatre was discovered on the site of the Art Gallery

by the use of the 'bridge', a wide corridor leading from the library to the art gallery. Here for the next eight years some half-dozen exhibitions were mounted, the first (1947–50) being on 'Bygone London'. The most popular of these proved, significantly, to be those on 'Recent archaeological finds from Walbrook' (1950, seen by nearly twelve thousand visitors) and on 'Roman London, with special emphasis on recent finds', which in 1953 attracted great interest in the national press and on the BBC.[27]

By that time the post-war archaeological challenge for London was approaching one of the most intense of its periodic crises. The buildings on more than 50 of the 350 or so acres of the ancient walled city had been destroyed by bombing, and an interval of several years elapsed between the end of the war and the start of rebuilding. A unique opportunity therefore presented itself for the scientific elucidation of London's origins and distant past, in conditions free (in Professor Grimes's words) 'from the cramping limitations of time and builders' needs which had prevailed formerly'.[28] For the City this was, without doubt, the most exceptional bargain offer of knowledge ever made by the Sibyl.

256 *Temporary exhibition on the 'bridge' at Guildhall*

257 *War devastation in the City of London as seen from the Golden Gallery of St Paul's Cathedral, looking east. On the right is Cannon Street, and parallel with it in the centre is Watling Street. Photograph taken in 1944–5 by Arthur Cross and Fred Tibbs for the City of London Police*

This opportunity had been foreseen by the Society of Antiquaries, which in 1944 had sent a deputation to the Lord Mayor in order 'to secure the support of the Corporation for a proposal to excavate sites in the City of London with a view to elucidating the lay-out of the Roman city'. A letter from the Antiquaries which was subsequently laid before the Court of Common Council had, however, received an unforthcoming answer – in the case of excavations desired to be made on the Corporation's own property they would 'extend their co-operation as far as possible', but elsewhere they had no control. So in the absence of any lead from the Corporation – in the absence, indeed, of any comprehension there of either the size or the essentiality of the work to be done – the Antiquaries themselves in 1945–6 took the initiative in establishing the Roman and Medieval London Excavation Council for the purpose of organizing a programme of systematic excavation. And the Corporation agreed that the librarian (Smith) and the museum curator (Oswald) should be allowed to serve on this new body.[29]

The inauguration of the RMLEC took place in September 1946 at the Mansion House at a meeting presided over by the Lord Mayor. Grimes,

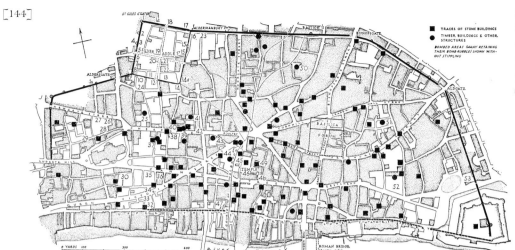

258 Sites within the City excavated by W F Grimes between 1946 and 1962. Bombed areas are shown without stippling. Reproduced from Grimes's book, 'The Excavation of Roman and Mediaeval London', 1968

who (as we have seen) had succeeded Wheeler in 1945 as keeper of the London Museum, became the honorary director of the impending excavations, and he and the Council readily agreed that all finds should (subject to the consent of the site owners) go to the Guildhall Museum initially, and subsequently 'when quantity permits', to the London Museum. After a short trial season in 1946, financed by the Antiquaries and directed by Grimes, the Council's operations began in July 1947 and (in their director's words) 'went on without ceasing, winter and summer, from then until December 1962'.[30]

These post-war excavations were, with only very minor exceptions, the first ever to be undertaken in the City for *purely* archaeological purposes, uninhibited by the exigencies of builders' timetables.[31] Their total cost, spread over fifteen years, amounted to some £40000. Well over half of this sum (£26300) was provided by an annual grant from the Ministry of Public Building and Works, and most of the rest came from banks, insurance companies, some of the City Livery Companies and many private individuals. The City Corporation itself gave £550 – equivalent to about 1.3 per cent of the total sum.[32]

The Corporation did, however, still concern itself with 'rescue' operations – the watching of builders' excavations – as it had since the days of Frank Lambert. This was now done by Adrian Oswald, through whose energy and vigilance part of a fine tesselated pavement of the third century was revealed and preserved on its site in Ironmonger Lane by the owners, Messrs Peat, Marwick, Mitchell and Company, the accountants.[33] As its honorary secretary Oswald also helped the RMLEC in raising funds and in negotiating site owners' permission for Grimes to dig, and in the museum's makeshift laboratory on the fourth floor of the Guildhall's main entrance porch he attempted to wash and process the constant stream of Grimes's finds. By 1948–9, however, the post-war rebuilding of the City was just beginning, and with all these other tasks (as well as the organization of the museum's exhibitions on the 'bridge' and in the Basinghall Street entrance) he and his one assistant, G W Lawrence (no relation of G F Lawrence, formerly of the London Museum) could not possibly give more than an occasional glance at the developers' excavations. So towards the end of 1949 they both resigned, Oswald having accepted the post of keeper of Birmingham City Museum's Department of Archaeology. Librarian Smith admitted that they had been 'quite overwhelmed' by the growing influx of new material, and added that by their resignation the work of the museum had been 'thrown into a state of near-chaos'.[34]

*259/260 Excavations on the site of St Swithin's House, Walbrook, 1949–50 (above)
With Ivor Noel Hume at work (top right)*

261/262 A Roman amphora in course of removal, and after cleaning (right)

Unfortunately for the Corporation, Oswald's departure coincided with the first really massive post-war building operation in the City; and the site, extending from St Swithin's Lane to Walbrook, was one of the potentially most important areas of Roman London. The person left to deal with this situation was Ivor Noel Hume, 'an unsuccessful playwright' (his own description of himself) who 'while waiting for someone to recognise [*his*] literary prowess . . . had passed the spring and early summer of 1949 picking up artifacts on the foreshore of the Thames and taking them to Adrian Oswald for identification'. Then he had become Oswald's 'honorary part-time potwasher' and 'volunteer shovel-carrier', and finally, in December 1949, with some six months' experience of archaeology, he became responsible for all the museum's outdoor site work. 'For better or worse', he later recorded, 'rescue archaeology in the City was in my hands for seven years beginning in December 1949.'[35]

Librarian Smith at once welcomed his new recruit with the news that there was a move afoot within the Corporation to dispense with the museum altogether, and hand the collections over to the London Museum. This was, however, to be averted by constantly reminding the members of the Library Committee that the museum was successfully performing a useful public function; and this in turn could best be achieved by showing as many new finds as possible at the monthly meetings of the Committee, and by immediately informing the press of all 'newsworthy' discoveries. So throughout the winter of 1949–50 hardly a week went by without a story in the newspapers or on the BBC of some remarkable find at the St Swithin's House site; and certainly never a month went by without the Library Committee being entertained with private views of pots (often heavily restored) and fibulae and stili and strigils. It hardly mattered that owing to his inexperience some of the information given by Noel Hume to eager reporters amid the roar of the bulldozers was not (as he himself afterwards admitted) always accurate, or that some of the restorations made for the benefit of the Library Committee 'resulted in some highly questionable vessels'. By the end of March 1950 the Corporation had, however, at last decided to provide a reasonable staff establishment for its museum. Three new posts were to be created, and in all there were to be five posts – keeper (filled by Norman Cook), assistant keeper (Ralph Merrifield), excavations assistant (Noel Hume), cataloguer (Lysbeth Webb) and repairer and technician (Audrey Baines).[36]

Norman Cook, the keeper of the Guildhall Museum, came from the Southampton Museum, of which he had been curator since 1946. During his twenty-one years at the Guildhall, from 1950 to 1971, he proved in many important ways to be the right man for the job. Genial and convivial by nature, he enjoyed the friendly relations which livery company and committee dinners engendered in the City and which often extended into the conduct of the Corporation's business. He was on easy terms with many influential members of the Corporation because he had frequently met them socially on such occasions; and in such a large assembly as the Court of Common Council, or even the Library Committee, where there were no party political caucuses, individual personalities were very important. Slowly he was able to raise the standing of the museum within the Corporation from the nadir at which he found it in 1950, and to convince the Corporation that, given proper facilities, it could and should provide a service of deep permanent value to the public. It was during his years that Common Council committed itself to the concept of amalgamation with the London Museum, and so Norman Cook will always be regarded as one of the founding fathers of the Museum of London.

Ralph Merrifield, the assistant keeper, came from the Brighton Museum, where (apart from six years in the RAF) he had been an assistant since 1930. He was first and foremost a museum man, with a wide knowledge of material objects, rather than an excavator, though he would always give help in the field whenever requested. He was also a very fine photographer. But above all he was a scholar – certainly the most distinguished scholar ever to serve on the staff of the Guildhall Museum – and the author of three fine books on Roman London, the first of which, *The Roman City of London*, published in 1965, was a landmark in the study of the whole subject. He remained with the Guildhall Museum until its fusion with the London Museum in 1975. Thereafter he was senior keeper of the Prehistoric and Roman Department, and latterly deputy director, of the Museum of London. His retirement in 1978 was honoured by the publication of a *festschrift, Collectanea Londiniensia,* containing nearly forty essays contributed by fellow scholars.

The arrival of these two experienced men made the year 1950 an important landmark in the history of the Guildhall Museum. By August an exhibition had (as previously mentioned) been mounted in the 'bridge' corridor on 'Recent Archaeological finds from Walbrook', and thereafter the displays at Guildhall were changed more frequently. The greater part of the museum's possessions, still down at their wartime home in Berkshire, were at last brought back, and a new Excavation Register was established to preserve notes made in the field and to create an improved numbering system.[37] The main emphasis of the museum's work continued, however, to be directed towards Noel Hume's 'rescue' archaeology – at any rate in the eyes of the Library Committee and the general public. In 1951–2 he was busy at the site of Lloyd's new building at the corner of Lime Street and Fenchurch Avenue, where a Roman hypocaust and several areas of coarse tesselated pavements were found. At the junction of Queen Street and Queen Victoria Street, on the site of the Bank of London and South America, he investigated over a dozen ancient wells ('he was always a great digger out of wells and rubbish pits', Ralph Merrifield later remarked), and the discovery of such 'newsworthy' objects as a Roman ladder and a Roman 'Bikini' (both now in the Museum of London) put him firmly back in the public eye in 1953. Here and on other sites where he was active he was supported by bands of voluntary helpers who for the next few years were prominent on many 'rescue' sites in the City, much of their work being done at weekends, when they were free and the builders were absent. The tools used on these forays had to be carried about on London Transport buses, for the Corporation provided no transportation of its own for such purposes; and finds had to be taken to Guildhall in paper bags or (when more plentiful) in coal sacks or even trundled along in a wheelbarrow. For very many people archaeology was, indeed, in the early 1950s becoming a matter of active interest, or at any rate curiosity; and it was no coincidence that in the summer of 1953 objects chosen from the Guildhall Museum were displayed on one of the BBC's television programmes entitled 'Animal, Vegetable or Mineral?' – a series that was just then beginning to exert its popularizing influence on all matters archaeological.[38] It was in this atmosphere of general inquisitiveness and expectancy that there occurred in September 1954 the famous Mithras incident.

Throughout all the post-war years of turmoil at the Guildhall Museum Grimes had on behalf of the Roman and Medieval London Excavation Council been quietly carrying on his small-scale, scientifically controlled and observed excavations on the bombed sites. He had already, in 1949,

263 *Ralph Merrifield*

264 *Roman ladder discovered in 1953 by Ivor Noel Hume in a first-century well near Queen Street*

made what is still the outstanding discovery of post-war investigation in London – the existence of the Cripplegate Fort – but very characteristically he had published this fact in a learned journal, and (apart from *The Times*) the newshounds of Fleet Street seem to have known nothing about it. Nor had the Corporation shown any interest (though the Librarian must have been aware of it), for hardly any 'finds' had reached the Guildhall Museum through it. Grimes, in fact, eschewed publicity. A very experienced and scholarly archaeologist, he was only concerned with one thing – the scientific elucidation of London's past – and the 'finds', though needed at Guildhall to keep the Library Committee happy, were of little interest to him unless they contributed to that end. It is therefore hardly surprising that he viewed the untrained Noel Hume's 'rescue' operations with some distaste.

Grimes had begun to make a series of cuttings across what was later to become nationally famous as the Mithras site in 1950–1. Here on the west side of Walbrook a block of one and a half acres had been devastated by bombing, but much of the ground was still deeply covered with rubble and other obstructions, and there was therefore very little room in which to work. Eventually further progress became impossible until the site was cleared by the developers, and so the digging had to stop. Through lack of means, both of facilities and of money, precious time was thus lost. When in 1954 archaeological work became feasible again it had to be done – despite the generous cooperation of both the site owners and the building contractors – in conditions not so very different from those of Noel Hume's 'rescue' operations. This was particularly so after the discovery of the head of Mithras on Saturday 18 September, and the feverish publicity which this at once evoked. During the next nine days at least 30000 people visited the site, many of them queueing for hours to do so, very much as they had in 1869 after the discovery of the mosaic pavement on the adjoining site in Bucklersbury. Questions were asked in Parliament, the Minister of Works visited the site, and the possibility of preserving the temple *in situ* was widely discussed. This would have entailed substantial modification of the plans for the proposed new building and would have cost around half a million pounds. But a public appeal produced only £6000 (of which the Corporation contributed £300), and ultimately the remains of the temple were 'reconstructed' at the cost of the owners on the forecourt of the gigantic office block known as Bucklersbury House which now stands upon the site. The result of this was, however, in Grimes's view 'virtually meaningless as a reconstruction of a mithraeum'.[39]

When the building contractors' bulldozers moved in to clear the whole site Noel Hume and his colleagues conducted one of their 'rescue' operations. This part of the Walbrook valley was 'literally bristling with Roman artifacts and structural remains preserved in immaculate condition', and hundreds of bags were filled with pottery, coins and other finds salvaged from the wreckage.[40] This work continued well into the spring of 1955. The extent of the evidence which scientific investigation, if given the chance, could have revealed and which was now destroyed for ever in this general holocaust can never be known. The appeal for such investigations which had been made in 1873 by John Edward Price in his report on the discoveries then recently made on the adjoining site of the National Safe Deposit Company's premises was still largely relevant: 'With the rapidity with which such a large quantity of earth has to be excavated and removed, and the dangers consequent on delay, there must naturally be a large number of objects which escape detection. . . . Such are conditions which must ever exist

unless an excavation in the city be undertaken *solely* on antiquarian grounds. This has never yet been done. We institute researches abroad, sometimes on doubtful sites, and critically examine every shovel-full of earth, often with no certain prospect of reward; but in a comparatively small space situate at home, and illustrative alike of the origin and progressive thought of this the chief city of the empire, sufficient interest has not yet been manifested to induce a properly organized investigation of any given site.'[41]

It was, in fact, almost a case of 'Plus ça change, plus c'est la même chose' – almost, but not quite. By 1962, when most of the bombed sites had been built upon and his investigations in the City had therefore come to an end, Grimes had been able to make over fifty scientific excavations, mostly small in scale; and though tragically handicapped by lack of resources, his findings at the Cripplegate Fort, the Walbrook Mithraeum and on many of the other sites had immeasurably advanced knowledge of London's distant past. He was the lonely forerunner of the better times which were to come a decade later. ◻

265 *The Mithras site in Walbrook during excavations, 1954*
(top left)

266 *The Temple of Mithras as seen from above*

269 *Silver canister and strainer, found by Grimes on the site of the Temple of Mithras, 1954.*
This is a most remarkable object: an extraordinary variety of animals is depicted including mythical griffins which are shown trying to tear open what appear to be coffins. The significance of the symbolism is not known
(right)

267 *Bastion 12 at the north-west corner of the Roman Fort, adjoining the churchyard of St Giles Cripplegate, in 1946. It was excavated in about 1900 and the upper part, at least, is medieval*

After the great Mithras commotion there were several years of quiet in the City's world of archaeological fieldwork. Developers had become extremely wary of archaeologists and were nervous of the heavy costs to which the presence of such people on their building sites might lead. There was little derelict bombed land still awaiting development and the great office building boom of the 1960s had hardly yet begun. In 1955 Noel Hume, in one of his last and most important operations, was able to recover the complete ground-plan of a Roman bath-house in Cheapside; but early in 1957 he left the museum and took up an archaeological post at Colonial Williamsburg in the United States of America.

So far as the museum itself was concerned Mithras had two important results – firstly, the acquisition of all the sculptures found at the temple, a series of outstanding pieces which in the words of Grimes himself (never given to boasting about his own achievements) 'as a whole can be claimed the equal of any so far recorded in the Western Roman Empire'.[42] Secondly, Mithras greatly enhanced the standing of the museum in the eyes of the Corporation, even though the principal 'finds' had not been made by the museum staff. The museum was suddenly perceived to be potentially capable of providing a service more and more demanded by the public and the media. By a fortunate chance the covered courtyard at the Royal Exchange was no longer being used for commercial purposes and the Gresham Committee (which administered the building on behalf of the joint owners, the Corporation and the Mercers' Company) was looking for a new tenant. In 1953 a member of the Library Committee had suggested that the empty courtyard might provide a permanent home for the museum,[43] and a few months before the onset of the Mithras hubbub the Gresham Committee had agreed to allow the museum to use the courtyard for five years, subject to certain conditions. Temporary offices and display cases were accordingly put up at the Exchange, the exhibition at the 'bridge' in Guildhall was closed in February 1955, and on 29 June 1955 the Lord Mayor opened the museum in its new home. The display included specimens relating to all periods of the City's past, but special emphasis was, of course, given to the finds at the temple of Mithras. In a rather over-enthusiastic comment about such an essentially makeshift arrangement librarian Smith told his Committee what they wanted to hear – the Corporation's possessions were at last being 'displayed with the dignity due to their importance'.[44]

But at any rate the museum was back in business, and by 1957 annual attendances had risen to the substantial figure of over 122000. Two years later the remains of the western gateway of Grimes's Cripplegate

268 *Brian Spencer, then assistant keeper at the London Museum, photographed at the Walbrook site by 'The Times', holding the recently discovered head of Mithras, 1954. Numerous other sculptures of Roman deities, expertly carved in good quality Italian marble, were also found. These now form an important exhibit in the museum*

270 *The western gateway of the Roman Fort was excavated by Grimes in 1956–8. Its remains have been preserved, underneath the modern street called London Wall*

271/272 *From 1955 to 1967 the Guildhall Museum had a temporary home in the courtyard and of the Royal Exchange*

Fort, now preserved under the modern street known as London Wall, were opened for public inspection and attracted thousands of visitors during the lunch-hour breaks.* Several booklets were produced, notably Noel Hume's *Discoveries on Walbrook 1949–50* (*ie* those at St Swithin's House), and Norman Cook's *Finds in Roman London 1949–52*. In 1958 there was a temporary exhibition on 'Treasure Trove in the City' – always a subject of concern to the City Fathers, particularly since the Cheapside Hoard affair – occasioned by the discovery of over seventy silver denarii on a site at Temple House. Treasure trove was also in the news at about this time through the inquest held on the beautiful silver canister found by Grimes at the Mithras temple, and which through his generosity ultimately found its home in the museum. Other additions to the museum's collection included a large deposit of leathercraft in 1957 and two years later the Robert Spence collection of gloves, lent by the Glovers' Company.[45]

Although the museum's sojourn at the Royal Exchange had never been intended to be more than temporary, 'the word "temporary"' had sometimes, as librarian Smith had once stated in another connection, 'to be given a long term perspective'. By 1959, when four of the five years originally granted by the Gresham Committee had elapsed, Smith's successor, A H Hall, reported that the accommodation was 'by no means satisfactory'. There was no heating except in the offices, no water and no cloakroom facilities. At frequent intervals the work and displays of the museum were interrupted by totally irrelevant exhibitions mounted with the permission of the Gresham Committee in the centre of the court-yard. On a typical such occasion in 1960, for instance, the museum was virtually closed for six weeks. In 1963 the whole courtyard was closed for three months for repairs to the roof, and in 1966 visitors were during the washing of the exterior of the building liable to be drenched with water at the entrance.[46]

By that time, however, negotiations for the amalgamation of the Guild-hall Museum with the London Museum, which had started in 1959, were exerting an increasing influence upon the Corporation's policy towards its own collections. There was no point, so the City Fathers perhaps thought, in spending money on providing better accommodation for the Guildhall Museum when a great brand new museum building was going to be put up on London Wall pretty soon. So nothing would probably have been done had not the press got to hear about the embarrassing plight of the museum staff. 'Long before the rush-hour starts each night', so the *Daily Mail* told its readers in December 1966, 'people hurry from the Guildhall Museum in the City to the nearest Tube station, Bank. They aren't catching early trains home. They are all going to the lavatory.'

* The permanent preservation of the west gate of the fort and much of the adjacent north-west wall of the City was largely due to the efforts of the Corporation's engineer, F J Forty.

And the man from the *Daily Sketch* watched members of the staff slip out of the Exchange 'clutching bits of paper and vanish into the Bank Underground station close by', where they presented their Corporation chitties to the attendant at the public 'wash-and-brush-up' (price 3d) and were admitted free of charge.[47]

The Corporation is often sensitive to criticism in the press but it might nevertheless have ignored facetious comments of this kind. Unfortunately, however, the Offices, Shops and Railway Premises Act of 1963 precluded any such indifference. An inspector called at the museum, and in due course declared that the accommodation was 'quite inadequate'. So something had to be done.[48]

The problem was solved when the Corporation took a seven-year lease of three vacant sites on the newly-built Bassishaw High Walk which had been intended for small shops; and there was also an office annexe in the adjoining new block known as Gillett House, on London Wall. This new home, to which the exhibits at the Exchange and the reserve collections there and at Guildhall were removed at the end of 1967, provided much better display possibilities, greatly improved working conditions and (for the first time in the history of the museum) adequate facilities for students working on the reserve material. Members of the public were first admitted on 4 January 1968, but there was an official opening ceremony on 1 April to coincide with the beginning of Museums Week in Britain.

This was the last of the Guildhall Museum's homes, for it remained here until it merged with the London Museum on 1 June 1975. During these years its considerably enlarged staff mounted a number of exhibitions, presented an entirely new display of the Roman collections, and started a much-needed campaign of conservation work. Owing to the layout of the galleries it proved impossible to count the number of individual visitors but in 1971 over one hundred and fifty organized groups were taken round the museum, and many thousands of postcards and booklets were sold at the entrance counter. In its final years the Guildhall Museum was, indeed, a well-run, active and efficient place.[49]

One of the reasons for this was that in 1966 the Guildhall Museum had at last become completely separate from the Guildhall Library; and as with the museum's departure from the Royal Exchange, this bifurcation was to some extent the result of the mandatory requirements of a recent Act of Parliament. Just as it was an Act of Parliament which had

273 *Norman Cook examining gloves from the Spence collection, deposited by the Worshipful Company of Glovers in 1959. He joined the staff as keeper of the Guildhall Museum in 1950, became its first director in 1966 and retired in 1971. With Donald Harden, he was much involved in the planning for the new Museum of London*

274 *Gillett House, Bassishaw High Walk, provided the last home for the Guildhall Museum before it amalgamated with the London Museum. It opened to the public in January 1968*

275 *A display in the museum at Gillett House*

obliged the Corporation to provide offices equipped with lavatories for its museum staff, so too another Act of Parliament helped to induce the Corporation to acknowledge the importance of its museum by separating it from the library. This event was no doubt facilitated by the personal distinction of its keeper, Norman Cook, for it was really rather ridiculous that the president of the Museums Association (a post held by Cook in 1964–5) was still not allowed to speak at meetings of the Library Committee except through his 'boss', the librarian; and no doubt also the separation was seen as an appropriate half-way stage towards the forthcoming absorption of the museum into the new Museum of London. Nevertheless the Public Libraries and Museums Act of 1964 confronted the Corporation with a new problem. Until 1921 the Guildhall Library, Museum and Art Gallery had been financed out of the City's cash, but in that year the Corporation had adopted the Public Libraries Act and so been able to finance all three institutions out of the rate funds. This meant that the Corporation became the public library authority for the City, but the Guildhall Library was still not a lending library. By the Act of 1964, however, library authorities were compelled to provide lending facilities, and in due course several new such libraries were set up in the City by the Corporation. But as none of the staff at the Guildhall Library had had any experience of lending libraries, an 'outsider' (Mr Godfrey Thompson, hitherto City librarian of Leeds) was brought in to organize and administer this greatly enlarged system. The museum could have no rational place in this new set-up; and so on A H Hall's retirement as librarian Norman Cook, hitherto the keeper of the museum, became on 1 April 1966 the first director of the liberated Guildhall Museum, at last entirely separate from the library.[50] And a few months later the Corporation set up a new 'Purchase of Exhibits Fund', to be used for acquisitions for either the art gallery or the museum. The generous sum of £10000 was provided in the first year and a similar amount in 1967 (though expenditure had been less than £1500), the Corporation's policy being to top the fund up each year to the maximum permitted for such funds by the Public Libraries and Museums Act of 1964.[51]

276 *Sir Mortimer Wheeler, Norman Cook and Peter Marsden (left) examining walls of the Blackfriars Monastery, found in 1960 on the site of the new 'Times' newspaper office in Queen Victoria Street*

In the final few years of the Guildhall Museum's separate existence the Corporation also moved towards recognizing and paying for its responsibilities for field archaeology within the City. But it had to be pushed all the way, mainly by its own increasingly capable museum staff and by the pressure of public opinion. After Noel Hume's departure in 1957 his successor in the watching of building sites was Eve Rutter, who located the ancient stream-bed of the Walbrook in two places. But the rising star in this sphere of activity was already Peter Marsden. At the age of fourteen he had through his grandfather, who was a quantity surveyor working at the Bucklersbury House project in Walbrook, obtained access to the Mithras site, where he had almost immediately found a Roman well or water tank. Thereafter he spent many weekends at numerous 'digs', and at the age of eighteen had caused a sensation by his discovery of a Roman ship at Guy's Hospital in Southwark. His persistence gradually won over Norman Cook, whose primary concern was not with archaeological fieldwork, and after Eve Rutter's departure in 1959 he was taken on as a museum assistant, later becoming the excavations assistant. Though totally unqualified, he had a natural flair for the work, and above all he knew how to get on with builders and developers. Until 1973 most of the archaeological fieldwork within the City was done by him.[52]

These were years of much building activity in the City. Numerous Victorian or later buildings were being cleared away for the erection of huge new office blocks, and near the waterfront a new dual carriageway was being driven from Blackfriars to the Tower. Grimes's fieldwork in the City had come to an end in 1962, and the Corporation was not yet providing any money to pay for the cost of excavations by its own museum staff. The archaeological situation was therefore extremely serious. Young Peter Marsden was, however, given a sense of direction by Ralph Merrifield's book, *The Roman City of London*, published after years of work in 1965. Future archaeological operations, it was clear, must somehow combine both the 'rescue' work previously done by Noel Hume on building sites and the scientific excavations hitherto done by Grimes – and all with very little money. It was a demanding programme.[53]

The 1960s, therefore, were the heyday of the volunteer excavations, when archaeology was kept alive in the City by the enthusiasm and devotion of scores of volunteers working for nothing, and mostly at weekends. The first scientific excavation (as opposed to 'rescue' operation) using volunteers was in 1960 in Bush Lane, east of Cannon Street Station, where massive walls later found to be part of a Roman palace were revealed. Other important sites in which volunteers were active included Blackfriars, where in 1962–3, during the construction of the Blackfriars underpass, Peter Marsden discovered a Roman ship in the river mud, part of which was removed to the Guildhall Museum. In 1964 the levelling by a bulldozer of a site in Huggin Hill, opposite Queenhithe, led to the finding of a Roman bath-house. Here the urgency of the situation was so great that the help of two neighbouring archaeological groups was successfully requested – the Wandsworth Historical Society led by Nicholas Farrant (by profession an officer at the Bank of England), and the West Kent Border Archaeological Group led by Brian Philp; and out of that strenuous August Bank Holiday weekend, in which a substantial portion of the plan of the building was recovered, there emerged the City of London Excavation Group, later the City of London Archaeological Society. With this more formal body to support him Peter Marsden was able to enlarge the size of his operations considerably, particularly in the recording of sites, which was always of primary

277 *Peter Marsden with the Roman ship found during excavations for the Blackfriars underpass and embankment in 1962–3*

importance to him. His painstaking work in searching for and recording even the most inconspicuous traces of Roman road metalling, for instance, has proved of lasting value in the reconstruction of the street-plan of Londinium. And starting in 1961 he even made time to publish summaries of his findings in the *Transactions of the London and Middlesex Archaeological Society.*[54]

Meanwhile, the Corporation had been considering what might be done about archaeology in the post-Grimes era. In October 1963 the Librarian, A H Hall, had recommended to the Library Committee that in considering planning applications for redevelopment the Corporation should have the archaeological potential of each site reviewed by the keeper of the museum; if important remains were expected, his opinion should be confirmed by an independent archaeological panel; and if his opinion were upheld, planning permission should then be made conditional upon time for excavation being allowed. Where the money for any such investigation was to come from was not stated, but it did not really matter, for the Corporation's lawyers advised that it was not legally possible to make archaeological excavations a condition of planning permission. The matter then lapsed; but on building sites where the Corporation itself had a financial interest excavations were given a legal basis by the insertion in the building agreements of clauses requiring the contractor during demolition to afford the keeper of the museum or his staff 'reasonable facilities to examine measure and record and remove any articles of historical or archaeological interest which may be disclosed'. In 1966, too, a map of 'Known Roman Sites of Archaeological Importance' was prepared in the Corporation's Department of Architecture and Planning, based on information supplied by the museum; and thereafter planning permissions for sites within the most important areas included an *advisory* clause stating that 'It is considered excavation of the site may uncover remains of considerable archaeological interest, and it is requested that the director of the Guildhall Museum be consulted in regard to this aspect of the matter.'[55]

One of the first occasions – indeed perhaps the very first occasion – on which the Corporation made a direct contribution towards the costs of the excavations carried out by its own staff was in 1965. Peter Marsden and Nicholas Farrant and their volunteers, working very near to Guildhall itself, had exposed a forty-foot length of the east wall of the Roman Fort; but at the end of this operation they had been left with a vast mound of spoil which had to be replaced, but which not even the most devoted volunteers could be expected to manhandle back with pick and shovel. So a bulldozer was hired to do the job, and the Corporation paid the bill. In the following year the Corporation agreed to spend £3000 on the clearance of land in its own possession which was needed for the extension of the Central Criminal Court at the Old Bailey. This was done under Peter Marsden's archaeological supervision and resulted in the uncovering of a number of medieval houses, but there was no matching grant for other archaeological work, which therefore still had to be done by volunteers. In 1967 there was £1300 for more navvying, again under Marsden's direction, to uncover the site of the gate at Aldgate; and at Billingsgate, where the demolition of the Coal Exchange in Lower Thames Street had made land adjacent to the Roman bath beneath available for excavation before the street was widened. But both these sums were administered by the Engineer's Department of the Corporation and were for the clearance of ground about to be built upon; and it was not until 1968–9 that any money was included in the Library Committee's estimates specifically for archaeological excavations.

278 *The Coal Exchange, Lower Thames Street.*
After the demolition of this notable Victorian building the site was excavated by Peter Marsden in 1967

In that year excavations were proceeding at the crucial Limebank site at the junction of Fenchurch Street and Gracechurch Street under the direction of Brian Philp, Peter Marsden being already fully engaged at the Billingsgate bath.* A sum of £1000 was voted for these works, and this was matched by £500 from the Ministry of Public Building and Works. But in the following year only £107 was actually made available, and the estimate for 1971–2 was reduced to £500.[57]

Progress was, in fact, still painfully slow, and Peter Marsden, writing in 1980, was later to recall that 'The years up to 1972 now seem like a bad dream, with missed opportunities and the ruthless destruction of large parts of Roman London.'[58] But with the arrival of Max Hebditch in May 1971 as director in succession to Norman Cook, things very soon began to change. At the age of only thirty-four he came from the City Museum at Bristol, where he had been curator in Agricultural and Social History, and was (in his own words) 'frankly amazed that such low sums were being spent on the archaeology of the most important urban site in Britain'. Norman Cook had, understandably, been reluctant to 'rock the boat' of the nascent Museum of London by asking the Corporation for more money for archaeology. But Max Hebditch immediately proposed a sum of £3000 in the estimates for the financial year 1972–3 for excavation purposes, towards which a grant of £1500 was expected from the Department of the Environment (previously the Ministry of Public Building and Works). In due course the Department did provide a grant of £1500 but the Corporation cut its allocation to only £500 – the same figure as for 1971–2.

Unabashed, however, by this temporary setback, the new director nevertheless proceeded to belabour the Library Committee in his first Annual Report, written in March 1972, and received by the Court of Common Council in the following month. 'It cannot be pretended that adequate time and resources were devoted to coping with the destruction of archaeological evidence in the City. Although the information recovered from excavation and observation was valuable to the history of the city, it was perforce piecemeal and scrappy. There is no substitute for proper excavation of more sites before construction work takes place. The decision not to excavate a site, whether forced on the Museum or consciously taken, is in many ways equivalent to destroying a portion of the documents in the City's archives.'[59]

The Corporation began to take notice, if only because it was not used to being addressed in such terms by one of its own officers. Furthermore it began to realize that the problem was not going to go away, for the number of planning applications for rebuilding which had been approved was steadily mounting.[60] The Corporation was concerned, too, at the contrast between its own record of support for archaeology within its own domains and that of the Government, whose grant for nationwide rescue work had been increased six-fold over the previous ten years, and was now to be nearly doubled. It was also in the spring of 1972 that the Rescue Trust for British Archaeology, a formidable new pressure group established for the purpose of saving Britain's ancient archaeological deposits, first became widely known to the public.[61]

In this rather uneasy atmosphere there suddenly occurred the Baynard's Castle affair, akin in many ways to both the St Swithin's House affair of 1949–50 and to the Mithras affair of 1954; but on this occasion the results were to be of lasting benefit to archaeological studies in London. This was largely due to the efforts of Max Hebditch. He was, of course, greatly helped by a powerful groundswell of public opinion moving strongly in favour of support for archaeology, conservation and matters

* These excavations uncovered vital evidence about the evolution of the great Roman forum in that part of the City. They were carried out with much tenacity by Philp and a large contingent of volunteers throughout the grim winter of 1968–9.[56]

environmental in general, and also by the impending establishment of the Museum of London; but nevertheless he succeeded within less than three years of his arrival in getting the Corporation to do what Wheeler and Grimes and many others had all wanted – set up a properly funded professional archaeological unit for the City. It was a remarkable achievement.

Baynard's Castle was originally a Norman fortress built at the south-west corner of the City, a little to the east of the modern Blackfriars Bridge, where it fulfilled the same defensive function as the Tower of London at the south-east corner. In late medieval times its site had become part of the precincts of Blackfriars and a new castle or palace with a turreted front to the river had been built. This was one of the two important sites selected by Max Hebditch and his colleagues for excavation in 1972, the other being at Duke's Place, Aldgate, where Hugh Chapman, then an assistant curator at the Museum and later deputy director of the Museum of London, was in charge. Much of the Baynard's Castle site was required for the new dual carriageway to be built along Thames Street, and archaeological excavations were planned to take place there between April and September 1972. But in February it was learnt that the site of the turreted façade would be required by the contractors on 1 April. Desperate measures were therefore needed. The director successfully demanded extra funds from the Library Committee, the Department of the Environment made an advance on its grant for the financial year 1972–3, and with Peter Marsden in charge an emergency excavation of the river frontage was mounted. The valuable archaeological deposits which were soon revealed near to the Thames were found to be extremely well-preserved, thereby arousing much greater interest in other sites further east along the waterfront; and the Easter weekend of 30 March to 3 April found large numbers of volunteers working desperately in the mud and silt to complete their records before everything was destroyed by the bulldozers – as indeed it was on 5 April.[62]

All this was happening within hardly more than a stone's throw of Fleet Street, and the remains disclosed commanded great visual interest for the layman, for whom one archaeological excavation usually looks much like another; here 'you could see that there was a castle'. So widespread public notice of the matter in the press ensued, much of it highly critical of the Corporation. This was particularly the case after Martin Biddle, the chairman of Rescue and director of the Winchester Research Unit, had visited the site on 21 March. He shared with Max Hebditch the confidence of youth, and within the next few days he generated much public comment about the inadequate organization of archaeology in the City and the slender contributions to it of the Corporation. As had happened during the Mithras incident, there were questions in the House of Commons; and the Corporation suddenly became aware that it was in an embarrassing predicament.[63]

Once again Max Hebditch successfully demanded extra funds, a revised sum of £3950 being quickly provided by the Library Committee for 1972–3, with the Department of the Environment making a grant of a similar amount. Later on, in September, the Department as part owner of the site, produced another £8500 for the cost of excavating the waterfront west of Baynard's Castle, where the Post Office was about to build a new telecommunications centre. The total expenditure on excavations (apart from the salaries of permanent staff, which totalled some £6250) in 1972–3 finally amounted (with an anonymous private donation of £1000) to £17695, of which the Corporation's contribution

279–281 Emergency excavations being conducted with volunteers' help at Baynard's Castle, spring 1972

was £3950. Still, this was a considerable improvement on all previous years.[64]

But the Corporation was far from having heard the last of Rescue, for in June 1972 it received a letter from Biddle 'indicating his organisation's dissatisfaction with the state of archaeology in the City of London', caused principally by the lack of both staff and money, and by inadequate consideration of the correct priorities in determining what fieldwork should be done. When this letter was placed before the Library Committee in July Max Hebditch had to tell the members that these criticisms were substantially correct – 'a single Field Officer to deal with the recording of all archaeology in the City of London . . . finance for archaeology in the City is inadequate, and compares very poorly with what is now available in many other towns' etc. And he went on to suggest that 'the solution might well lie' in the immediate enlargement of the resources of the Guildhall Museum, while in the longer term there should be a special Department of Urban Archaeology within the Museum of London.[65]

The upshot of this meeting was that the Library Committee called for a report from the City architect and planning officer and the museum director into all the implications of the problem. This provided Max Hebditch with the moment to produce the draft of a short booklet entitled *Archaeology in the City of London: an Opportunity*. Prepared by all the museum staff, it showed how much of the City's archaeological deposits were already lost or inaccessible, how important were the (carefully defined) areas that remained, and the extent of impending redevelopments which threatened these areas. 'If this opportunity is not grasped now, it will be lost for ever', the booklet concluded, '. . . success in seizing this opportunity depends on the co-operation of developers, archaeologists and planners. There is no second chance. What is lost today is lost for all time.'

This powerful statement, intended to form a basis for public discussion of the whole matter, was presented to the Library Committee early in November 1972 together with a separate report on what action was required from the Corporation if it was to make an adequate contribution to seizing the 'opportunity'. This report proposed the formation of a Department of Urban Archaeology within the Guildhall Museum, an excavations and publications fund to attract outside contributions as well as grants from the Corporation and the Department of the Environment for excavations, and the circulation of *an Opportunity* among property owners, developers, architects and builders 'so that they at least understood what the archaeologists wanted'. The additional cost to the rates was estimated at around £25 000 per annum, of which some £11 000 would be for staff salaries and the remainder for the Corporation's contribution to the on-site costs of future excavations.[66]

The Library Committee proved 'sympathetic to the proposals indicated in the report', and referred the whole matter to a sub-committee. Numerous such sub-committees, and later Grand (*ie* full) Committees, were involved in the prolonged huddle into which the Corporation now retreated for several months. Throughout these crucial times it was well known in the corridors of power at Guildhall that Martin Biddle and his colleagues at Rescue were preparing their own report demanding an independent City Archaeological Unit separate from the Guildhall Museum – an idea also supported by the influential Council for British Archaeology – and expenditure by the Corporation much larger than that proposed by Max Hebditch. In order to pre-empt this alarming scenario, and also in the interests of good public relations – a subject of great importance at Guildhall in matters archaeological at this time – it

282 *Hugh Chapman*

therefore became essential for the Corporation to make public its own decisions about its future policy for archaeology before Rescue was able to fire off its impending cannonade.[67]

This it just managed to do, but only by the skin of its teeth. On 28 June 1973 the Court of Common Council approved the issue of the booklet *Archaeology in the City of London: an Opportunity* in promoting goodwill, and endorsed the need for proper archaeological endeavour. This received widespread press coverage. The Court also agreed to receive a further report containing detailed staffing and financial proposals, and a few days later the Establishments Committee agreed to Hebditch's request for the setting up of a Department of Urban Archaeology in Guildhall Museum with a permanent staff of four archaeologists and one draughtsman. This small nucleus was to be supported as occasion required by staff employed on a fees and subsistence basis, which was to be paid out of the grant from the Department of the Environment. Unfortunately, however, the Establishment Committee's approval was made subject to the observations of the Planning and Communications and of the Library Committees as to 'the effective integration of archaeological research with planning decisions' (by which, apparently, was meant the matter of the future Museum of London involvement); and this qualification prevented the staffing matters going before the Court of Common Council for approval at its last meeting before the summer recess. By that time the publication of Rescue's dreaded *The Future of London's Past* was imminent, and on 22 July 1973 it received lengthy attention in *The Sunday Times*. On the very next day, therefore, the chairman of the Library Committee, Francis F Stunt (who had proved a good friend to the museum) met the chairman of the Planning and Communications Committee privately. They agreed that the Establishment Committee's qualification should not be allowed to delay the setting up of the Department of Urban Archaeology, and that the advertisement for the post of chief urban archaeologist might be placed in *The Times* at once. So the Corporation had its riposte ready for Rescue's formidable programme, which included a demand for expenditure by the Corporation of no less than an estimated £93000 per annum. But it had been a very close run thing.[68]

The Times, in a leading article entitled 'The Death of the Past' which appeared on the day after the Rescue report, considered that the Corporation's decisions for archaeology were 'certainly inadequate'.[69] Whether this view has been proved to be right or wrong is a matter of personal opinion. It is, however, certain that when the Sibyl made her final offer of knowledge in 1972–3, the price to be paid, by the creation of the Department of Urban Archaeology, had become very high indeed. But at all events when Brian Hobley, the chief urban archaeologist in the Guildhall Museum's new Department, took up his post in December 1973 and within three days began excavations at New Fresh Wharf, close to Billingsgate, there could be no doubt that a new and welcome phase in the bumpy story of the City's archaeology had begun. This most recent phase can better be described in the next chapter, for within less than two years of the inauguration of the Department of Urban Archaeology the Guildhall Museum had on 1 June 1975 fused with the London Museum to form the Museum of London, thereby bringing to a close the one hundred and forty-nine years of its independent existence under the Corporation.

283 *Mudlarks scouring the Thames foreshore for finds in 1948. The introduction of metal detectors revolutionized this practice in the 1970s*

284 *Foreshore finds in recent years have included pilgrim badges. These mid or late fourteenth-century examples are all associated with St Thomas Becket; top left, returning from exile; top right, the sword that killed him; lower left, a head of the saint; lower right, the shrine to his memory*

285 *The medieval gallery, Museum of London, 1980. The chronological sequence of the new museum's galleries tells a complex story about the growth of a great metropolitan city. The mixture of every type of material, on open display and in enclosed cases, is intended to inform visitors and lead them to further personal exploration throughout London*

THE MUSEUM OF LONDON: ITS FORMATIVE YEARS
1965 to 1987

The Museum of London's permanent galleries are arranged on two floors around a central garden court. On the upper level reconstructions, such as the Roman living and kitchen areas (286), prepare the visitor for later rooms incorporating oak panelling from a house in Wandsworth and contemporary artifacts from the sixteenth century (287). The upper level ends with the Great Fire of London in 1666, and a ramp of metal and glass leads to the lower floor (288).

287   288

Chapter 7
THE MUSEUM OF LONDON: ITS FORMATIVE YEARS
1965 TO 1987

291 *The early third-century tombstone of Vivius Marcianus was found in 1669 at Ludgate Hill and is on permanent loan from the Ashmolean Museum, Oxford. Throughout the galleries the museum's displays are considerably enhanced by loans from public institutions and private individuals*

289/290 *Displays illustrating Victorian Imperialism contrast with the detailed and carefully re-assembled interiors of offices and shops, of which the Edwardian hairdresser's is a typical example (left)*

The Guildhall Museum and the London Museum were finally amalgamated on 1 June 1975 – 'vesting day', when the two collections and their management were vested in the Board of Governors of the new Museum of London. This event was the culmination of sixteen years of complicated negotiation between the Treasury, the City Corporation, the Trustees of the London Museum and the London County Council (which in 1965 was superseded by the Greater London Council). It marked a great triumph of common sense, and was a notable red-letter day in the history of London.

Relations between the two museums had not always been easy. The City Corporation had been rather huffy at being ignored when the London Museum was founded in 1911. Two years later Guy Laking had hoped that the impending removal of the London Museum from Kensington Palace to its much larger semi-permanent new home at Lancaster House might provide an opportune moment for amalgamation with the Guildhall. He had discussed the feasibility of this idea with the Mayor of Westminster, who had a talk with the Lord Mayor of London about it. The Lord Mayor favoured the proposal but was fearful of what members of the Court of Common Council might say, and so nothing came of it.[1] In 1916 there was dissension between the City Corporation and the Trustees of the London Museum over the ownership of the Cheapside Hoard, and at the end of this episode Lewis Harcourt told the City Solicitor that 'I have often thought that it is a pity the two London Collections cannot be combined, but as this is obviously impossible, we must continue to suffer and enjoy our mutual emulation'.[2]

During the inter-war years, mutual suspicion prevailed. Dr Mortimer Wheeler's vigorous efforts to persuade the Corporation to do more about its archaeological responsibilities have already been described in a previous chapter; and doubtless his public criticism of the City Fathers in the London Museum's *Roman London Catalogue* (1930) was long remembered at Guildhall. When he gave oral evidence in 1928 to the Royal Commission on National Museums and Galleries, he was questioned about dealings between the two museums. He replied that it would be useful if the Lord Mayor were to be *ex officio* a Trustee of the London Museum (an idea implemented soon afterwards). It was possible, indeed, that the two museums might 'ultimately be persuaded to pool their resources, illustrating one period, perhaps, in the City of London and another period' at Lancaster House, and he looked forward rather vaguely to 'a day when the two Museums will work in affiliation'.[3] But the idea of amalgamation was not even mentioned, and the bickering which later broke out between Wheeler and J L Douthwaite (the Guildhall librarian), although conducted with the utmost politeness, nevertheless revealed an underlying distrust on both sides.[4]

Things might have drifted on indefinitely like this but for the war of 1939–45, by which both museums were made homeless. The Guildhall Museum, it will be recalled, was converted into a bookstore for the Guildhall Library, while Lancaster House had become a conference centre for the Foreign Office. So, if they were to avoid total extinction, both museums needed a permanent new abode, and therefore for the first time they shared a basic common aim. Amalgamation of the two largely complementary collections had, of course, always been a matter of common sense, but now it became almost inevitable as well. Some thirty years, counting from the end of the war, were nevertheless required to achieve the final union.

The long laborious process began early in 1944, when Douthwaite's successor as librarian and curator at the Guildhall, Raymond Smith, stated in his first annual report that 'much closer collaboration is desirable between the London Museum and the Guildhall Museum'. At about this time the chairman of the Corporation's Library Committee discussed the matter with someone at the London Museum, but Dr Wheeler had gone off to India and his successor had not yet been appointed, so nothing could be done.[5] By early 1946, however, W F Grimes, the new director of the London Museum, was starting his excavations in the City. He regarded this work as 'a very good opportunity for establishing close and friendly relations' with the Guildhall Museum, to which he passed all his archaeological finds made within its territory. And later in the same year he was writing to his chairman of the Board of Trustees (Lord Harewood) about amalgamation of the two museums, and pointing out that the City Corporation would have to provide a new building for its Guildhall collections 'in due course'.[6]

Nothing definite happened, however, for some years. Both museums moved into 'temporary' new homes, at the Royal Exchange and at Kensington Palace, and museum-building did not command a high priority in the post-war years of 'austerity'. We have already seen that so far as the London Museum was concerned neither the Treasury nor the London County Council was prepared to pay for a new building, and in the case of the Guildhall Museum the City Corporation had many other things on its mind.

But in the later 1950s things did at last begin to move. In 1956 Mr Duncan Sandys, Minister of Housing and Local Government in Mr Anthony Eden's Conservative administration, rejected a scheme for the commercial redevelopment of some fifty acres of land between Aldersgate Street and Moorfields, where hardly a single building had survived the bombs of 1940–1. In a public letter to the Lord Mayor he had stated that he was 'convinced that there would be advantage in creating in the City a genuine residential neighbourhood, incorporating schools, shops, open spaces, and other amenities, even if this means forgoing a more remunerative return on the land'.[7] It was from the seed sown by this decision that there slowly germinated what eventually took shape as the Barbican Estate and the Barbican Centre for the Arts. During the early 1960s there was, indeed, a distinct change of attitude within the City Corporation about its policy towards the arts, leisure and generally towards what is now called 'heritage' matters. The wider views which it now began to take resulted in the building, at great cost, of the Barbican Centre; and the Corporation also gave its steady support to the proposed amalgamation of the two museums.

In 1959 the Treasury invited the Trustees of the London Museum and representatives of both the London County Council and (for the first time) the City Corporation to talks about the future of the two museums.[8] By that time nine of the fifteen years granted by King George VI to the London Museum for the use of part of Kensington Palace had elapsed, while over in the City only one of the five years granted by the Gresham Committee to the Guildhall Museum for its sojourn at the Royal Exchange was still to come. Talks which had previously taken place between the Treasury and the London County Council about a permanent home for the London Museum on the South Bank had come to a halt, and now the outlook for both collections was bleak in the extreme. In all the circumstances it was clearly a moment for the Treasury to take the lead – and if, in the process, it could get rid of all or at least some of its responsibility for London's Museum (as it had always wanted to do ever since Lewis Harcourt had first foisted the museum on to a reluctant Lloyd George), so much the better.

The site of the Museum of London's eventual home was at the junction of Aldersgate Street and Falcon Street. This area, recorded in the Ordnance Survey map of 1873 (294) and in Henry Hodge's depiction of buildings demolished in the 1880s (292), was devastated by enemy bombing in the Second World War (293)

The first step was taken by Mr Jocelyn Simon, Financial Secretary to the Treasury (later Baron Simon of Glaisdale) in Mr Harold Macmillan's administration. In February 1959 he invited Lord Esher (Oliver Esher), as chairman of the Trustees of the London Museum, to the Treasury for an exploratory talk on 'general policy' about the museum. At that time the fifth report of the Royal Commission on National Museums and Galleries was about to be published, and this recommended resumption of discussions between the Treasury and the LCC about the long-term future of the London Museum. 'I feel sure he wants to push us, if he can, into the arms of the L.C.C.', Lord Esher told Dr Harden, then the director of the London Museum. And so, of course, he did; but Simon also told Lord Esher that as well as talking to Isaac Hayward, the leader of the controlling Labour group on the LCC, about the matter, he was going to bring in the City Corporation too. Within a short while he had actually done so, and by September 1959 he had paid a personal visit to both the London Museum and the Guildhall Museum to see things for himself. But at that juncture a General Election was called, and after it Mr Simon moved on to become Solicitor General in Mr Macmillan's second administration.

Thus it was under the guidance of the next Financial Secretary, Sir Edward Boyle, who held this key position for nearly three years, that the future Museum of London was largely fashioned. At a meeting at the Treasury in November 1959 attended by the 'top brass' of the LCC, the City Corporation and the London Museum he put forward the proposition that the two museums should be united. In March 1960 he suggested a constitution for the new museum on basically the lines afterwards agreed upon by all parties. There was to be a new building to be erected in the City, to house the two collections, and to be paid for jointly by the Government, the LCC and the City Corporation. The management of the new museum was to be by a body of trustees or governors, to be nominated by the three authorities, which would share the annual running costs. The financial and administrative functions hitherto discharged in the case of the London Museum by the Treasury and the Ministry of Works were to be taken over by the Corporation. The City's objection to a body of independent Trustees – the town clerk, Sir Edward Nichols, had wanted the management to be by a Corporation Museum Committee subject to the control of the Court of Common Council – was with difficulty overcome. In 1961 all three parties approved the draft constitution in principle, the site was settled, and by the time of Sir Edward Boyle's departure from the Treasury in July 1962 (promoted to be Minister of Education) a Parliamentary Bill was being prepared and the first meeting of the Interim Board of Governors of the Museum of London (eighteen in number, one third nominated by each of the three parties) had been held. It was a remarkable achievement, in which Sir Edward Boyle's consistent aim had been 'not only that the museums should be amalgamated, but that the resulting institution should not be just another municipal one but something greater and better . . .', with the Treasury still involved, as was only fitting that it should be in the capital city of the nation.[9]

The principal projector of the Museum of London was, however, Lord Harcourt, only son of Lewis Harcourt, the founder of the London Museum, who when only fourteen years old had succeeded his father as William, second Viscount Harcourt, in 1922. Like Sir Edward Boyle, he had been educated at Eton and Christ Church, but unlike Sir Edward he had gone straight from Oxford into the City, where at the age of twenty-three he had become managing director of the family firm of merchant bankers, Morgan Grenfell and Company. In 1958 he had been nominated a Trustee of the London Museum (in the same year as he had also become chairman of one of the biggest insurance companies in the City, Legal and General Assurance) and in 1961 he had succeeded Oliver Esher as chairman of the Museum's Board. He had in fact been 'groomed' for this succession, and with Lord Esher had since 1959 attended all the crucial meetings between Sir Edward Boyle, the LCC and the City Corporation. In 1962 he became chairman of the Interim Board of Governors of the Museum of London, and after the passing of the Museum of London Act in 1965, first chairman of the full Board. On 2 December 1976 it was he who welcomed the Queen at the opening ceremony, and he continued as chairman of the new museum until his death early in 1979. Thus of all the people actively involved at the highest level in the formation of the Museum of London, Lord Harcourt was the only one to have been there in the centre of things throughout, from the first inception of the idea in 1959 to its consummation in 1976. He had, in fact, finally achieved the aim of his father, Lewis Harcourt, who in 1910 had first set out to present the great panorama of the history of London in its entirety and in a single museum.

295 *Lewis, second Viscount Harcourt, 1908–79.*
The only son of one of the two creators of the London Museum, Lord Harcourt became chairman of the Trustees of the London Museum in 1961 and in 1965 chairman of the Board of Governors of the Museum of London. A patrician, taciturn man of great strength of purpose, he was respected rather than liked by museum staff

Lord Harcourt did, however, have a very difficult time of it all. The creation of a new, expensive institution dependent upon three separate public paymasters, each responsible to its own separate constituency, was a very formidable undertaking. It was one thing for the three authorities – the Government, the LCC and the City Corporation – to agree in principle to the idea of the union of the two collections and to the equal sharing of the costs, but much harder to get them to implement this idea, step by step. Everything of importance – and particularly all financial matters – recommended or decided by the Interim Board of Governors, and after 1965 by the Board itself, had to be submitted to and approved by each of the three authorities, much of this important work being done by Geoffrey Rowley, deputy town clerk of the City Corporation and deputy secretary of the Board. No fewer than six drafts of the Parliamentary Bill embodying the outline agreement negotiated in 1961–2 by Sir Edward Boyle were, for instance, needed before the Bill could even be presented to Parliament.[10] Other delays were caused by the need in 1964–5 to get the agreement of the newly elected Greater London Council to take on the commitment to the Museum of London entered into by its predecessor, the London County Council;[11] and due to pressures on the parliamentary timetable there was difficulty in having the Bill submitted at all. Thus three years elapsed before the Bill was at last passed, in 1965.

Some things were, however, easily decided. The name of the new museum, which might have caused much dissension, was quickly settled after the first proposal, the 'Royal London Museum', had fortunately not found favour at Buckingham Palace.[12] So too was the location of the museum, for after Isaac Hayward of the LCC had told Lord Esher early in 1959 that there was no chance of a site on the South Bank being available before the end of the century,[13] the only other acceptable place was bound to be in the City; and the Corporation was able to offer a site, which both the Treasury and the LCC accepted.

This site, which was later to present the three authorities and their architects with a formidable problem, consisted of some three acres of ground, mostly already in the Corporation's possession, at the southwest corner of the Barbican Redevelopment Area. It was situated at the intersection of the City Corporation's new Route 11 (now known as London Wall) and Aldersgate Street, and on its eastern side it faced one of the largest surviving stretches of the City's ancient defensive wall – a

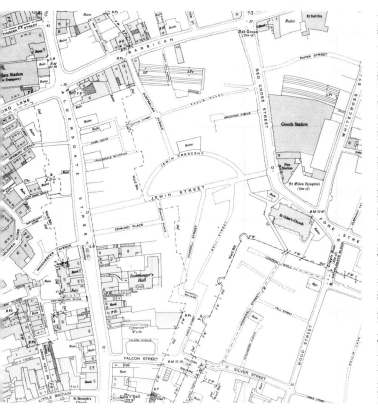

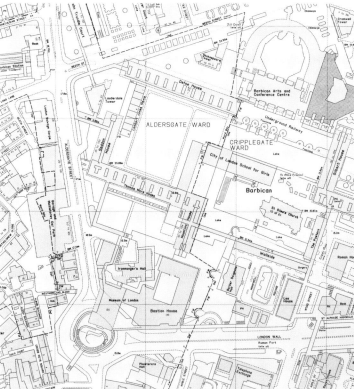

297/298 *Ordnance Surveys of 1951 and 1980 demonstrate the considerable changes that took place in this area of the City.*

The views of St Paul's Cathedral and St Martin's-le-Grand (299), Aldersgate Street looking north (300) and the west end of London Wall, with Ironmongers' Hall in left background (301), indicate the 'look' of this area when work began on the museum building

296 *The war-damaged City of London was reconstructed with modern roads and office buildings. Route 11, now known as London Wall, provided a fast dual carriageway from Moorgate in the east to the junction with Aldersgate Street in the west. The western junction (far background in this photograph of 1959) provided the eventual site for the Museum of London (left)*

wonderful bonus for the Museum of London. In 1962, however, the site was severely curtailed when the Ministry of Transport decreed that there should be a large roundabout at the junction of the two streets.[14] The Interim Board of Governors then decided that the site would not be large enough unless a piece of ground to the north, upon which stood the Hall of the Worshipful Company of Ironmongers (built in 1922–5 in the Tudor style to designs by Sydney Tatchell), could be added to it. Accordingly the Board consulted the Corporation, as ground landlord of most of the rest of the land needed for the museum, about the cost and feasibility of acquiring the Ironmongers' site. Favourable assurances were evidently given, for in the autumn of 1963 the consultant architects for the museum were instructed to prepare plans on the assumption that this ground would in fact be available; and soon after the Museum of London Act[15] had become law the Corporation applied to the Ministry of Housing and Local Government for a compulsory purchase order for the acquisition of those few interests not already in its possession, including the site of the Ironmongers' Hall.[16]

The museum's accommodation was to be in a low podium building surmounted by a multi-storey block of commercial offices, the rents from which would, of course, be paid to the Corporation as ground landlord. In due course the consultant architects, Messrs Powell and Moya, had got as far as presenting sketch plans and a model of the proposed museum and office block, that firm having been appointed by the Interim Board of Governors from a short-list of four chosen on the advice of the President of the Royal Institute of British Architects (Professor Sir Robert Matthew).[17] By the early 1960s Philip Powell and John Moya already had a formidable list of distinguished buildings to their credit, including flats, houses, hospitals, numerous works at both Oxford and Cambridge, the Skylon for the Festival of Britain (1951), and most recently, the Chichester Festival Theatre. They were already working in close consultation with Dr Harden, director of the London Museum, and Norman Cook, keeper of the Guildhall Museum, whom the Interim Governors had appointed as director and deputy director respectively of the Museum of London. In 1962–3 architects and directors made several joint tours of inspection of museums in the Rhineland, Vienna and North Italy, and later there was another, to the United States of America and Mexico, when John Cantwell, a senior member of the firm of Powell and Moya who was much concerned with the design of the Museum of London, also came. In all these forays it was Lord Harcourt's firm view that as the building of the museum was going to cost millions, it was worth spending a few extra thousands on travel 'in order to get it right'.[18]

For some time after the preliminary agreement of principle had been reached between the three authorities in 1961–2, things did, indeed, go well, though more slowly than had been expected. But in the winter of 1964–5 the first blow fell when Mr Harold Wilson's new Labour administration banned all office building in London unless expressly allowed by a Government licence. Without such a permit this precluded the building of the tower block (which was crucial to the Corporation's involvement), and even that of the museum itself, whose own office requirements fell within the terms of the new Control of Office Development Act. In Dr Harden's words, the whole project had suddenly, and quite unforeseeably, entered into 'a state of suspended animation'.[19]

Worse was to follow, however, for in May 1966, after some eighteen months' delay, Lord Harcourt was informed that the Board of Trade had decided to refuse an office development permit for the tower block. The Board would, however, hold up official notification of its decision until Lord Harcourt had been able to take the matter up with the Prime Minister (still Mr Wilson). Quite what Lord Harcourt subsequently did is not clear, but he certainly achieved the desired result, for at their next meeting he told the Trustees of the London Museum that he had seen Miss Jennie Lee, Minister for the Arts, who had promised to take the matter up with the Board of Trade; and in December 1966, after two years' delay, the licence was finally issued.[20]

But in that same month another crucial event took place which was to have lasting consequences for the museum. This was the public inquiry into the City Corporation's application to the Minister of Housing and Local Government for a compulsory purchase order for the acquisition of those interests in the proposed site of the museum not already owned by the Corporation; and one of the interested parties was the Worshipful Company of Ironmongers. The inquiry, conducted by one of the Ministry's inspectors, lasted four days, and the objectors – the Ironmongers in particular – contested the issue more strongly than had been expected.[21] Nevertheless everybody, including even the Ironmongers, seems to have

302/303 *The two models of the Museum of London. The first was designed on the premise that Ironmongers' Hall at the corner of Aldersgate Street and London Wall would be demolished. The second model designed the Museum around the Hall, which was 'hidden' within the overall redevelopment of the site but with access to Aldersgate Street, far left*

assumed that the Minister would uphold the Corporation, and whilst his judgment was awaited much discussion took place between the Company and the City authorities about another site for a new Hall and about the amount of compensation to be paid to the Ironmongers for the loss of their existing premises.[22] So the decision of the Minister (Mr Anthony Greenwood), announced early in July 1967, to overrule his own inspector's recommendation and to exclude the site of the Ironmongers' Hall from the compulsory purchase order (the rest of which he allowed), came as a bolt from the blue.[23]

This second setback produced a very rapid and positive response, however. Despite its previous decision that without the site of the Ironmongers' Hall the site would not be big enough, the Board of Governors instructed its architects to prepare a 'feasibility study' to see whether by change of plan a viable museum of the same size as before might be built on the remainder of the land. Within less than four months Powell and Moya had produced revised outline designs which were accepted by the Board, despite the reservations of one of its members, Lord Esher (Lionel Esher, son of Oliver Esher, formerly chairman of the Trustees of the London Museum), past president of the Royal Institute of British Architects; and the general view was that, provided no further delays occurred, the loss of the Ironmongers' Hall part of the site would put back the completion of the project by only about fifteen months.[24]

In the new design the museum buildings were wrapped around the Ironmongers' Hall, which now projected deeply into the north-western part of the site. The lecture hall, education department and administrative offices were placed in the western wing of the museum, separated from the exhibition galleries by the Hall yet linked to them by the museum's own entrance hall and shop. This arrangement has the advantage of isolating the noise and hustle of numerous school parties from the quieter atmosphere required in the galleries, though at the cost of providing the staff with constant exercise in walking to and fro along the corridors. The galleries, and the tower block of offices above, were moved fifty feet eastward, thereby preventing any loss of depth through the exclusion of the site of the Hall. The galleries still retained their visual association with both the internal garden courtyard and, externally, with the City's wall; and they were still on only two floors. Changes were also made in the approaches to the museum which, after over ten years' experience, have perhaps not proved to be altogether satisfactory.[25] But at the time many people thought that the new design had many excellent features of its own, and that its internal plan was at least as good as, if not better than, that of its predecessor.[26]

Meanwhile, and throughout all the ups and downs of fortune caused by the need for an office development permit and by the loss of the Ironmongers' Hall site (both, it may be noted, the result of unhelpful actions by the central government), another problem was still rumbling on, and doing so with ever growing intensity. This obstacle was the refusal of the Greater London Council to agree to a date for vesting – *ie* to a firm date when, as laid down in the Museum of London Act, the management of the staff and collections of the London Museum and of the Guildhall Museum should be transferred from, respectively, the Trustees of the former and the Library Committee of the Corporation, to the new Board of Governors of the Museum of London. The GLC did, however, have some case for its apparently perverse policy – at any rate at first. Once vesting had taken place the expense of running the united collections would be shared equally between the three authorities; but whereas the Government in 1971–2, for instance, spent around £170000 on running the London Museum,[27] and the Corporation some £68 000 on the Guildhall Museum,[28] the GLC had hitherto spent nothing under this head (except indirectly through a small contribution from the Inner London Education Authority to the London Museum's educational activities). So whereas vesting in that year would have saved the Government some £90 000,* and would have cost the Corporation only about an extra £10 000, the GLC would have had to meet a new item of expenditure of around £80 000. Thus very soon after the passing of the Museum of London Act in the summer of 1965 both the Treasury and the Corporation (and, of course, the Board of Governors) agreed that vesting should take place as soon as possible, and preferably on 1 April 1966. But the GLC objected; and it persisted in this objection for nearly nine years.[29]

This objection was first made, reasonably enough, by the GLC's Labour administration, under the leadership of Sir William Fiske, the Government itself having in August 1965 requested all local authorities to slow down expenditure on capital projects.[30] But after the local government elections of April 1967, when the Conservatives won control of County Hall, the Council's objection was continued under the auspices of the new leader, Sir Desmond Plummer. At first the Council refused to agree to an early vesting date unless the Government was prepared to continue for the time being to pay the full cost of running the London Museum.[31] But in 1968 Sir Desmond told Lord Harcourt that the GLC would not agree to vesting until the construction of the new museum building was well under way.[32] A meeting of all the interested parties convened in November of the same year by Miss Jennie Lee as Minister for the Arts failed to budge the GLC,[33] and Sir Desmond even suggested that the Council might have to reconsider taking part in the scheme at all.[34] A year later Lord Harcourt described the position of the museum as 'frustrating beyond belief'. He was, however, 'determined to get the amalgamation through, and to see the new Museum built, but the antics of the GLC are really making life almost impossible'.[35]

Discussions in ever greater detail about the design of the new building, and about staffing matters did, nevertheless, continue between the three authorities; and a fresh matter of disagreement with the GLC, about the level of the ground rent of the site of the museum, was regarded as an encouraging sign that the Council did intend eventually to proceed with the scheme.[36] In the summer of 1970, however, there was still doubt about whether it would go ahead at all,[37] and little real progress was made until the arrival (after the Conservatives' victory in the General Election of June 1970) of Lord Eccles as Paymaster General with responsibility for the arts. In October he summoned Sir Desmond Plummer to an interview, and on 2 February 1971 he took the chair at a meeting of the three authorities at which a general consensus was reached.[38] The GLC confirmed that it would honour its obligations under the Museum of London Act of 1965, but the ground rent was to be fixed at £70 000 per annum instead of being based, as the Corporation had wanted, upon the prevailing office-use rate for the site. And the Government agreed that it would increase its long-promised grant of £150 000 for the furniture and fittings of the museum. So all three parties made concessions, and the whole project could move forward again.[39]

But so far as the date for vesting was concerned, the GLC's attitude actually hardened, for in March 1971 it decided that vesting should not take place until the building was completed.[40] And this policy was continued for over three more years, for after the Labour Party had regained control of County Hall in the elections of April 1973 the Council still refused to agree to vesting in 1974; and it was not until 1 June 1975,

304 *The coat of arms of the Museum of London.*
Authorization for the museum to acquire a coat of arms was given by the Earl Marshal on 30 September 1968. The charter incorporating the arms was witnessed and sealed by Garter, Clarenceux, Norroy and Ulster Kings of Arms on 16 July 1973

* £170 000 + £68 000 = £238 000
÷ by 3 = £79 333.
£170 000 − £79 333 = £90 667

when building work had been going on for over four years, that the great landmark of amalgamation was at last reached.[41]

The GLC's consistently unhelpful attitude, maintained from 1965 to 1974 by the successive controlling groups of both political parties at County Hall, had not, in fact, greatly delayed the project, for the architects, Powell and Moya, had not been ready to go out to tender until the autumn of 1970. But it had provided a constant anxiety, particularly for the staffs of the Guildhall and London Museums, whose future often seemed uncertain; and it had wasted long hours of negotiations (mainly conducted by Geoffrey Rowley) over pay and conditions for the staff contracts. At times, indeed, the GLC's obduracy had appeared to threaten the very foundations of the whole project. Even as late as January 1971 Norman Cook, director of the Guildhall Museum, thought it necessary for the Corporation's Library Committee to consider its policy 'if the Museum of London did not proceed . . .'.[42]

The agreement reached by the three authorities on 2 February 1971 enabled the City Corporation as ground landlord to go ahead and enter into a building contract for the construction of the museum, the office tower block (named Bastion House) and the associated elevated walkways. The Corporation took this step at some risk to itself, for the other two authorities would only agree to meet one third each of the cost set out in the building contractors' tender and had not agreed to meet the increases in costs which would inevitably arise through inflation or through alterations in the interior design of the museum; and so in due course the Corporation had to negotiate all such changes with the other two parties separately.[43]

The agreement of 2 February 1971 also enabled the Corporation to sign a building agreement with the Board of Governors of the Museum of London for the grant of a ninety-nine-year lease to them of the museum premises. The loan charges on the capital cost of building the museum were to be repaid to the Corporation by the Governors over a period of sixty years. Work on the site began in April 1971.[44]

The main contractor was G E Wallis and Son Limited, whose tender for the museum, tower block and walkways was for £5.4m, of which £3.1m was in respect of the museum. In practice, however, things worked out rather differently, as they often do with large building projects and as they always do in times of high inflation. The final cost of the museum, offices and walkways eventually amounted to a little over £12m, of which some £7m was in respect of the museum. This was roughly double the original estimate – an increase which might well have been larger, considering the inflation then rampant – the cost of the exhibition and display work in particular having proved greater than expected, despite the doubling (from £150000 to £300000) of the grant from the Government for furniture and equipment.[45] The annual running costs of the museum during the first three complete financial years of its existence (ie 1976–7 to 1978–9) averaged a little over £2m, which was paid for by an average annual contribution from each of the three authorities of some £684000.[46] In the case of the Corporation, however, this sum was partly offset by the annual rent of £70000 payable to it by the Governors. The Governors also paid an amount equivalent to the Corporation's annual loan charges (about £1m) in respect of the capital cost of construction of the museum premises, and all outgoings in respect of the running and maintenance of the building.[47]

So far as the tower block was concerned, the commercial rents received by the Corporation from its tenants in the offices at Bastion House proved considerably higher than originally estimated, and by the

305 *Aerial view of the construction of the museum building in the early 1970s, looking south west towards London Wall, with St Botolph's Church at the centre top of the photograph*

H M Queen Elizabeth, the Queen Mother, laid the foundation stone of the museum on 29 March 1973. She is seen inspecting the model with Lord Harcourt and the architect, (Sir) Philip Powell (306); making a speech (307) and laying a trowel of cement (308). Her interest in the project continued the tradition of royal involvement which had characterized the London Museum since its inception

end of 1978 they produced a net annual income of £785950 (offset, of course, by the loan charges arising from the capital cost of erecting the tower block.)[48] All in all, the Corporation made a satisfactory bargain out of the formation of the Museum of London, though of course it could have done better if it had used the museum's site solely for commercial purposes. And the Government did not do too badly either, for its one-third contribution to the running costs of the Museum of London was partly offset by the loss of the costs of the London Museum, which in its last years amounted to well over £200000 per annum.[49] So it was only the GLC that had to foot the bill for an entirely new item of expenditure, amounting initially to well over half a million pounds per annum.

Over five and a half years elapsed between the commencement of work on the site in April 1971 and the opening of the museum in December 1976. By January 1972 building had reached lower ground-floor level, and the rotunda at the roundabout was taking shape. On 29 March 1973 the foundation stone was 'laid' by Queen Elizabeth the Queen Mother.* By that time the building had actually been formed up to the topmost level, and nearly half the roof was in place. The programme was, however, already about six months behind schedule, which by the summer of 1974 had risen to twelve months. So it was not until June 1976 that the office accommodation of the top floor of the museum could be occupied. Two months later the galleries were handed over with, by this time, the Board of Governors committed to the opening by Her Majesty the Queen on 2 December 1976.[51]

* The start of building work had already been unofficially commemorated by two of the museum's own staff. Peter Marsden and John Clark had felt that a traditional 'foundation offering' ought to be made to whichever Muses might concern themselves with the future well-being of the museum. In 1971 they had accordingly thrown a handful of current coins of the realm into one of the pile shafts about to be filled with concrete, where some archaeologist of the distant future may one day be glad to rediscover them.[50]

309 *Thomas (Tom) Hume, director of the Museum of London 1972–7*

Meanwhile the staff and administrative sides of the museum had also been taking shape. Secretarial, financial and legal services for the Board of Governors were supplied by the Corporation's own staff, led by Mr Rowley; and the Corporation's staff also maintained the building, all these activities being, of course, paid for by the Governors. Until his retirement in June 1970 Dr Harden acted as director of the Museum of London as well as of the London Museum. He was succeeded by Norman Cook, who had been keeper or director of the Guildhall Museum since 1950. It was under this experienced pair that most of the consultation with Powell and Moya over the planning of the building had been done; and in Norman Cook's time discussions with the exhibition designers had also made progress. But he retired in February 1972, and it was under his successor that all the plans made by so many different people over a period of so many years were at last brought to life.

This successor was Tom Hume, director for the crucial years 1972 to 1977. He was a Northumberland man who had served as curator successively of museums at Leeds and Aylesbury, and latterly as director for twelve years of the large and important City of Liverpool Museums, where he had carried out extensive rebuilding and refurbishment works. He had, in fact, got an unrivalled record as a museums organiser, and this was precisely the qualification required by the Museum of London from its director in 1972 – as Lord Harcourt, who was chairman of the Governors' selection committee, did not fail to perceive.

Tom Hume took up his duties in the summer of 1972 at the height of the Baynard's Castle affair which (as we have already seen) led on, under Max Hebditch's skilful management, to the creation by the City Corporation of a Department of Urban Archaeology within the Guildhall Museum. This took well over a year to achieve, however, and uncertainty about the future size of the Guildhall Museum's staff added to Mr Hume's difficulties, he being at this time engaged in detailed discussions with the establishment officers of the three contributing authorities about his proposals for the number, structure, grading and pay of the staff of the Museum of London. The assimilation of the staff of the two previous museums and the establishment of negotiating and consultative machinery for that of the new museum were also delicate and time-consuming yet vital matters. By October 1973 his plan for a staff structure of 109 posts was nevertheless ready, and had even been approved by the Governors and by the Corporation;[52] and general agreement was reached in the following year.

The upshot of all these efforts was that the Museum of London started its life with an extremely able staff, in which the long experience in the London and Guildhall Museums of such men as Ralph Merrifield, Brian Spencer and Arthur Trotman was well balanced by the youthful enthusiasm of many new or more recent recruits. The departmental structure was derived from the allocation of senior staff responsibilities, but in addition to the four curatorial departments which had existed at the London Museum since at least W F Grimes's time (Prehistoric and Roman, Medieval, Tudor and Stuart, and Modern) there were now more recent off-shoots, notably Costume and Textiles, Prints, Drawings and Paintings, Reserve Collections, as well, of course, as the Department of Urban Archaeology (City) and the Greater London Archaeology Section. Education, Communications, Conservation, Photography, Administration, Workshops and Security Services completed the list of the new museum's multifarious activities.

It was with the aid of this formidable new engine that Tom Hume was able to keep pace with the building work and get the Museum of

310 *Tom Hume discussing the new building with Sir Mortimer Wheeler, keeper of the London Museum 1926–44*

London open. The design of the exhibition had started in 1969, some three years before Tom Hume's appointment, when Higgins, Ney and Partners had on the recommendation of Powell and Moya, the architects, been appointed as design consultants for the internal layouts and displays.[53] In the winter of 1971–2 they provided the designs for Brian Spencer's London Museum exhibition on 'Chaucer's London', held at Kensington Palace. Much of this work was done by Jasper Jacob, who soon afterwards turned his attention to the display areas of the Museum of London. He had wide design experience and a great gift for sketching ideas or alternative possibilities on paper in a few seconds. He quickly earned the respect of the curators, who in the latter part of 1972 were set to work directly alongside Higgins, Ney's staff in premises made available within the London Museum at Kensington Palace.[54] At about the same time preliminary plans were presented to the Governors.

Frequent meetings now ensued between the curatorial staff of both the Guildhall Museum and the London Museum (including a number of key people recruited at the latter by John Hayes) on the one hand, and Peter Ney and his colleagues Chris Hutton and Jasper Jacob on the other, to discuss the appearance and content of the exhibition. The curators selected and ordered the material to be displayed. They also wrote the entire texts and captions, amounting to over a quarter of a million words and arranged on a three-tier system of labelling which provided the visitor with three different levels of perspective – general background, specific subject and individual object. And they closely involved themselves in determining the visual character of the galleries.[55]

At first, however, two important issues had to be resolved. These were firstly, the proportion of space to be allocated within the primary chronological galleries to each period of London's history; and secondly, whether this primary historical narrative should be supplemented by 'special rooms' devoted to such subjects as royal palaces, national Government, 'Civic', City company crafts, theatre, fire fighting, insurance and police, toys and games, education, transport etc. In the first scheme of things the Roman and medieval periods were to have had more space than was allocated to the whole modern period from 1700 to the present day; and the subject rooms were to have had almost as much space as the combined total of the primary galleries, from which they were to be physically separate.[56]

The challenge to this view came from John Hayes (until he left in 1973) and from all the keepers (though with slightly differing approaches), the two 'old hands', Ralph Merrifield and Brian Spencer, being supported by Philippa Glanville and a newcomer, Colin Sorensen, who at the beginning of 1971 had been appointed keeper of the Modern Department at the London Museum. Colin Sorensen brought to this his first museum job a varied experience in, amongst other things, teaching, art historical research, publishing, organizing exhibitions and the study of the London theatre. Above all, he had ideas, which he could expound with great persuasiveness. One of these was that as the Museum of London was presenting the biography of London, and that as at least two-thirds of all the people who had ever lived in London had done so during the last two hundred and fifty years or so, this period must be fully represented in the galleries. At the London Museum the Modern Department was (apart from its collections of costume and of prints, paintings and drawings), in fact, the weakest, while at the archaeologically oriented Guildhall Museum modern times were virtually unrepresented. To Colin Sorensen, however, the then still widely accepted axiom in museums that 'If you haven't got an object, you can't deal with the subject' was anathema.

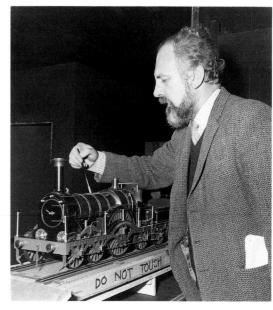

311 *Colin Sorensen, keeper of the Modern Department, preparing a model for display*

314 *The collection of contemporary and near-contemporary material was an important element in the work of the Modern Department under Colin Sorensen's guidance. Complete shopfronts and interiors were painstakingly dismantled by the museum's conservation and technical staff for possible re-use in the new galleries (right)*

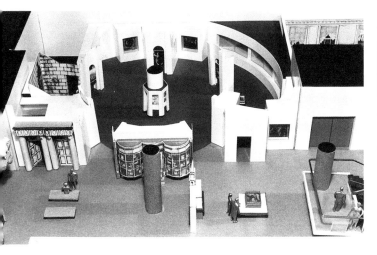

312/313 *Powell and Moya, the architects of the new museum, worked closely with Higgins, Ney, the consultant designers, to provide innovative solutions to the curatorial requirement for lively and informative displays. These models of part of the lower floor indicate ideas for the late Stuart and eighteenth-century galleries which, with minor alterations, were used*

The Sorensian attitude was that 'If you haven't got an object, you either go and get one, or you find another way of dealing with the subject – you do *not* just ignore or exclude it.' So he asked himself what the museum *ought* to have in it for his period, compared this with what the collections actually had, and then went out and begged, borrowed or bought what was needed. The proportion of exhibition space allocated to the modern period was accordingly much increased, and when the museum opened about three quarters of the objects displayed in the nineteenth-century galleries, and virtually everything in the twentieth-century rooms, had been obtained by Colin Sorensen and his able departmental colleagues within the last five years.

This total rethink of the exhibition approach was not, however, confined to the modern period. Additional space was also allocated to the Tudor and Stuart and medieval periods under the powerful advocacy of Philippa Glanville and Brian Spencer, the latter being ably supported by John Clark. All this extra space was found by the virtual elimination of the special subject rooms, which would have cut across and confused the chronological arrangement of the primary galleries. The later more detailed designs incorporating these revised ideas were the result of a triangular tussle involving curators, designers and architects; and from all this shared expertise there gradually emerged a consensus on the general policies and styles to be applied throughout the whole museum. In the end these provided an elaborate set of environments and contexts for the objects which, while not using the latest devices such as audio-visual presentations, was nevertheless the finest exposition of traditional display techniques and the first big comprehensive exhibition of the development of a geographical area from the earliest times to the present.

In 1974 the sub-contract for building the exhibition galleries was let to Russell Bros of Paddington Ltd.[57] Work on the structure of the exhibition began early in 1975, and the first of the large exhibits, the prison cells from Wellclose Square – one of Guy Laking's early acquisitions for the London Museum in 1911 – was installed in its new home soon afterwards. Other architectural exhibits were built-in during the spring of 1976, but it was not until 1 June that (as previously stated) it became possible for staff to begin to occupy the office floor of the new museum; and by that time the Governors had arranged for the opening by the Queen to take place on 2 December. The galleries were not handed over for the installation of all the graphics, case linings and small exhibits until 1 August. The period of nine months originally planned for this stage of the operation was thus condensed into four, and a season of desperate rush ensued. Nevertheless on 2 December the galleries emerged

The conservational and technical problems posed during the setting up of the museum's new galleries were complex and demanding. The removal of the Bucklersbury tesselated pavement from Guildhall (315), the installation of massive artifacts (316), the repair of all manner of objects, ranging from a Victorian street lamp to one of the London Museum's models (317, 318), or the final placement of the royal coat of arms (319), all required the highest professional skills

looking remarkably complete.* Lord Harcourt – very uncharacteristically nervous on the great day (so it was afterwards recalled) – escorted Her Majesty around on her tour of inspection, just as his father had conducted King George and Queen Mary around the infant London Museum at Kensington Palace on that far-away day in the spring of 1912. And on 3 December the Museum of London at last opened its doors to the public.

* One of the most popular of all the exhibits, the London Museum's old model of the Great Fire of 1666, was not finally ready until 4am on the day of the opening. Under Philippa Glanville's auspices it had been renovated by its makers, Thorp's, new and greatly improved lighting effects had been installed, and a recording of appropriate background noise and the voice of Michael Hordern reading Pepys's description of the conflagration had been provided by the BBC.

320–322 The publicity for the new museum was an important element in its early success. Advertising and clear sign-posting overcame the difficulties posed by a site which, initially, was awkward. The highwalk system within the City did not allow a street-level entrance to the museum, a feature which has caused difficulties for visitors unused to this concept. However, once inside the building, the chronological sequence of galleries is relatively straightforward

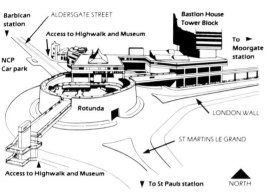

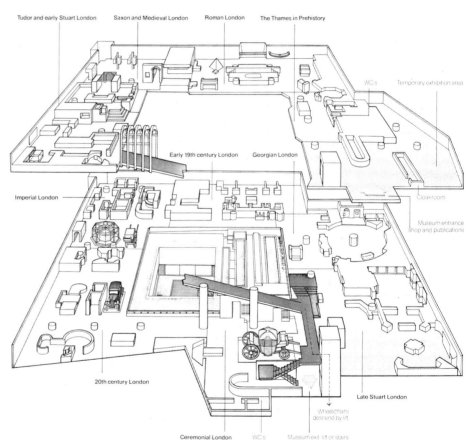

323 In 1978 the Museum of London was awarded the United Kingdom Museum of the Year Award as joint-winner with Erddig, the National Trust's house in Wales

During the first ten years of its public life the museum welcomed over six million visitors. It greatly extended its activities and the services which it provided, particularly in the fields of archaeology, the Docklands, exhibitions and education; and the quality of its work was recognized by numerous public awards, including that of United Kingdom Museum of the Year in 1978, and in 1982 Museum of the Year in *The Good Museums Guide*. It became world famous, and London suddenly realized that it had a new museum, fully worthy of the capital city.

But these successes were only won in the face of great difficulties.

Within little more than two years of its opening the museum lost both its top two men. Tom Hume retired in June 1977 at the age of sixty, with a richly deserved CBE. During the five years of his directorship the museum had risen from the designers' drawing boards and the contractors' huge hole in the ground to become a fully working institution; and much of the later renown of the museum must be due to the foundations which he laid during those critical years.

Only eighteen months later, on 3 January 1979, Lord Harcourt died, aged seventy. Ever since he had first become a Trustee of the London Museum in 1958 he had promoted the work of that museum and of its successor with what his fellow Governors called 'selfless dedication, diplomacy and zest'. In all those years, in which he was chairman of both the Trustees of the London Museum from 1961 to 1975 and of the Governors of the Museum of London from 1965 onwards, he attended all but a very few of the 120 meetings held by the two Boards, habitually arriving early and (as far as possible unobserved) spending a few minutes on his own, scrutinizing changes in the galleries and appraising new acquisitions. On other occasions successive directors had found him easily accessible by telephone at the partners' room at Morgan Grenfell's in Great Winchester Street, where he spent much of his time. The particular problem needing his attention would be explained by the director, a short decisive answer would be given, and the receiver promptly replaced. He had faced every impasse in the development of the Museum of London with resilience, patience and persistence, and when matters had seemed to reach deadlock he had unobtrusively taken those difficulties to the highest level. He had, in fact, displayed the same qualities as had enabled his father to establish the London Museum in 1910–12; and it may be doubted whether either that museum or the Museum of London would ever have come into being without these two most impressive men.

The new director was Max Hebditch, who had been director of the Guildhall Museum from 1971 to 1974. There his achievement in getting the City Corporation to set up a properly funded archaeological unit had attracted Lord Harcourt's notice; and after a short spell as deputy director of the Museum of London he succeeded Tom Hume in the top job. And Mr Michael Robbins, who had been a Trustee of the London Museum from 1970 to 1975 and a Governor of the Museum of London since 1968, was elected as chairman of the Board in succession to Lord Harcourt. His working career in London Transport had given him a wide knowledge of the intricate ways in which large public bodies and their associated trade unions operate. As chairman of the Middlesex Victoria County History Council he knew all about the problems of funding a project of historical scholarship out of the rates annually voted by a whole gaggle of separate local authorities; and he was also a scholar of great distinction, his major work being (with professor T C Barker) the two-volume *History of London Transport*.

The main difficulty confronting the museum throughout its short life has been caused by the less than adequate funding provided by the three (or latterly two) contributing authorities. Ever since the first year's budget, for 1976–7, was drawn up (which was done before the museum was even in operation, and so was conjectural), the ability of the Governors and director to plan for development has been restricted by the injunction of the three authorities, repeated every year until 1986–7, that it was inadmissible to propose any increase in expenditure, in real terms, over that approved for the previous year.

So the museum has had to set to and so far as possible earn its own living; and its success in doing so is its most impressive single achievement at the present time. Twenty years ago sponsorship or organized financial support from outside bodies were virtually unknown in the

324 *R M Robbins, chairman of the Board of Governors 1979–90.*
A distinguished public servant and considerable scholar, he provided the experience and stability which the new museum required in a chairman

325 *Max Hebditch, director 1977–*

328 *The London Wall Walk, sponsored by local businesses, provides a handsomely and informatively signed route around the City walls. This 'outreach' activity has proved popular with thousands of visitors to the City (right)*

326/327 Valerie Cumming (left) first chairman of the 'Friends of Fashion' with their 1989/90 patron, Lady Bidwell (centre). The Friends assist with purchases such as that of the Peter Pan stage costume (below), publications and displays

museum world. Nowadays they permeate much of the museum's work and provide fuel for many of its activities. The Museum of London Trust Fund (mainly financed by visitors' contributions to the collecting box in the main hall) provides money for the purchase of additions to the collections and for other developments. The Friends of Fashion have (amongst other things) done much the same for the costume collection. The Cripplegate Foundation paid for the provision of the external information boards describing the Roman and medieval remains in the vicinity of the museum. The Corporation and Members of Lloyds and Lloyds Brokers helped in 1982 to purchase the South Sea Company's splendid silver-gilt plate. The Worshipful Company of Shipwrights financed an exhibition on Shipbuilding on the Thames, and Whitbread and Company presented 'Paintings, Politics and Porter', to mention only two of the more important of the numerous exhibitions sponsored in one way or another by outside bodies. The London Wall Walk, which by means of twenty-one permanent ceramic panels enables the public to follow the route of the City's defences from the museum to the Tower of London, was devised by the museum but entirely paid for by various City businesses and charities. In 1981 an induction loop system for the hard of hearing was provided in the lecture theatre by Marks & Spencer Limited, and soon afterwards a similar apparatus was installed in the Fire of London Experience with money raised on a Lenten project by pupils of the London Oratory School. The City of London Archaeological Trust, the Midland Bank, *The Observer* and Wiltshier (London) Limited provided a public viewing platform overlooking the important excavations which were being conducted in 1982 at Billingsgate by the museum's Department of Urban Archaeology, Ilford Limited and AV Distributors (London) Limited provided materials and camera equipment needed for the compilation of the museum's photographic record of London in the mid-1980s. Nomura International Limited, a leading Japanese finance house, sponsored several of the museum's film seasons entitled 'Made in London', which in addition to displaying the art of an important London industry also provided valuable extensions of what the museum tries to do in its galleries. And although this list could be continued almost ad infinitum, even the shortest catalogue should not omit the generosity of such old stalwarts as the Pilgrim Trust and the National Art-Collections Fund, supplemented in more recent years by Grants in Aid from official Government funds for special acquisitions provided through the Victoria & Albert and the Science Museums and from the National Heritage Memorial Fund.

The museum's greatest success in obtaining funds to supplement the basic support provided by the three contributing authorities has, however, been in the field of archaeology. Here the three authorities made clear to the Board of Governors that they did not feel that they should bear all the costs of field archaeology in London merely by virtue of happening to be partners under the Museum of London Act. So additional money had to be found elsewhere.

At the end of the last chapter we saw how in 1973 the City Corporation had established a Department of Urban Archaeology within the Guildhall Museum, with a permanent staff of four archaeologists and one draughtsman. This small nucleus was to be supported as occasion required by staff to be paid out of grants from the Department of the Environment and from any other available source; and the first Chief Urban Archaeologist had started work in December of the same year.

This was Brian Hobley, who came to the Guildhall Museum (and thence after vesting in 1975 to the Museum of London) from Coventry, where, after several years' experience in business he had become the Corporation's field officer and later keeper of field archaeology in the museum there. During his dozen or more years in London he has put archaeology in the City on a sound basis at last. Since 1973 the DUA has carried out over two hundred major investigations, published over six hundred reports on this work, and enriched the museum's archaeological collections beyond anyone's wildest hopes. The results of all this work amount to a transformation of knowledge of a number of important aspects of Roman and Saxon London.[58]

All this has, of course, cost a great deal of money, and will continue to do so for many years. At first most of the money was provided by grants from the Department of the Environment and the Manpower Services Commission, and much of it was used to pay a large staff recruited on a short-term basis. Originally the DUA's base was at Gillett House (previously the home of the Guildhall Museum), but after a while it moved to the Library's old basement store at Guildhall, and only in 1980 was permanent space for the Department found within the museum. By that time the staff of the DUA numbered over fifty (over and above the nucleus of five permanent staff paid for by the museum).

By that time, too, Brian Hobley was supplementing the resources at his disposal by very substantial grants made by private developers – over £81 000 in 1979–80, amounting to some 22 per cent of the whole income of the DUA. He realized that getting the support of developers, in terms of both time and money, was of critical importance for the success of archaeology in the City. Since its establishment in 1973 not a single site wanted by the DUA for a 'dig' has been refused by any developer, nor has any 'find' been denied to it. Responsibility for paying full archaeological costs (excluding long-term post-excavation research work) has become generally accepted by developers in the City; and in the financial year 1986–7 they contributed over £1m for this purpose – equivalent to 50 per cent of the total income of the DUA.

So despite being a late-comer in the field of urban archaeology – later than its counterparts in such cities as, for instance, Winchester, Lincoln or York – the Museum of London's DUA has become the largest and the acknowledged leader. The extra workers who are taken on for short contracts related to particular projects sometimes bring the total staff up to well over one hundred and fifty, its *Site Manual*, published for internal use in 1980 as a guide to the compilation of written site records, now serves as a model elsewhere, and the Department has initiated new methods of conservation and computerized post-excavation analysis. This latter is already leading to the creation of an archaeological archive which in such fields as types of pottery-fabric and London building materials will soon provide primary evidence for archaeological research. Brian Hobley, in conjunction with the British Property Federation, has produced a nationwide *Code of Practice* to be followed, it is intended, by both archaeologists and developers on sites where excavation in advance of building work is to be done. And recently the Department has persuaded the Corporation to include a special section on archaeology in the written statement of its *City of London Local Plan* (1986). There it is stated that 'the Corporation recognises that archaeological evidence is an important, but finite, historical resource and that modern development is almost inevitably destructive of archaeological deposits'. It is therefore, it continues, the Corporation's aim 'to prevent the destruction of potentially valuable archaeological remains when sites are redeveloped'.

The DUA is a descendant and extension of the old Guildhall Museum, and therefore only concerns itself with the area of the City. But in the

329/330 *The excavations at Billingsgate in 1982 provided the public with a sponsored viewing platform and introductory talks to the work in progress. Amongst distinguished visitors to the site was H R H the Prince of Wales. The excavations revealed a series of Roman and medieval waterfronts*

332/333 *In 1986 the museum staged an exhibition about London's early history, 'Capital Gains', which displayed some of the new evidence and finds made by the museum's archaeological departments during the preceding fifteen years. The Minister for the Arts (1985–90), Richard Luce, the director and the chairman of the Governors view the reconstructed waterfront timbers (right)*

London Museum there was latterly (as we have seen in Chapter 5) a small department of field archaeology, the two officers of which did their best to keep an eye on matters archaeological throughout the whole of the rest of London. They concentrated much of their activity in West Middlesex, and when the two museums merged in 1975 these two posts were continued within the Museum of London, where they formed the nucleus of the Greater London Archaeology Department.

Here the first archaeology officer was (and still is) Harvey Sheldon, who had previously been and continued to be the field officer of the Southwark and Lambeth Archaeological Excavation Committee. This was one of a few voluntary local groups most of which had been formed in the early 1970s when Rescue, under Martin Biddle's leadership, was greatly increasing public awareness of the destruction of archaeological deposits and of the need to do something about it. Each of these groups was funded in greater or lesser degree by grants from the Department of the Environment, local councils and local developers, while the Museum of London through Harvey Sheldon endeavoured to provide some degree of coordination.

In 1976 a working party of the Department of the Environment, the GLC and the Museum of London published a survey of archaeological needs in Greater London entitled *Time On Our Side?*. This was conceived on lines analogous to those of Rescue's *The Future of London's Past* (1973), and advocated a single archaeological agency for Greater London in order to provide a framework within which full-time and part-time excavation teams might operate to the best advantage. Archaeological work in Greater London remained, however, uneven and uncoordinated until in 1983–4 the GLC made a new grant of £200000 for the provision of a Greater London Archaeological Service to cover the whole of Greater London and to be run by the Museum of London (apart from in the five north-eastern boroughs, where the service was to be provided by the Passmore Edwards Museum). Twenty-five staff, paid for at first mainly by the GLC and the Department of the Environment, supplemented by grants from local authorities and private developers, were taken on. This has made it possible for the museum to provide a permanent team to direct rescue operations and to publish the results throughout most of Greater London.* After its abolition in 1985 the responsibilities of the GLC for the Greater London Archaeological Service were transferred to the Historic Buildings and Monuments Commission (*ie* English Heritage).[59]

Two other of the museum's activities are now also financed largely by English Heritage. First, there is the computerized bibliography of all published material relating to the archaeology of Greater London, which was started in 1981. And second, there is the Sites and Monuments Record (also computerized, and started in 1983), which when completed will contain a vast bank of up-to-date information about all buildings listed as of historic or architectural interest, about open spaces and of course about archaeological sites. The results of all these labours will be open for use by the public.

During the last twenty or thirty years London's archaeology has in one way or another seldom been out of the public eye for very long. But now that its organizational and financial problems seem at last to have been placed on a reasonably satisfactory basis, public attention has begun to shift to a new branch of the same science – Industrial Archaeology. In London this field has, at any rate so far as the museum is concerned, been dominated by Dockland. Due to increased containerization and the use of ever-larger ships the working Port of London has throughout the

331 *The DUA's excavations at Leadenhall Court in 1986 presented an unique opportunity for the controlled scientific excavation of the Roman basilica. They were jointly funded by the developers and the Historic Buildings and Monuments Commission*

* In the four south-eastern boroughs the work is carried out for the museum by the Kent Archaeological Rescue Unit on an agency basis.

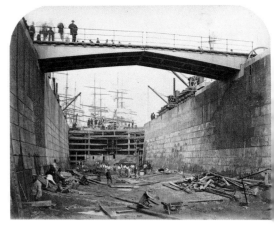

334 *Aerial view of the Port of London, part of the Upper Pool, the Lower Pool and the five up-river dock systems, 1960*

335 *Completing the cut between the newly built Canada Dock and Albion Dock, c.1875. From an album recording the building alterations to the Surrey Commercial Docks (above)*

337 *Thames spritsail barge 'Henry' in the Royal Albert Dock, c.1956 (top right)*

1960s and 1970s moved downstream to Tilbury, leaving empty docks and warehouses and vast areas of derelict land. In 1981 the Government set up the London Docklands Development Corporation to plan and organize the regeneration of what at the present time is the largest single area of urban redevelopment in the whole of Europe.

Before he had even come to the old London Museum in 1971 Colin Sorensen, now keeper of the Modern Department in the Museum of London, had drawn attention in a broadcast talk to the need to record the social, industrial and physical scene in Dockland before these colossal impending changes took place. In 1980 his colleague in the Modern Department, Chris Ellmers, began, with the cooperation of the Port of London Authority, to rescue and record information about Dockland, chiefly from the West India, Millwall and Royal groups of docks. Two warehouses at the Royal Victoria Dock were made available for storage, and here an enormous collection of cargo-handling material of all periods has been assembled, while other objects too big to keep there, such as a tug and a quayside crane well over a hundred feet in height, have been found safe havens elsewhere.

In 1982 the Board of Governors proposed the formation of a major new museum – The Museum in Docklands – dealing with the story of London as the nation's greatest industrial and commercial centre. After discussions with the London Docklands Development Corporation, buildings were tentatively earmarked at the north-west corner of the West India Docks, these being the very first of London's trading docks to be built in the early nineteenth century. Here stands a range of monumental warehouses which would form a splendid home for the capital city's industrial museum. Here the boats, cranes and dock equipment already collected could be exhibited and even used in the habitat for which they were made; and here the Museum of London's other industrial, commercial and technical collections illustrating the development of London as a world centre of trade and manufacture could be adequately displayed on a site close to the new Docklands Light Railway linking the area with the City. The Museum in Docklands should, in the view of the Governors of the Museum of London, be administered by its own Trustees, to whom

336 *Painters working on the telescopic funnel of Paddle Steamer Crested Eagle. This photograph forms part of the Port of London Authority's collection of some 25000 items, now in the care of the museum*

339 *Museum publications included popular, inexpensive but factual introductions to collections or topics, written by or in conjunction with the museum's curators (right)*

338 *The Museum in Docklands project team has introduced oral history recording into the museum. Louise Brodie was in charge of this work and is here seen in discussion with David Challis, the museum's Design Officer 1979–88*

the Museum of London would offer advice and lend its collections; and the whole project would have to be financially self-supporting.

A substantial grant given by the London Docklands Development Corporation to the Museum of London in 1983–4 made possible the establishment of a 'Museum in Docklands Team', now around a dozen strong in number, which has continued the task of collecting, restoring, interpreting and presenting material relating to the docks, the river and 'working' London generally. In 1985 consultants commissioned by the London Docklands Development Corporation to prepare a feasibility study on The Museum in Docklands reported very favourably on the financial viability of the idea, and forecast that by 1998 the number of visitors would exceed 750 000.[60]

However, the very success of the commercial regeneration of the Isle of Dogs makes it now unlikely that the museum can be located at the West India Docks. The land is now worth too much, and quite how this enormous and ambitious scheme will work out still remains to be seen.

The sheer scale of the activities of The Museum in Docklands and of the Museum of London's two archaeological departments sometimes seems to overshadow the equally important but less glamorous work of the rest of the museum. The little home-based remainder of the Tudor and Stuart and Modern Departments, whose brief extends from 1485 to the present day, have to keep a watchful eye on all the other evidence of London's past, and need an organization on a large scale. They have nevertheless (and amongst scores of other activities) extended the collection of Tudor and Stuart decorative arts, assembled material relating to some forty different London-based trades and skills, recorded the daily life of Billingsgate Market before its closure, salvaged material from a number of obsolescent suburban cinemas of the 1930s, and so on and so on. In conjunction with students of the London College of Printing the Modern Department is at present recording the life and environment of London in the mid 1980s, and would like to have its own film unit to do such work on a much larger scale, film being a vital source of archaeological evidence for the twentieth century as well as a major social influence. Similarly the costume collection (which is now an independent department separate from the Modern Department, as befits one of the four major collections in Britain, comparable in range and completeness with any in the country) has inevitably been under-used for display purposes in a museum whose main object in its galleries is to present a balanced picture of London's history. Ever since 1979 the Governors have been hoping to provide space somewhere to show more of the costume, but so far, lack of funds has prevented this; and to date the only relief available has been that provided by temporary exhibitions. And the collection of paintings, prints and drawings (also recently separated from the Modern Department) is in much the same situation, being in urgent need of a permanent exhibition gallery of its own.

All the work of the curatorial departments depends, of course, very greatly upon the back-up services provided by the staff concerned with such crucial matters as conservation, technical and design services, public relations, library, shop, administration and security. In larger and older institutions activities of this kind sometimes become fossilized by immutable routines and procedures, but at the Museum of London – still young and comparatively small and a place where everybody can still know everybody else by name – the support staff at all levels are ingenious and professional. Thanks in large measure to them, the public face of the museum is an agreeable one. The attendants do not wear dark police-style uniforms, politeness always prevails, and there is a general commitment to communicating an interest and enthusiasm for London to all the museum's visitors.

One of the main means of arousing such interest is by mounting special exhibitions, which have been a constant feature of the museum ever since it first opened. The very first of these, held in the museum's 'Treasury' adjoining the Lord Mayor's coach, was on the history of the Coronation, for which Kay Staniland, then curator of costume and textiles, was responsible, and which included items from the museum's own permanent collection and the temporary loan of the Queen's own coronation dress. Normally two, or sometimes three, such major exhibitions have been held every year, either in the Treasury (*eg* 'Pavlova', 1981 or 'Fans', 1986) or in the Special Exhibition Gallery provided for this purpose near the museum shop. Notable presentations here have included 'King's Cross and St Pancras: A Tale of Two Stations', in 1982–3, and 'The Quiet Conquest: The Huguenots 1685–1985', in 1985. Some exhibitions have been prepared entirely by outside bodies such as the GLC or the Middlesex Polytechnic; and there have also been numerous smaller exhibitions temporarily fitted into the displays in one of the permanent galleries.

Some of these exhibitions have simply used material from the museum's own collections – 'Looking at London', 1980, is a case in point. Others, such as 'London Craftsmanship 1680–1780', in 1979, have supplemented the museum's possessions with loans from elsewhere, and yet others, like 'London Silver 1680–1780', in 1982–3, have consisted exclusively of loaned material. All these exhibitions have, however, got at least one thing in common – they cost a great deal of money to produce. So far, the museum has only once levied a charge for admission. 'London's Flying Start', in 1981–2, recreating London's major part in the early days of the aviation industry (much of the material of which was later incorporated into the museum's permanent display on this theme), was the only occasion on which this was done. But increasingly the exhibitions at the museum have had to rely more and more on outside sponsorship. We have already seen that in 1982–3, for instance, the Shipwrights' Company financed the exhibition on 'Shipbuilding on the Thames', while soon afterwards Whitbread and Company presented 'Paintings, Politics and Porter'. And in 1985 'The Quiet Conquest', one of the finest exhibitions yet seen at the museum, depended not only on the labours of its own staff and of many members of the Huguenot Society, but also on the financial support of over thirty outside bodies.[61]

This dependence has its dangers, for in 1983–4 three special exhibitions had to be cancelled because of the lack of a sponsor and the absence of public funds; and in consequence both the Treasury and the Special Exhibition Gallery stood empty throughout most of 1984. Sponsorship, in fact, does have disadvantages; and the opportunities for the in-house curatorial and other departments to earn other forms of income are severely limited compared with those of the archaeological field departments. It is, however, the Governors' intention to develop the marketing side specifically to improve the museum's ability to generate more of the financial resources needed. Nevertheless it seems unlikely that this will be able to earn enough money to finance the Governors' capital programme for either the fuller development of the main building, where new galleries for the collections of costume and of paintings, prints and drawings are envisaged, or for the provision of better storage of the collections, which are at present scattered in many places. So it seems that unless the museum's contributing authorities permit some further increase in real terms in the level of the budget, the central core of the museum's activities is bound to suffer in the long term.

340–342 'London's Flying Start', the major exhibition of 1981–2, displayed the pioneering early days of aviation, when the industry was based in the capital. The principal exhibit was a replica of the Roe triplane built in London in 1908. The exhibition was opened by the distinguished aviator Lord Balfour of Inchrye, seen here with Barrington Gray (right) and Colin Manton (centre), who had done the research

343 *The exhibition 'London Silver 1680–1780' was based upon two major collections lent to the museum for a year-long display in 1982–3*

344/345 *Sponsorship was essential in the presentation of large-scale exhibitions in the museum in the mid and late 1980s. 'The Quiet Conquest' (1985) displayed the Huguenot contribution to London, the funds for its production being raised by the Huguenot Society. In 1987 'Londoners', an exhibition of paintings, prints and drawings devised by Dr Celina Fox (centre background), was sponsored by Chase Manhattan Bank. The chairman of the Bank is seen with H R H Princess Margaret, as they pause before another display of that year which marked the coronations of 1838 and 1937*

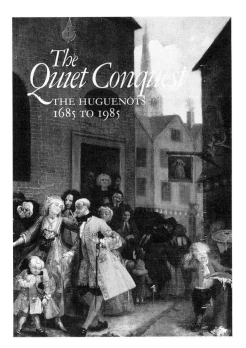

It is greatly to be hoped, however, that this will not happen, and particularly so in the case of that essential aspect of the museum's work, the Education Department. Here people of all ages and many different levels of intellectual attainment are catered for. Here in particular the Museum of London tries to perform its fundamental purpose of explaining to its visitors, the community, where it (the community) is and where it has come from. In the post-war era of standardization, anonymity and loss of individual identity, a measure of understanding of the why and the wherefore of the modern urban condition must be of ever growing importance. Many people do, indeed, feel a need for such an understanding, and this feeling is closely allied to their need for 'roots', or ancestors, or for a sense of 'belonging'. So in these times of declining religious awareness, a museum of social history like the Museum of London finds that it has a very powerful role, which if it is to satisfy many of its visitors' perhaps unconscious cravings, even includes a partly spiritual content.

The schools service of the Education Department can trace its ancestry back to the improbable person of Colonel Maurice Brett, who in 1921 had become the London Museum's first guide lecturer, part-time. (The Guildhall Museum never employed anyone specifically for teaching.) During and after the war the post was in abeyance but in 1957 it was revived as a full-time position under the title of Schools Officer, and when the two old museums merged in 1975 the then incumbent, Mary Speaight, became the Museum of London's first education officer. It was she who had in large measure created the educational service at the London Museum, and who in the early 1970s laid the foundations of the new and greatly enlarged service at the Museum of London. In 1977 she retired and was succeeded by Geoffrey Toms, who with the assistance of five colleagues still runs the Department, the scope of which has expanded to develop programmes for organized groups of adults and college students as well as primary and secondary school pupils.

The aim of the Education Department is to interpret and to extend the information contained in the galleries. The Department is fortunate in having its own specially designed accommodation, separate from the galleries. It includes a large reception area, where the five hundred children who often arrive here daily in successive school parties can prepare themselves before going into one of the two large classrooms or the seminar room. There they can personally handle real objects from the museum's educational collection – always important for all visits, but particularly so for children aged between about eight and thirteen, who form well over half the museum's schools clientele. Then, under the control of their own school teacher, and usually equipped with one of the museum's numerous 'worksheets', they go down to the galleries, or more probably to one particular gallery to look, perhaps, at one particular subject displayed there, such as, in the Victorian galleries, 'Transport', 'Shopping', or 'The Day's Work'. Here, at the most receptive years of childhood, they will be presented, often for the first time, with new impressions of their city, London, and even of themselves and of their own origins, which may well colour their still malleable attitudes throughout the whole of their lives. So the importance of the schools service can hardly be exaggerated.

Some two thousand school parties, consisting of some 75 000 children, visit the museum each year. Many of them come from as far away as Wales or Scotland or indeed from abroad, it being a surprising fact that there are now more schools visiting from France than from the whole of Greater London. About a third of these school parties receive some tuition from the Education Department's own staff. Teaching the teachers, both in the history of London and in how best to use the facilities provided by the museum, is also provided, and few parties come without careful preparation for their visit having been made beforehand. And in the school holidays there are specific programmes for children, or for family groups, which have proved very popular. In 1983, for instance, 'Summer Specials' provided handling sessions, gallery talks, walks, demonstrations and films; and in the Department's workroom 450 masks were made by children and their parents in practical activities linked to the current exhibition entitled 'Masquerade'.

There is no hard and fast line between the interpretation and the extension of the information contained in the galleries, but in general the Department's activities for children are more concerned with interpretation and those for adults with extension. In the latter field the numerous lunch-time lectures, given in the museum's fully-equipped and comfortable 270-seat lecture theatre, provide the basic ingredient. These are given by members of the museum's curatorial and other staff or by outside speakers, and are often concerned either to amplify the current exhibition or to provide a commentary on some aspect of the museum's permanent themes or prevailing activities. There are also lunch-time 'workshops', or informal talks, where visitors can meet specialist staff and see objects from the collections at close quarters. Evening classes held in conjunction with the London University Department of Extra-Mural Studies are held at the museum, conferences related in some way to the work of the Museum of London take place here, and the Friends of Fashion have their lectures here.

The museum has also led the way in the regular use of film, particularly full-length feature films, as a means of presenting the recent past. The moving photographic image, especially when accompanied by sound, has added a new dimension to the capacity of all social history museums to project the infinite variety of life in modern times, and with the vital collaboration of the National Film Archive of the British Film Institute, fourteen seasons of 'Made in London' films have been presented in the early evening in the museum's lecture theatre.

In recent years the demand for adult education activities has been growing steadily. In addition to the public programme of lectures and workshops many organized adult groups such as members of the Townswomen's Guild or the National Trust receive teaching sessions. City business houses which run week-long induction courses for their newly recruited executives include a half-day session at the museum as an

346 *School children under instruction in one of the galleries*

347 *Family holiday activities included, in 1984, the opportunity to dress-up and experience the lengthy process of being photographed in the Victorian period. Museum staff were persuaded to participate, producing formidable and almost unrecognisable results*

348 *Commander Greenhalgh demonstrating the principles of pre World War I flying with contemporary models in the lecture theatre during the exhibition 'London's Flying Start', 1981–2 (top right)*

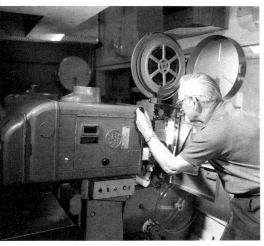

349 *The 'Made in London' film seasons, devised by Colin Sorensen in association with the British Film Institute and sponsored by Nomura, present the diverse achievements of the British film industry (principally London based) to enthusiastic audiences. The projection quality is expertly maintained by George Clarke*

* The Treasury mandarins of the old school, who in the days of the London Museum had always viewed with distaste the use of taxpayers' money for a metropolitan function, and who had at last managed to get this museum obligation shared with the GLC and the City Corporation, would certainly never have proposed such an arrangement.

† This was the fund shared by the metropolitan local authorities on an equal rate poundage basis, and into which such rich authorities as the City Corporation had to pay large sums for the use of their poorer neighbours.

essential part of this training. Many foreign groups come to the museum for 'London orientation tuition', this being particularly popular with students from American universities who come to Britain for six- or twelve-month courses and who regard an educational programme at the museum in the first two weeks of their stay as the best way of obtaining an understanding of the capital city.

Nowadays hardly a day in the working week passes without an educational event of some kind taking place. All in all, the museum has made itself an Institute of London Studies in its own right, providing a 'local museum' service in a national and international context.

In 1986 the Conservative Government headed by Mrs Thatcher abolished the Greater London Council. For the Museum of London the unexpected assassination of one of its contributing authorities by another of the three partners presented tricky problems. Where was the GLC's tranche of one third of the costs to come from now? How, too, was the museum's Greater London Archaeological Service, which since its inception in 1983–4 had depended almost exclusively upon an annual grant of over £200000 from the GLC, to be paid for? And no less importantly, how was the museum's formal link with the whole of Greater London, hitherto provided by the GLC's appointment of one third of the Board of Governors, to be protected?

The threat to the GLC had first become clear early in 1983. After the Conservatives' victory in the general election of that year the Government's new Office of Arts and Libraries (which had recently taken over the responsibilities for museums hitherto discharged by the Treasury) produced a consultation paper which proposed that the Corporation should take over the GLC's share of responsibility for the museum. However, this idea, by which the Corporation would have assumed two thirds of both the costs and the control of the museum, aroused so much alarm and despondency in all quarters that the Office of Arts and Libraries was forced to retreat. Instead, it was decided in the corridors of Whitehall that the Local Government Bill (by which the GLC and other metropolitan counties were to be abolished) should contain clauses to make a fifty-fifty split between the Government and the Corporation.

But unfortunately the parliamentary lawyers then ruled that this provision would make the whole abolition bill 'hybrid', with alarming prospects for the progress of this important item of Government business. So the Office of Arts and Libraries was instructed to draft a simple clause by which the Government, rather than the Corporation as originally proposed, should take over the GLC's one third share;* but it was indicated that this was only a technical device to get the Government out of an awkward situation, and that the whole matter would quickly be put to rights by a specific Museum of London Amending Bill.

This measure, which became law as the Museum of London Act of 1986, reverted to the earlier proposal of an equal partnership, and provided that the cost and control of the museum should be shared half-and-half by the Corporation and the Government. The Corporation, which had very naturally thought that the Government's wish to do away with the GLC was no reason why it should have to increase its share of the cost of the museum from one third to a half (or, at any rate, not without adequate compensation), finally did agree to pay half, but only on condition that this extra cost, amounting to about £800000 per annum, should be offset against its contribution to the Extended London Rate Equalisation Scheme.† The number of Governors to be appointed by the Prime Minister and by the Corporation respectively was therefore raised from six to nine. Both the Prime Minister and the Corporation did, however, in making these extra appointments, have regard to the interests of Greater London as a whole, thereby maintaining the museum's formal link with the entire metropolis. The Act also defined the museum's position in regard to archaeology and authorized the Historic Buildings and Monuments Commission to make grants to the Board of Governors for archaeological purposes – *ie* for the museum's Greater London Archaeological Service, which as we have already seen had hitherto been heavily dependent on a grant from the GLC.[62]

Under these new arrangements the museum has been given a good second start, both the Office of Arts and Libraries and the Corporation having agreed in the Museum of London estimates for 1986–7 to a figure six per cent above the rate of inflation. The reconstituted Board of Governors has, however, some formidable problems to solve, the most important, perhaps, being that of space. The storage of most of the collections will, it is hoped, be transferred in due course to a new 'support centre' elsewhere, leaving the existing premises as the main exhibition and public service building. Here, current proposals for the redevelopment of a site adjoining the museum in Little Britain (on the west side of Aldersgate Street) and the western end of London Wall (one scheme even involving the demolition of the rotunda and the museum's offices) may provide the Board with a unique opportunity to obtain a better entrance and extra exhibition space.

Whatever the future may hold, the new diarchal Board certainly has in its charge a museum which despite its youth has already built up a proud tradition of activities. Notwithstanding all the uncertainty and apprehension caused by the impending abolition of the GLC, 1985–6 – the last year under the tripartite dispensation – had proved to be a good year for the museum. More exhibitions were mounted, more sites excavated, more publications produced, and more sponsorship obtained than in any previous year. And attendances went up by 24000 to 547000, an increase of over four per cent. The words written long ago by Sir Guy Laking, first keeper of the London Museum, may appropriately be recalled – 'London can never be exhausted'. And nor, evidently, can be the need for the services of its museum.

350 *In November each year the Lord Mayor's Show takes the Lord Mayor's coach out of the museum and on to the streets of the City. In 1981 and 1986 the museum celebrated its fifth and tenth anniversaries by producing a float for the Show*

351 *'Londinio', as scratched upon a late first-century writing tablet, probably found in Lothbury in the bed of the Walbrook Stream in 1927*

352 *Aerial view of the museum looking south towards St Paul's, 1976*

Chapter 1
HISTORICAL CONTEXTS

Pages 1 to 4

1 MOL, Exhibit files, A14000–14367, Harcourt to City Solicitor, 10 April 1916
2 N G Brett-James, *The Growth of Stuart London*, 1935, pp226–7, 244; T F Reddaway, *The Rebuilding of London after the Great Fire*, 1940, pp42–7. See also I G Doolittle, *The City of London and its Livery Companies*, 1982, pp5–8
3 Standing Commission on Museums and Galleries, *Survey of Provincial Museums and Galleries*, 1963, p3

ABBREVIATIONS

CLRO
Corporation of London Records Office, Guildhall, London

Co Co
Common Council of the Corporation of London

Esher Papers
Esher Papers at the Churchill Archives Centre, Churchill College, Cambridge

GLC
Greater London Council

Harcourt Papers
Harcourt Papers at the Bodleian Library, Oxford

LCC
London County Council

MOL
Museum of London

PRO
Public Record Office

RA
Royal Archives at Windsor Castle

Chapter 2
THE GUILDHALL MUSEUM
1826 TO 1911

Pages 5 to 30

1 *Reminiscences of the Public Life of Richard Lambert Jones*, 1863, pp2–3, 105: *The Town*, 11 May 1839: Boase, *Biographical Dictionary*
2 CLRO, Library Committee Journals, 21 April, 3, 7, 14 May, 9 June 1824, 26 January, 17 May 1828, 29 January 1832, 16 May, 2 June 1843
3 Library Committee Journals 1, 17 August 1833, 7 February 1835. See also W Sedgwick Saunders, *Guildhall Library: Its Origins and Progress*, etc, 1869, p24
4 Library Committee Journals, 25 April 1829, 25 February 1839
5 *Ibid*, 21 January 1826
6 *Ibid*, 1 October 1829
7 *Ibid*, 25 February, 16 December 1826
8 *Ibid*, 16 July, 1 October 1829
9 *Ibid*, 1 June 1833, 6 August, 13 October 1835
10 Charles Roach Smith, *Collectanea Antiqua*, vol I, 1848, p138
11 Library Committee Journals, 9 May 1840
12 Saunders, *op cit*, p55
13 Library Committee Journals, 1 February, 9 May 1840
14 CLRO, Minutes of Committee to carry into execution the Act of Parliament for the rebuilding of London Bridge etc, 11 May 1840
15 Charles Roach Smith, *Illustrations of Roman London*, 1859, pI
16 *Reminiscences of the Public Life of . . . Jones*, pp37–41, 45–7
17 British Museum, Dept of Medieval and later Antiquities, Journals of Charles Roach Smith, 19 July 1835
18 Charles Roach Smith, *Retrospections, Social and Archaeological*, vol I, 1883, p118
19 Roach Smith's Journals, vol II, pp5, 128
20 *Ibid*, vol II, 1836, pp63, 87
21 *Archaeologia*, vol 27, 1838, pp140–52; vol 28, 1840, pp38–46; vol 29, pp367–8, 400–4
22 Roach Smith's Journals, 1836, vol II, 28 October–22 December 1836, 22 Feb, 22 March 1838; vol III, 26 February 1839
23 Society of Antiquaries, Council Minutes, 7 May 1839
24 Roach Smith's Journals, 7 July 1835; vol III, 1840–1, 2 February 1841, letter to the Gresham Committee
25 *Ibid*, 29 March, 8 July 1835
26 *Ibid*, 26 November 1836, 23 July 1838
27 *Ibid*, 3 March 1836, pp38–9
28 2 and 3 Vict c 107, local, Act for Further Extending the Approaches to London Bridge
29 Roach Smith's Journals, vol III, 1840–1, letter to the Gresham Committee
30 *Ibid*, vol III, 1840–1, p136 for figure of £583; CLRO, Minutes of Committee to carry into execution the Act . . . for the rebuilding of London Bridge, 11 May 1840
31 Roach Smith's Journals, vol III, 1840–1, 11 May 1840: *Retrospections*, vol I, pp120–1
32 CLRO, Minutes of Committee for . . . London Bridge, 21 January 1839
33 Roach Smith's Journals, 4 October 1840
34 *Ibid*, vol III, 1840–1, 16, 24 November 1840
35 William Tite, *A Descriptive Catalogue of the Antiquities found in the Excavations at the New Royal Exchange*, 1848, ppxxxvii–xxxviii
36 Roach Smith's Journals, vol III, 1840–1, 1, 2 Feb 1841, pp190, 192, 199–201, 203
37 Roach Smith, *Retrospections*, vol I, p131
38 Roach Smith's Journals, 2 February 1841, pp193–204
39 *Ibid*, p194
40 Roach Smith's Journals, vol III, 1840–1, 17 February, 27 April 1841
41 *Archaeologia*, vol xxix, 1842, p145
42 *The Westminster Review*, vol xxxvi, 1841, pp404–24; Roach Smith, *Retrospections*, I, pp122, 131
43 *The Gentleman's Magazine*, vol 17, 1842, p79
44 Roach Smith's Journals, 1842, vol V, 27, 28, 29 April, 11, 12, 16 May 1843
45 Roach Smith, *Collectanea Antiqua*, vol I, 1848, p4. For the date of publication see also the Preface, and Joan Evans, *A History of the Society of Antiquaries*, 1956, p231n
46 *The Builder*, 22 November 1845, p558
47 *Ibid*, 22, 29 November, 6, 13, 20, 27 December 1845, pp557–8, 569–70, 582–3, 585, 595–6, 612, 621
48 *Ibid*, 29 November 1845, p570
49 *Ibid*, 13 December 1845, p596
50 Roach Smith's Journals, 1842, vol V, 14 August 1842; 1842, 1851 etc, p142
51 *Ibid*, 1842, 1851 etc, p142
52 Charles Roach Smith, *Catalogue of the Museum of London Antiquities*, 1854, ppv–vi
53 Roach Smith, *Retrospections*, vol I, p119
54 Library Committee Journals, 11 September 1841, 4 September, 14 November 1843, 3 June 1844

55 *Ibid*, 3 March 1845; Library Committee Minute Papers, 3 March 1845, letter of 19 February 1845

56 *The Builder*, 22 November 1845, p557

57 8 and 9 Vict c 43: See also Thomas Kelly, *A History of Public Libraries in Great Britain 1845–1975*, 1977, pp9–10

58 *The Builder*, 1 February 1845, p55

59 Library Committee Journals, 3, 31 March 1845

60 *Ibid*, 3, 31 March, 7 April, 6 October, 13, 20 November, 1, 18 December 1845, 6 April 1846

61 *Ibid*, 2 March, 6 April, 2 November 1846

62 *Ibid*, 1 February 1847

63 *Ibid*, 27 January, 3 February 1845, 7 February, 6 March 1848, 4 June 1849

64 *Ibid*, 6 December 1847, 24 January 1848

65 *Ibid*, 5 October 1846, 1 May, 5 June 1848, 4 April 1853

66 *The Times*, 24 February 1849, p7; Roach Smith, *Retrospections*, vol II, 1886, pp207–8; Roach Smith, *Illustrations of Roman London*, 1859, pp47–8 and Plate v

67 *The Times*, 24 February 1849, p7

68 Tite, *op cit*, pxlv: Library Committee Journals, 2 April 1849

69 *The Times*, 1 June 1849, p7; 6 June 1849, p2; 8 June 1849, p3

70 Library Committee Journals, 3 June, 1 July 1850

71 Principal Probate Registry, Somerset House, will of Richard Lambert Jones, 1863. Jones was still attending meetings of the Library Committee in December 1852

72 Roach Smith, *Retrospections*, vol II, 1886, p224; Roach Smith, *Collectanea Antiqua*, vol IV, 1857, Appendix, p64

73 Roach Smith, *Collectanea Antiqua*, vol IV, 1857, Appendix, pp17–19, 32: Library Committee Journals, 5, 14 February, 12, 26 March 1855

74 Roach Smith, *Collectanea Antiqua*, vol IV, 1857, Appendix, p17

75 *Chambers's Journal*, 1855, pp355–8; Dafydd Kidd, 'Charles Roach Smith and his Museum of London Antiquities' in *British Museum Yearbook 2*, 1977, pp105, 126–30

76 Library Committee Journals, 7 June 1847, 5 April 1852

77 18 and 19 Vict c lxx, public general

78 Library Committee Journals, 7 May 1845: Roach Smith, *Collectanea Antiqua*, vol iv, 1857, Appendix, p20: Thomas Kelly, *A History of Adult Education in Great Britain*, 1962, p177

79 Roach Smith, *Collectanea Antiqua*, vol IV, 1857, Appendix, pp20–32, 61–75

80 Kidd, *op cit*, pp105, 133

81 Principal Probate Registry, Somerset House, will of Charles Roach Smith, 1890

82 Sedgwick Saunders, *Guildhall Library: Its Origins and Progress*, 1869, pp37–8

83 CLRO, Library Committee Minutes, 6, 20 February 1860

84 John Summerson, *The London Building World of the Eighteen-Sixties*, 1973, p7

85 Roach Smith, *Retrospections*, vol II, 1886, p199

86 Library Committee Minutes, 3, 6, 10 April 1865, 1, 9 April, 6 May 1867

87 Sedgwick Saunders, *op cit*, pp13, 39, 55

88 Library Committee Minutes, 7 December 1863

89 Sedgwick Saunders, *op cit*, pp50–3

90 CLRO, Common Council Minutes and Reports, Report of City Lands Committee presented 22 October 1868, Report No 40

91 Library Committee Minutes, 6, 13, 31 May, 13 June 1867

92 Sedgwick Saunders, *op cit*, pp14, 17

93 *The Builder*, 15, 19 May 1869, pp392, 424

94 *The Illustrated London News*, 29 May 1869, p550

95 Library Committee Minutes, 7 June 1869

96 CLRO, Common Council Minutes, 15, 22 July 1869, pp165, 174–5; Charles Welch, *A Brief Guide to the Guildhall Museum*, 1901, p7

97 CLRO, Minutes of Select Committee for the Erection of a New Library and Museum, *passim*

98 Select Committee, *passim*; Library Committee minutes, 3, 17 November 1873; *Catalogue of the Collection of London Antiquities in the Guildhall Museum*, 1903, p iv; *The Builder*, 27 August 1870, pp684, 686, 9 November 1872, pp878–9

99 Select Committee, 24 March 1874

100 *Ibid*, *passim*

101 *Ibid*, 17 July 1871, 3 June 1872; Library Committee Minutes, 5 February 1872

102 Library Committee Minutes, 17 November 1873, 14 July 1875, 6 October 1884, 5 October 1891

103 *Ibid*, 10 December 1883, 9 April, 7 May 1888, 4 May 1896

104 *Transactions of the London and Middlesex Archaeological Society*, vol I, 1860, p7

105 John Edward Price, *On a Bastion of London Wall . . .*, 1880, p5

106 John Edward Price, *Roman Antiquities Illustrated by Remains Recently Discovered on the site of The National Safe Deposit Company's Premises . . .*, 1873, pp2, 79

107 Library Committee Minutes, 3 May 1875: Welch, *Brief Guide*, pp9, 17

108 Price, *On a Bastion of London Wall*, pp80–1

109 Library Committee Minutes, 7 March, 4 April 1881

110 Guildhall Library, MS 17,151, vol I, Catalogue of Antiquities by John Walker Baily: *Journal of the British Archaeological Association*, vol XXX, 1874, pp349–51

111 Guildhall Library, MS 17,151, vol I, cutting from *The City Press*, 21 May 1881

112 Library Committee Minutes, 10 April 1893, 9 December 1898, 6 February 1899; Welch, *Brief Guide*, pp6, 12, 13

113 Library Committee Minutes, 15 February 1877, 7 March 1881, 3 July 1899: Welch, *Brief Guide*, pp9–10, 13–14

114 Library Committee Minutes, 2, 18 July, 5 November 1888, 4 February 1889

115 CLRO, Common Council Minutes, 1904, Report No 33

116 Library Committee Minutes, 1 April, 22 December 1889, 11 December 1891, 7 March 1904

117 *Ibid*, 2, 25 February, 2 March, 6, 29 April 1891: Boase, *Biographical Dictionary*

118 Library Committee Minutes, 2 February 1891, 1 February 1892, 24 September 1897; CLRO, Common Council Minutes, 13 January 1898, p26

119 Common Council Minutes, 21 April 1898, p106, 8, 15 December 1898, pp397, 413

120 Library Committee Minutes, 7 May 1900, 1 April 1901

121 *Ibid*, 6 April 1891: Principal Probate Registry, Somerset House, will of G F Lawrence, 1939

122 Library Committee Minutes, 2, 10 February, 6 April, 8 June, 13 July 1903, 14 March 1904

123 *Ibid*, 26 April 1893, 21 April, 4 June 1904: *Catalogue of the Collection of London Antiquities in the Guildhall Museum*, 1903, pix

124 Library Committee Minutes, 8 June 1903; Library Committee Papers, July 1903

125 Common Council Minutes, 1904, Report No 33; Library Committee Minutes, 14 March 1904. Attendance figures from librarian's annual reports

126 Library Committee Minutes, 20 June, 1, 22 October, 5 November 1906, 16 September 1909

127 Common Council Minutes, 1907, Reports Nos 13, 14

128 Library Committee Minutes, 2 Dec 1907

129 *Ibid*, 6 July, 2 November, 7 December 1908, 3 April 1911

ABBREVIATIONS

CLRO
Corporation of London Records Office, Guildhall, London

Co Co
Common Council of the Corporation of London

Esher Papers
Esher Papers at the Churchill Archives Centre, Churchill College, Cambridge

GLC
Greater London Council

Harcourt Papers
Harcourt Papers at the Bodleian Library, Oxford

LCC
London County Council

MOL
Museum of London

PRO
Public Record Office

RA
Royal Archives at Windsor Castle

Chapter 3
FOUNDATION OF THE LONDON MUSEUM
1910 TO 1912

Pages 31 to 66

1 Harcourt Papers 531/59, Lord Harcourt's passport particulars; MOL, DC11/6, p24

2 Esher Papers 10/16, Harcourt to Esher, 23 January 1902; Principal Probate Registry, Somerset House, will of Viscount Harcourt, 1922

3 Esher Papers 10/16, Harcourt to Esher, 24 November 1904

4 MOL, DC11/6, p177

5 A G Gardiner, *The Life of Sir William Harcourt*, 1923, vol I, pp118, 242, 305–6, 336, 386–7

6 Harcourt Papers 192, f50

7 *The Times*, 7 May 1908, p8

8 Peter Fraser, *Lord Esher. A Political Biography*, 1973, p9. For a more personal account see also James Lees-Milne, *The Enigmatic Edwardian. The Life of Reginald 2nd Viscount Esher*, 1986, *passim*

9 Gardiner, I, p339

10 Harcourt Papers 424, *passim*; Esher Papers, 10/16, *passim*

11 Esher Papers 10/16, Harcourt to Esher, 22 February 1895

12 Harcourt Papers 424/104,183

13 Esher Papers 10/16, 10 December 1905; typescript catalogue of Esher Papers, Curriculum Vitae of Reginald Esher

14 Harcourt Papers 456, *passim*

15 *Ibid*, 453, p55

16 *Ibid*, 455, pp69, 82

17 *Ibid*, 458, p2; *The Times*, 7 May 1908, p8

18 Harcourt Papers 455, p92

19 *Ibid*, 1984 Deposit, 30, 15 June 1908

20 RA, W35/78, Harcourt to Knollys, 26 April 1910

21 Information kindly supplied by the Musée Carnavalet

22 Esher Papers 10/16, 4 April 1890

23 LCC Minutes, 28 March 1911, p744

24 *Survey of London*, vol I, 1900, *The Parish of Bromley-by-Bow*, p xxxi

25 LCC Minutes, 10 May 1910, pp1028–30, 17–18 December 1912, pp1663–4

26 *The Times*, 25 March 1911, p8, 4 September 1911, p6

27 Information kindly supplied by Mr John Phillips

28 *The Times*, 14 June 1909, p14

29 MOL, DC3/6, p645

30 Harcourt Papers 439, ff 92–3; *The Times*, 25 July 1906, p8

31 Patrick Geddes, 'A Suggested Plan for a Civic Museum . . .' in *Sociological Papers*, vol 3, 1906, p231

32 For much of this paragraph I am much indebted to Mr Andrew Saint

33 *The Times*, 11 April 1910, p12

34 *Ibid*, 4 Oct 1924, p13; *Who Was Who 1916–28*; information kindly supplied by Ms Priscilla Greville, granddaughter of Sir Harry Waechter

35 Information kindly supplied by Ms Priscilla Greville

36 Esher Papers 5/38, Trippell to Esher, 26 Oct 1911

37 *Ibid*, 5/42, undated, *c.*December 1912, Waechter to Esher; *The Times*, 22 May 1929, p10; *Who Was Who 1929–40*; Information from Ms Priscilla Greville

38 Esher Papers 10/54, Harcourt to Esher, 14 March 1910

39 *Ibid*, 5/34, Harcourt to Esher, 16 April 1910

40 RA, w35/78, Harcourt to Knollys, 26 April 1910

41 CLRO, Common Council Minutes, 26 April 1923, p134, 1 May 1924, p150; Common Council Papers, 26 April 1923, 1 May 1924, 23 April 1925

42 MOL, DC11/6, p118

43 Esher Papers 5/39, Harcourt to Esher, 25 July 1910

44 *Ibid*, 5/39, Harcourt to Esher, 27 October 1910

45 *Ibid*, 6/4, Queen Alexandra to Esher, 19 March 1911; *The Times*, 25 March 1911, p8

46 *Journals and Letters of Reginald Viscount Esher*, ed. Oliver Viscount Esher, vol 3, 1938, pp11–12

47 Esher Papers 6/4, Queen Alexandra to Esher, 30 July 1910

48 *Ibid*, 6/7, Queen Mary to Esher, 4, 7 August 1910

49 Esher Papers 5/35, 15, 16 July 1910, Harcourt to Esher; *Journals and Letters of Reginald Viscount Esher*, vol 3, pp15–17

50 *The Times*, 3 August 1910, p8, 17 September 1910, p11

51 Esher Papers 5/39, Harcourt to Esher, 10 October 1910

52 *The Times*, 15 October 1910, p13, 29 October 1910, p13

53 *Ibid*, 7 Nov 1910, p11, 8 November 1910, p10; Esher, 5/39, Harcourt to Esher, 27, 29 October 1910

54 *The Times*, 7 November 1910, p11

55 Esher Papers 5/36, Harcourt to Esher, 3 April 1911; 5/39, same to same, 10, 27 October 1910; MOL, DC3/3, p80, Laking to Harcourt, 17 January 1912; Harcourt Papers 519, Harcourt to Johnson, 10 February 1913. See also M E Ogborn, *Staple Inn*, 1980 edition

56 Esher Papers 2/12, 28 October 1910

57 *The Times*, 2 January 1911, p10

58 Esher Papers 5/39, Harcourt to Esher, 5 January 1911

59 Harcourt Papers 448, Harcourt to Child's Bank, 17 July 1917; MOL, DC3/13, pp100−2

60 MOL, DC3/3, p80

61 *Ibid*, DC3/7, p77, Laking to Harcourt, 6 January 1914

62 Esher Papers 5/37, Harcourt to Esher, 1 August 1911

63 *Ibid*, 5/39, Harcourt to Esher, 5 January 1911

64 *Ibid*, 6/5, King George to Esher, 19 March 1911

65 *Ibid*, 6/4, Queen Alexandra to Esher, 19 March 1911

66 *Ibid*, 6/7, Queen Mary to Esher, ND (February or March 1911)

67 MOL, DC11/1, *Standard*, 25 March 1911

68 Esher Papers 5/36, Harcourt to Esher, 3 April 1911

69 LCC Minutes, 1−2 Aug 1911, p637

70 MOL, DC11/1, *Daily Express*, 25 March 1911

71 *Ibid*, DC2/01, correspondence with J J Bisgood, March−April 1911; DC3/1, pp65−6, Laking to Harcourt, 4 April 1911

72 *Ibid*, DC11/6, p135, *Daily Telegraph*, 24 November 1919

73 The quotations in this paragraph are from 'Sir Guy Francis Laking' by John Hayward in *Armi Antiche* (Bolletino dell'Accademia di S Marciano, Turin), 1964, pp266−70. See also *Daily Telegraph*, 24 November 1919, *The Times*, 24 November 1919, 23 April 1920, p19 and *Who Was Who 1916−28*

74 MOL, DC3/5, pp249, 252, 492, 760

75 Esher Papers 5/36, letters of Laking and Asquith to Esher, January−March 1911

76 MOL, 2/01, Laking to Harcourt, 7 October 1911

77 PRO, WORK 19/222, 19/1132

78 MOL, DC3/1, *passim*

79 *Ibid*, DC3/1, p41, Laking to Lawrence, 3 April 1911

80 *Ibid*, DC3/4, pp97−100, Laking to Harcourt, 24 April 1912

81 *Twenty-Five Years of the London Museum*, 1937, p8

82 MOL, DC3/1, p165, Laking to Harcourt 25 April 1911

83 *Ibid*, DC3/1, pp353, 405, Laking to Harcourt, 18, 29 August, 4 September 1911; DC2/01, Laking to Harcourt, 7 October 1911

84 *Ibid*, DC3/1, pp122, 161, Laking to Harcourt, 11, 22 April 1911; DC3/2, p460, Laking to McDonnell, 2 November 1911; PRO, WORK 19/1132

85 MOL, DC3/1, p263, Laking to McDonnell, 20 June 1911; DC3/2, pp460, 594, 900, same to same, 2, 17 November, 20 December 1911; DC3/2, p95, Laking to Harcourt, 14 September 1911

86 *The Times*, 25 March 1911, p8

87 MOL, DC3/1, pp161, 266, Laking to Harcourt, 22 April, 26 June 1911; Esher, 5/37, Laking to Esher, 8 June 1911

88 *Ibid*, DC3/1, p321, Laking to 'Fitz', 8 August 1911; p354, Laking to Harcourt, 18 August 1911; pp351, 365, Oates to Steele, 18, 21 August 1911

89 *Ibid*, DC3/1, pp256, 353, Laking to Harcourt, 14 June, 18 August 1911; DC3/2, p959, Laking to Joubert, c.January 1912

90 *Ibid*, DC3/1, pp161, 256, 276, Laking to Harcourt, 22 April, 14 June, 7 July 1911

91 *Ibid*, DC2/01, Harcourt to Laking, 6 April 1911, and Harcourt to Gomme, 11 April 1911; DC3/1, p205, Laking to Harcourt, 8 May 1911

92 *Ibid*, DC2/15, Murray to Oates, 7 March 1924; DC3/1, p309, Laking to Murray, 3 August 1911; DC3/4, pp97−100, Laking to Harcourt, 24 April 1912; DC4/1934, Murray to Wheeler, 21 August 1934; G F Laking, *Wallace Collection Catalogues. Oriental Arms and Armour*, 1964 ed, p x

93 MOL, DC3/4, pp97−100, 618, 648, Laking to Harcourt, 24 April, 20, 22 June 1912; DC3/13, pp25, 32, Laking to Treasury, 12 March, 27 April 1914; information kindly supplied by Mr Martin Holmes

94 MOL, DC3/1, pp310, 337, 426, Laking to Lawrence, 3, 14 August, 2 September 1911; DC3/2, p145, Laking to Harcourt, 22 September 1911

95 *Ibid*, DC2/01, Cooper to Laking, 3 April 1911; DC3/1, p297, Laking to Harcourt, 26 July 1911; p344, Laking to Mrs Parbury, 16 August 1911; p496, Laking to McDonnell, 7 September 1911

96 *Ibid*, DC3/1, pp401, 443, Laking to dealer, 29 August, 2 September 1911; Laking to Lawrence, 29 August 1911

97 *Ibid*, DC2/01, Laking to Harcourt, 6 September 1911; DC3/1, Laking to Harcourt, 4 September 1911; p417 Laking to Joubert, 1 September 1911; DC3/2, p145, Laking to Harcourt, 22 September 1911

98 *The Times, The Morning Post*, 25 August 1911

99 Esher Papers 5/36, Harcourt to Esher, 3 April 1911

100 LCC Minutes, 1−2 August 1911, p637

101 MOL, DC3/1, pp306−8, Laking to Esher, 3 August 1911

102 *Ibid*, DC3/1, p366, Laking to Harcourt, 21 August 1911; p416 Oates to Riley, 31 August 1911

103 *Ibid*, DC2/04, 05, correspondence with Office of Works, 1912−13

104 *Ibid*, DC11/1, pp43−65, *passim*

105 *The Museums Journal*, vol XI, 1912, pp295−6

106 MOL, DC3/3, pp139, 160, Laking to Harcourt, 23, 26 January 1912

107 Information kindly supplied by Mr Arthur Trotman

108 MOL, DC3/1, p405, Laking to Harcourt, 29 August 1911

109 *Ibid*, DC3/2, p104, September 1911; DC11/1, pp107−10

110 *Ibid*, DC3/2, p71, Laking to Ingram, 12 September 1911

111 *Ibid*, DC3/2, p370, Laking to Ward, 21 October 1911

112 *Ibid*, DC11/1, p73, *Daily Mail*, 4 September 1911

113 Information kindly supplied by Mr Martin Holmes

114 MOL, DC3/2, p331, Laking to Esher, 16 October 1911

115 *Ibid*, DC3/1, p370, Laking to Queen Mary, 22 August 1911; pp418, 424−5, same to Mrs Clarke, 1 September 1911

116 *Ibid*, DC2/01, Esher to Laking, 8 October 1911; Esher Papers 5/38, Harcourt to Esher, 2 September 1911; *Journals and Letters of Reginald Viscount Esher*, vol 3, pp59−64

117 MOL, DC3/2, p275, Laking to Queen Mary, 10 October 1911; pp348−9, same to Esher, 19 October 1911

118 *Ibid*, DC3/2, p504, Laking to Harcourt, 7 November 1911

119 Esher Papers 6/7, Queen Mary to Esher, 6 November 1911; 5/38, Harcourt to Esher, 4 November 1911

120 MOL, DC3/2, pp127, 213, Laking to Cust, 20 September, 3 October 1911; p211, Laking to Esher, 3 October 1911

121 *Ibid*, DC3/2, pp331, 333, Laking to Esher, 16 October 1911; Esher Papers 6/7, Queen Mary to Esher, 28 October 1911

122 MOL, DC3/2, pp566, 632, Laking to Harcourt, 15, 24 November 1911

123 *Ibid*, DC3/2, pp922–3, 985, Laking to Harcourt, 22 December 1911 6 January 1912; p968, Laking to Esher, 3 January 1912; DC3/3, p39, Laking to Harcourt, 11 January 1912

124 *Ibid*, DC2/02–03, McDonnell to Esher, 13 December 1911; DC3/3, p284, Laking to McDonnell, 8 February 1912; p343, Laking to Harcourt, 13 February 1912

125 MOL, Exhibits files, c66–74

126 Information kindly supplied by Lord Joicey and by the John George Joicey Museum, Newcastle upon Tyne; Principal Probate Registry, Somerset House, will of John George Joicey, 1919

127 MOL, Exhibits files, A9700–9912

128 *Ibid*, DC3/2, p553, Laking to Alexander, 14 November 1911

129 For this and the next three paragraphs, see MOL DC11/1–4 *passim*, except where otherwise stated

130 MOL, DC2/02–03, Mrs Enthoven to Laking, 4 January 1912

131 *Ibid*, DC3/3, pp15, 29, 602, Oates to Mrs Enthoven, 8, 10 January, 14 March 1912

132 *Ibid*, DC3/4, pp933–5, Laking to Mrs Enthoven, 16 August 1912

133 *Ibid*, DC3/3, p80, Laking to Harcourt, 17 January 1912

134 *Ibid*, DC3/2, pp511, 901, 922–3, Laking to Harcourt, 9 November, 20, 22 December 1911

135 *Ibid*, DC3/3, pp4, 139, 201, Laking to Harcourt, 8, 23, 30 January 1912

136 *Ibid*, DC3/3, p378, Laking to Harcourt, 19 February 1912

137 *Ibid*, DC3/3, p340, Laking to Lady Eve Dugdale, 13 February 1912

138 Esher Papers 6/7, Queen Mary to Esher, 10 March 1912

139 MOL, DC11/2, p93, *Daily Telegraph*, 19 March 1912

140 Antonia Raeburn, *The Militant Suffragettes*, 1973, p169. I am indebted for this reference to Mr Michael Robbins.

141 *The Times*, 19 March, 4, 9 April 1912

142 MOL, DC3/3, p378, Laking to Harcourt, 19 February 1912

143 *Ibid*, DC3/3, p599, Laking to Ingram, 13 March 1912

144 *Ibid*, DC3/3, p565, Laking to Cook, 9 March 1912

145 *Ibid*, DC3/3, p665, Oates to District Railway Co, 20 March 1912

146 PRO, T1/11564/17176, 22 February, 11 March 1912

147 MOL, DC2/02–03, McDonnell to Laking, 4 April 1912

148 All information in this and the next two paragraphs is unless otherwise stated taken from MOL, DC11/3, press cutting book

149 MOL, Exhibits files, A9700–9912; *The Times*, 22 March 1912

150 *The Building News*, 22 March 1912

151 *The Times*, 9 April 1912, p5; 25 May 1912, p7; *Daily Mirror*, 9 April 1912; MOL, DC3/4, p476, Oates to Jerningham, 1 June 1912

152 MOL, DC3/3, p987, Laking to Harcourt, 13 April 1912

153 *Ibid*, DC11/4, pp43, 51

154 *The Museums Journal*, vol XI, 1912, pp290–7

155 MOL, DC11/4, p52, *The Antiquary*, May 1912

156 *Ibid*, DC11/5, p13, *The Observer*, 5 December 1912

157 *Ibid*, DC11/5, p21, *Knowledge*, January 1913

158 *Ibid*, DC11/4, p51, *Nash's Magazine*, May 1912

ABBREVIATIONS

CLRO
Corporation of London Records Office, Guildhall, London

Co Co
Common Council of the Corporation of London

Esher Papers
Esher Papers at the Churchill Archives Centre, Churchill College, Cambridge

GLC
Greater London Council

Harcourt Papers
Harcourt Papers at the Bodleian Library, Oxford

LCC
London County Council

MOL
Museum of London

PRO
Public Record Office

RA
Royal Archives at Windsor Castle

Chapter 4
THE LONDON MUSEUM
1912 TO 1926

Pages 67 to 98

1 MOL, DC3/4, 331–2

2 *Ibid*, DC3/4, 331–2, 603–4; also 97–100, 618, 648, Laking to Harcourt, 24 April, 20, 22, June 1912; 665, 798, Laking to Beauchamp, 25 June, 16 July 1912

3 *Ibid*, DC3/4, 608, Laking to Beauchamp, 20 June 1912; DC11/4, 66

4 *Ibid*, DC3/4, Oates to Tilling, June to November 1912, *passim*; DC3/6, 535, same to same, 16 August 1913

5 Information kindly supplied by Mr Martin Holmes

6 MOL, DC3/4, 612, 879, Oates to Gas Light and Coke Co, 31 July 1912; DC11/5, 15

7 *Ibid*, DC3/5, Oates to Crisp and Laking to GPO, *passim*; DC11/5, 7

8 *The Times*, 27 September 1912, 7

9 Except where otherwise stated this and the following paragraph are based on MOL, Exhibits files A9700–9912

10 MOL, DC2/02–03, Joicey to Oates, 1, 13 June 1912

11 *Ibid*, DC2/02–03, Steele to Oates, 16 October 1912 and note on Harcourt to Laking, 16 October 1912

12 *Ibid*, Exhibits files, 46.78/1–74

13 *The Times*, 14 June 1912, 10

14 Harcourt Papers 443, 3, 5, 6, correspondence between H L Tangye and Harcourt, July 1912

15 *The Times*, 19 March 1914, 6

16 Except where otherwise stated this and the following five paragraphs are based on MOL, Cheapside Hoard file, A14000–14367

17 MOL, DC3/4, 621, Laking to Beauchamp, 20 June 1912

18 *Ibid*, DC3/4, 648, Laking to Harcourt, 22 June 1912

19 *Ibid*, DC3/4, 695, Oates to Lawrence, 26 June 1912

20 *Ibid*, DC3/6, 548, Oates to Lawrence, 15 August 1913

21 *Ibid*, DC3/4, 842, Laking to Harcourt, 24 July 1912

22 *Ibid*, DC3/4, 738, Oates to Harcourt's secretary, 5 July 1912

23 *Ibid*, DC3/4, 816, Laking to Harcourt, 18 July 1912

24 *The Times*, 14 March 1914, 5

25 CLRO, Common Council Papers, 19 April 1917, Librarian's report for 1916

26 MOL, DC3/3, 987, Laking to Harcourt,
13 April 1912

27 *Ibid*, DC2/04–05, Lever to Laking,
24 March 1914; Harcourt Papers 519,
179, 180, 186

28 H M Colvin, *A Biographical Dictionary
of British Architects 1600–1840*, 1978, 92,
938

29 *Twenty-Five Years of the London
Museum*, 1937, 7

30 MOL, DC11/5, 5

31 PRO, T1/11564/17176

32 Harcourt Papers 519, 45–6

33 *Survey of London*, vol XL, 1980, 271

34 Harcourt Papers 519, 5, 11–12; PRO,
T1/11564/17176

35 PRO, T1/11564/17176

36 *Ibid*, T160/77/F2686, T160/81/2947/1;
Harcourt Papers 519, 11–12

37 Harcourt Papers 519, 11–12

38 *The Times*, 1 January 1913, 10

39 *Ibid*, 7 January 1913, 7

40 *Ibid*, 16, 21, 24, 28, 29, 31 January 1913

41 *Ibid*, 1 August 1913, 13

42 RA, GV, R108, Asquith to the King,
20 March 1913

43 Harcourt Papers 519, 36–7

44 *Ibid* 519, 47–9

45 *The Times*, 29 March 1913, 8

46 *Ibid*, 3 May 1913, 8, Lever to Asquith,
26 April 1913

47 Harcourt Papers 519, 54–9, 71–5

48 *The Times*, 3 May 1913, 8

49 Harcourt Papers 519, 71–3

50 *Ibid*, 519, 50, 87

51 PRO, T1/11564/17176, Harcourt to
Heath, 12 July 1913

52 *Ibid*, deed of 1 July 1913

53 Harcourt Papers 519, 81

54 PRO, T1/11564, Heath to Masterman,
12 September 1913

55 *Ibid*, Harcourt to Chalmers, 5 May 1913

56 *Ibid*, note by Harcourt of 5 June 1913,
and separate sheet initialled LC

57 Harcourt Papers 519, 33, 154; MOL,
DC3/6, 555; DC11/5, 86

58 Harcourt Papers 519, 144; MOL,
DC11/5, 79

59 MOL, DC3/6, 511, Laking to Harcourt,
11 August 1913

60 Harcourt Papers 519, 131–2

61 *Ibid* 519, 189; MOL, DC3/6, 511, Laking
to Harcourt, 11 August 1913

62 MOL, DC3/6, 591–4, 718, 776, Laking
to Harcourt, 3 September, 6, 18 October
1913; 655, Oates to Wells,
20 September 1913

63 Harcourt Papers 519, 91

64 *Ibid* 519, 89

65 RA, GV, PSIO, 440/1, Stamfordham to
Earle, 9 May 1913

66 Harcourt Papers 519, 172

67 *Ibid* 519, 163, 172

68 RA, GV, PSIO, 440/1–36, *passim*;
Harcourt Papers 519, 87–172 *passim*;
PRO, T1/11564/17176, Beauchamp to
Heath, 24 April 1914

69 RA, GV, PSIO, 440/13

70 MOL, DC3/6, 499, Laking to Esher,
31 July 1913

71 *Ibid*, DC3/7, 689, 724, Laking to
Harcourt, 2, 7 April 1914

72 RA, GV, PSIO, 440/21–7

73 MOL, DC3/8, 544, Laking to Harcourt,
7 November 1914

74 *Ibid*, DC2/07, Office of Works to Laking,
18 January 1916

75 *Ibid*, DC3/6, 699, Laking to Harcourt,
30 September 1913

76 *Ibid*, DC3/6, 773, Laking to Esher,
18 October 1913

77 *Ibid*, DC11/6, 29

78 *The Times*, 14 October 1913, 3, 16,
19 March 1914, 10,6

79 MOL, DC11/6, 22

80 *Ibid*, DC3/6, 526, Oates to Chisholm,
14 August 1913

81 *The Times*, 16, 19 March 1914, 10,6

82 MOL, DC11/6, 72

83 *Ibid*, DC3/6, 524, 660, Oates to Office of
Works and Fire Brigade, 14 August,
22 September 1913

84 *Ibid*, DC3/7, 939, Laking to Treves,
13 May 1914

85 *Ibid*, Exhibits files, A9700–9912,
Laking to Joicey, 20 September 1913

86 *Ibid*, DC11/6, 62

87 *Ibid*, DC3/6, 815, Laking to Harcourt,
28 October 1913

88 *Ibid*, DC3/7, 68,77, Laking to Harcourt,
3, 6 January 1914

89 *Ibid*, Exhibits files, A9700–9912,
Laking to Joicey, 20 September 1913;
DC3/6, 815, Laking to Harcourt,
28 October 1913; DC11/6, 14

90 *Ibid*, Accessions file 'Models of Old
London', correspondence with Godfrey
and Maginnis

91 *Ibid*, file 'Models of Old London', Joicey
to Oates, 21 January 1914

92 *Ibid*, DC3/8, 508, Oates to Harcourt's
secretary, 27 October 1914

93 *Ibid*, DC3/7, 580, 624, Laking to
Harcourt, 23, 24 March 1914; file
A9700–9912, Joicey to Laking, 11 July
1914

94 *Ibid*, DC2/05, Works to Laking,
22 December 1914

95 *Ibid*, DC2/06, Joicey to Laking, 7 April
1915; DC3/9, 296, Oates to Joicey, 18
Oct 1915

96 *Ibid*, DC3/7, 87, Laking to Nathan,
7 January 1914

97 *Ibid*, DC2/05, Nathan to Laking,
22 January, 1 April 1914

98 *Ibid*, DC3/7, 51, 408, Oates and Laking
to New Scotland Yard, 23 Dec 1913,
6 March 1914; Harcourt Papers 519,
139

99 MOL, DC3/7, 349, Laking to Esher,
3 March 1914

100 *Ibid*, DC3/7, 488, Laking to Harcourt,
13 March 1914

101 *Ibid*, DC3/7, 292, Laking to Esher,
23 Feb 1914; *The Times*, 21 March
1914, 8, 10; 23 March 1914, 4

102 Harcourt Papers 444, 111

103 MOL, DC11/6, 43, 44, 55

104 *Ibid*, DC3/7, 928, Laking to Harcourt,
12 May 1914

105 *Ibid*, DC3/8, 686

106 PRO, T145/1

107 MOL, DC3/8, 337, Laking to Civil
Service Commission, 11 August 1914;
DC3/9, 687, 695, Laking to Murray,
13, 23 September 1916

108 *Ibid*, DC3/9, 368, Oates to Osmond,
24 November 1915; DC3/13, 38, 194,
197

109 *Ibid*, DC3/9, 527 and 738–9, Laking to
Harcourt and J G Read, 25 October
1916

110 *Ibid*, DC3/2, 215–16, Laking to
Harcourt, 3 October 1911

111 *Ibid*, DC3/4, 293, 8 May 1912

112 *Ibid*, DC3/8, 536, Laking to Treves,
6 November 1914

113 *Ibid*, DC3/9, 51, Laking to Harcourt,
7 June 1915

114 *Ibid*, DC3/9, 182, 188, Laking to
Harcourt, 9, 14 August 1915

115 *Ibid*, DC3/9, 296, Oates to Joicey,
18 October 1915; 314, Laking to
Harcourt, 20 October 1915

116 *Ibid*, DC3/10, 171, 183, Laking to
Harcourt, 15 April, 17 May 1918

117 *Ibid*, DC3/10, p218, Oates to Gardner,
8 August 1918

118 *Ibid*, DC3/10, p275, Oates to
Metropolitan Museum, New York,
30 November 1918

119 *Ibid*, DC2/06, Harcourt to Laking,
17 September 1915

120 *Ibid*, DC2/06–09, *passim*

121 *Ibid*, DC2/09, War Office to Laking,
12 August 1919

122 *Ibid*, DC2/08, *passim*; DC3/10, p326,
Oates to Harcourt, 15 February 1919

123 *Ibid*, DC2/06–07, December 1917;
DC3/10, p169, 11 April 1918

124 *Ibid*, DC3/08, Harcourt to Earle,
15 November 1918

125 *Ibid*, DC3/10, p326, Oates to Harcourt,
15 February 1919

126 PRO, T160/787/F6139/08

127 *The Times*, 21 October 1919, p16

128 Principal Probate Registry, Somerset House, will of John George Joicey, 1919

129 MOL, DC3/4, pp461–3, Laking to Harcourt, 31 May 1912

130 *Ibid*, DC3/10, p633, Laking to Earle, 24 October 1919

131 *Ibid*, DC3/10, p685, Lady Laking to Queen Alexandra, *c*.18 November 1919; *The Times*, 24 November 1919, p17

132 *Ibid*, DC11/5, p75, *Great Thoughts*, 7 June 1913

133 *The Times*, 16, 20 January 1914

134 *Ibid*, 18 April 1914, p4

135 *Ibid*, 25, 28 November 1919; 23, 24 April 1920

136 Information kindly supplied by Ms Priscilla Greville, granddaughter of Sir Harry Waechter

137 MOL, DC3/13, p78, Treasury Minute, 9 December 1919, and p83, Oates to Treasury, 15 Dec 1919; PRO, T145/1, 26 January 1920

138 MOL, DC3/13, p100, Oates to Esher, 3 March 1922

139 *Ibid*, DC3/13, p89, Dawson to Oates, 10 December 1920; Esher Papers, 6/8, Queen Mary to Esher, 18 December 1920

140 Information kindly supplied by Mr Walter Henderson

141 MOL, DC11/6, p139

142 Information kindly supplied by Mr Martin Holmes

143 RA, W35/78

144 MOL, DC11/6, p176, *Evening Standard*, 28 February 1922

145 *The Times*, 2 March 1922

146 Esher Papers 5/59, 60, *passim*

147 Harcourt Papers 424, p310

148 MOL, DC3/13, pp100–4, correspondence of 28 February–3 March 1922 between Walker, Martineau and Co, Lord Esher and Harman Oates

149 *Ibid*, DC3/7, pp780, 794, 937, Laking to Harcourt, 21, 22 April, 13 May 1914; DC3/8, p451, same to same, 26 September 1914

150 *Ibid*, DC3/8, p744, Oates to Armstrong, 13 February 1915; pp789, 799, 825, Oates to Joubert, 27 February, 2, 8 March 1915

151 *Ibid*, DC3/10, pp711, 861, Oates to Harcourt, 10 December 1919, 20 April 1920; p720, Oates to Lawrence, 15 December 1919; DC3/11, p89, 30 September 1920

152 Harcourt Papers 448, p64

153 Esher Papers 10/54, Harcourt to Esher, 11 March 1919

154 MOL, DC2/05, Laking to Harcourt, 6 March 1915

155 *Ibid*, DC2/07, Harcourt to Laking, 8 November, 11 December 1916

156 *Ibid*, DC2/09, Hooke to Harcourt, 18 July 1919

157 *Ibid*, DC2/04, Kenyon to Esher, 17 June 1913; DC3/6, p699, Laking to Harcourt, 30 September 1913

158 *Ibid*, Exhibits files, A13406–35; DC3/6, pp699, 736, Laking to Harcourt, 30 September, 9 October 1913

159 Information kindly supplied by Mr Walter Henderson

160 Harcourt Papers 519, p215

161 *Ibid*, 519, p215; *The Times*, 21 October 1919, p16; DC2/11, Harcourt to Oates, 11 January 1921

162 This and the following two paragraphs are based upon Esher Papers 10/54, Harcourt to Esher, 11 March 1919, and MOL, DC3/13, pp100–4 (cited above at reference 148)

163 See, for instance, Esher Papers 7/8, Maurice Brett to Esher, 30 March 1925

164 Harcourt Papers, Additional Papers 39, notes of 18 July 1913 and January 1917. See also MOL, DC2/08–10, Harcourt to Oates, 24 November 1920

165 Esher Papers 7/35, Esher to Maurice Brett, 25 February 1922

166 MOL, DC1/1, 8 February 1923

167 Esher Papers 7/35, Esher to Maurice Brett, 7, 10 April 1922

168 *Ibid*, 7/33, same to same, 1 January 1920

169 For Wheeler's ignorance of the Fund, see DC2/15, Wheeler to Esher, 28 June 1928

170 MOL, DC3/13, p211

171 Dr Wheeler's memorandum is in *Royal Commission on National Museums and Galleries. Oral Evidence, Memoranda and Appendices to the Interim Report*, 1928, pp237–8. His oral evidence is in ditto, *Oral Evidence, Memoranda and Appendices to the Final Report*, 1929, pp7–14. (The British Library Pressmark for both documents is BS4/2)

172 Parliamentary Papers 1929–30, vol XVI, *Royal Commission on National Museums and Galleries Final Report, Part I, General Conclusions and Recommendations* (Command 3401), pp512–16

173 *Ibid*, *Final Report, Part II, Conclusions and Recommendations Relating to Individual Institutions* (Command 3463), p582

174 MOL, DC4/1930, correspondence about new Trustees

175 Esher Papers 7/55, Maurice Brett to Oliver Esher, 13 May 1930

176 MOL, DC1/1, 5 June 1930, pp34–5

177 *Ibid*, DC1/1, 2 December 1937, pp92–3, and 22 March 1938, p97

178 PRO, T160/787/F6139/08; MOL, DC11/6, p181

179 PRO, T160/787/F6139/08, and T145/1, 16 August 1921

180 Information kindly supplied by Mr Walter Henderson

181 Esher Papers 7/8, Maurice Brett to Esher, *passim*; 7/34–37, *passim*, Esher to Maurice Brett

182 MOL, DC3/11, p1, Oates to Police Pensioners' Assoc, 3 July 1920

183 Information kindly supplied by Mr Arthur Trotman

184 MOL, DC3/10, p942, Oates to Civil Service Commissioners, 21 June; pp453, 987, Oates to Corps of Commissionaires, 27 June, 16 July 1920; DC3/11, pp236, 780, Oates to Civil Service Commissioners, 2 February 1921, 15 May 1922; information kindly supplied by Mr Walter Henderson

185 *Ibid*, DC11/6, *Daily Telegraph*, 30 October 1920

186 *The Times*, 7 May 1920, p11; 17 November 1920, p9; 2 April 1923; 27 July 1923, p7; 5 May 1925, p11

187 MOL, DC11/6, p192; John Hayes, *Catalogue of the Oil Paintings in the London Museum*, 1970, pp126–9

188 *The Times*, 17 Nov 1920, p9; 20 July 1921, p10; 14 December 1921, p7; MOL, DC11/6, p166

189 *The Times*, 2 April 1923, p5; MOL, DC11/6, p192

190 MOL, DC3/12, p182

191 *Ibid*, DC11/6, p199

192 *Ibid*, DC11/6, p159

193 *Ibid*, DC11/5, p26

194 *Ibid*, DC3/7, pp596, 883, Laking to Blair, 23 March, *c*.6 May 1914

195 *Ibid*, DC3/10, p627, Oates to LCC, 22 October 1919

196 *Ibid*, DC2/11, Harcourt to Oates, 11 January 1921

197 Harcourt Papers 519, Oates to Harcourt

198 MOL, DC11/6, p159

199 *Ibid*, DC3/11, p575, Oates to Bloomfield Road Society, 1 November 1921; *The Times*, 30 March 1921, p13

200 MOL, DC3/11, pp610, 721, 728, 962, Oates to LCC, 28 November 1921 to 12 December 1922; DC3/13, p122

201 *Ibid*, DC3/13, pp122, 126, 190

202 PRO, T1/11564/17176, Beauchamp to Heath, 24 April 1914

203 MOL, DC3/11, pp302, 324, 328, Oates
to Conway Davies, 16, 29, 30 March
1921
204 *Ibid*, DC2/14, Esher to Oates, 1 April
1924
205 PRO, T160/787/F6139/08
206 MOL, DC3/10, p482, Laking to War
Office, 28 July 1919
207 *Ibid*, DC2/09, War Office to Laking,
12 August 1919
208 *Ibid*, DC2/10, Reith to Brett, 13 May
1920
209 *Ibid*, DC3/10, p896, Oates to Reith,
17 May 1920
210 *Ibid*, DC2/10, Hampton to Oates,
31 May 1920

ABBREVIATIONS

CLRO
*Corporation of London Records Office,
Guildhall, London*

Co Co
Common Council of the Corporation of London

Esher Papers
*Esher Papers at the Churchill Archives
Centre, Churchill College, Cambridge*

GLC
Greater London Council

Harcourt Papers
Harcourt Papers at the Bodleian Library, Oxford

LCC
London County Council

MOL
Museum of London

PRO
Public Record Office

RA
Royal Archives at Windsor Castle

Chapter 5
LATER YEARS OF
THE LONDON MUSEUM
1926 TO 1975

Pages 99 to 130

1 PRO, T162/549/E3009/1
2 MOL, DC3/13, p198, Oates to HMSO,
29 April 1925; p220, Oates to Davies,
12 February 1926
3 Esher Papers 7/37, Esher to M Brett,
15 October 1925
4 MOL, DC1/1, p21, 15 January 1926
5 Quoted in Jacquetta Hawkes,
*Mortimer Wheeler. Adventurer in
Archaeology*, 1982, p104
6 MOL, DC4/1926
7 *Ibid*, DC1/1, p22, 3 February 1926
8 PRO, T162/549/E3009/1
9 Esher Papers 7/8, Brett to Esher,
25 August 1926
10 MOL, DC4/1926, Esher to Wheeler,
24 August 1926
11 Esher Papers 5/60, Wheeler to Esher,
30 August 1926
12 MOL, DC1/1, pp26, 28, 30 June,
3 December 1926
13 Sir Mortimer Wheeler, *Still Digging*,
1955, pp83, 84
14 *Royal Commission on National Museums
and Galleries. Oral Evidence,
Memoranda and Appendices to the
Interim Report*, 1928, pp237-8
15 *Ibid, Oral Evidence, Memoranda and
Appendices to the Final Report*, 1929,
pp7-14
16 *Final Report of Royal Commission on
National Museums and Galleries,
Part II. General Conclusions and
Recommendations*, 1929-30 (Command
3463), XVI, pp581-3
17 MOL, DC4/1930, 1931
18 *Ibid*, DC1/1, p42, 11 December 1930
19 PRO, T160/787/F6139/08
20 Information supplied by Mr Walter
Henderson
21 Information supplied by Mr Martin
Holmes
22 MOL, Accession Number A27278
23 MOL, DC2/15, Wheeler to Esher,
25 June 1928
24 Wheeler, *Still Digging*, p86
25 MOL, DC1/1, p26, 30 June 1926
26 *Ibid*, DC4/1928; personal file,
'Makower'
27 *Ibid*, DC4/1929, Wheeler to Esher,
11 July 1929
28 *Ibid*, DC1/1, 6 December 1932, p56;
DC4/1933, *passim*
29 *Ibid*, DC1/1, 2 December 1937, p93;
22 March 1938, p96; DC4/1938, *passim*
30 Wheeler, *Still Digging*, p86

31 *Royal Commission on National Museums
and Galleries. Oral Evidence,
Memoranda and Appendices to the Final
Report*, 1929, p8
32 MOL, DC1/1, 25 June 1928, pp29-30
33 *Ibid*, DC1/1, 27 March 1931, p46
34 *Ibid*, DC1/1, 8 April 1932, p54
35 *Ibid*, DC4/1937
36 *Ibid*, DC4/1932, 31 May 1932
37 *Ibid*, DC1/1, 25 June 1928, p31
38 *Ibid*, DC1/1, 25 March 1931, pp46-7
39 *Ibid*, DC4/1931
40 *Ibid*, DC1/1, 8 May 1936, p82
41 Wheeler, *Still Digging*, p86
42 MOL, DC4/1933
43 *Ibid*, personal file, 'Makower'
44 *Sixth Report of the Standing Commission
on Museums and Galleries*, 1961, p64
45 MOL, DC1/1, 3 December 1926, p28
46 Harcourt Papers 519, p50, Waechter to
Harcourt, ND
47 *Ibid* 519, p81, Harcourt to Lever, 5 May
1913
48 PRO, T1/11564/17176
49 A I Dasent, *The Story of Stafford House*,
with introduction by Viscount Esher,
1927, pix
50 MOL, DC1/1, 28 June 1937, p89
51 Hawkes, *Mortimer Wheeler*, pp196-8
52 MOL, DC1/1, 9 May 1940, p103
53 Information kindly supplied by Miss
Beatrice de Cardi
54 MOL, DC1/1, 2 December 1937, p92
55 *Ibid*, DC4/1941; DC1/1, 11 February 1943,
p107
56 *Ibid*, DC1/1, 11 February 1943, pp107-9;
13 January 1944, p116
57 *Ibid* DC1/1, 13 January 1944, pp113-16
58 PRO, WORK 17/356
59 MOL, DC4/1945, Harewood to Portal,
26 August 1944
60 *Ibid*, DC4/1945, Eates to Peers, 9 June
1945
61 *Ibid*, DC4/1945, Batch to Eates,
14 August 1945
62 *Ibid*, DC4/1945, Esher to Ministry of
Works, 20 August 1945; Eates to
Esher, 10 September 1945
63 *Ibid*, DC4/1945, Eates to Esher,
10 September 1945; Eates to de
Normann, 11 October 1945
64 *Ibid*, DC4/1945, Eates to Fox,
20 November 1945; DC1/1, 20 March,
24 October 1945, pp121-5; PRO,
T214/18
65 MOL, DC1/1, 13 December 1945, p128
66 PRO, WORK 12/239
67 *Ibid*, WORK 17/356
68 MOL, DC1/1, 24 October 1945, p124
69 *Ibid*, typescript note by Dr Harden,
1957
70 *Ibid*, DC1/1, 28 May 1947, p141
71 *Ibid*, DC1/1, 27 November 1946, p138

72 *Ibid*, DC1/1, 28 May 1947, p141; Keeper's Report
73 *Ibid*, DC1/1, 2 July, 26 November 1947, pp143, 146
74 PRO, WORK 19/1099
75 MOL, DC4/1945, Eates to Fox, 20 November 1945; DC4/1946, Grimes to Harewood, 26 February 1946
76 *The Times*, 26 January 1946, p29
77 MOL, DC4/1946, Grimes to Harewood, 12 June 1946
78 *Ibid*, DC1/1, 25 February 1948, pp149–50; Director's Report
79 *The Times*, 26 January 1946, p29; *Hansard*, vol 418, 25 January 1946, cols 512–18
80 *Hansard*, Lords' Debates, vol 140, 14 March 1946, cols 189–90
81 MOL, DC4/1946, Harewood to Grimes, 18 February 1946
82 *Ibid*, DC1/1, *passim*; PRO, T214/18; WORK 17/356
83 PRO, WORK 19/1099, de Normann to Alexander, 3 November 1948
84 *Ibid*, WORK 19/1099
85 MOL, DC1/1, 20 December 1950, p175; DC1/2, 14 March 1951, p1
86 Information supplied by Professor W F Grimes
87 MOL, Director's Report, 4 March 1955
88 *Ibid*, DC1/1, 11 February 1943, pp107–8: 13 January 1944, p116
89 *Ibid*, DC1/2, 31 October 1951–4 July 1956, pp7–47, *passim*; Director's Report, 26 June 1956, and draft Annual Report for 1957
90 *Ibid*, Director's Report, 10 October 1952; John Hayes, *Catalogue of the Oil Paintings in the London Museum*, 1970, *passim*
91 MOL, Director's Report, 10 October 1952
92 *Ibid*, DC1/2, 29 September 1954–26 November 1956, pp32–52, *passim*
93 This and the remainder of this chapter are based on the Director's Reports and author's personal knowledge

Chapter 6
LATER YEARS OF THE
GUILDHALL MUSEUM
1911 TO 1975

Pages 131 to 158

1 Ralph Merrifield, *The Roman City of London*, 1965, p25
2 *Ibid*, p7; Michael Rhodes, 'Methods of Cataloguing Pottery in Inner London: an Historical Outline', in *Medieval Ceramics* (Bulletin of the Medieval Pottery Research Group), vol 3, 1979, pp83,97, 101
3 CLRO, Library Committee Minutes, 2 March 1914
4 Merrifield, pp8–9; Rhodes, *loc cit*
5 Library Committee Minutes, 1 April, 6 May, 1 July 1912; CLRO, Librarian's Annual Reports, 1912–14
6 Librarian's Annual Reports, 1910–22
7 *Ibid*, 1915, 1919, 1921
8 *Ibid*, 1924, 1945, 1946
9 MOL, DC4/1926, Wheeler to Smith, 2 July 1926
10 Librarian's Annual Report, 1930
11 PRO, AE1/2 and AE1/25
12 Merrifield, p11; *Royal Commission on Historical Monuments (England), London Vol III, Roman London*, 1928
13 MOL, DC4/1926
14 *Ibid*, Wheeler to Smith, 2 July 1926
15 CLRO, Library Committee Minutes and Papers, 6 October 1926
16 MOL, DC4/1927, *passim*; Library Committee Minutes, 25 November, 6 December 1926, 11 April 1927
17 MOL, DC4/1927, *passim*
18 *Ibid*, Lord Crawford's note on Guildhall Conference, 24 May 1927
19 *Ibid*, Wheeler to Lord Crawford, 3 June 1927
20 *Ibid*, Wheeler to Buxton, 4, 9 August 1927
21 Society of Antiquaries, Executive Committee Minutes, 23 February 1928
22 *Ibid*, Council Minutes, 19 November 1930–27 January 1932, *passim*, and Executive Committee Minutes, 9 February 1928–18 January 1934, *passim*; Merrifield, pp12–13; Jacquetta Hawkes, *Mortimer Wheeler*, 1982, p112
23 Librarian's Annual Reports, 1939, 1940; Merrifield, p13
24 Librarian's Annual Reports, 1924–39
25 *Ibid*, 1940, and notes therewith on the fire by A H Hall and J F Bromley
26 *Ibid*, 1944–7
27 *Ibid*, 1945–53
28 W F Grimes, *The Excavation of Roman and Mediaeval London*, 1968, p1
29 *Ibid*, p1; Librarian's Annual Reports, 1944, 1945
30 Grimes, p1; Librarian's Annual Report, 1946
31 W F Grimes, 'Excavations in the City of London' in *Recent Excavations in Britain*, ed R L S Bruce-Mitford, 1956, p111
32 Grimes, *The Excavation of Roman and Mediaeval London*, pp1–2, 222, 245–51
33 Merrifield, p234; Ivor Noel Hume, 'Into the Jaws of Death . . . Walked One', in *Collectanea Londiniensia*, ed Joanna Bird, Hugh Chapman, John Clark, 1978, p11
34 Hume, pp9–11; Librarian's Annual Reports, 1948, 1949
35 Hume, pp10–11
36 *Ibid*, pp11–12; Librarian's Annual Reports, 1949, 1950
37 Hume, p22
38 *Ibid*, pp16–17; Merrifield, pp215, 290; Librarian's Annual Reports, 1950–3
39 This paragraph is based entirely on Grimes, *The Excavation* etc, pp92–117, 229–37
40 Hume, p19; Librarian's Annual Reports, 1954, 1955
41 John E Price, *Roman Antiquities Illustrated by Remains Recently Discovered on the Site of the National Safe Deposit Company's Premises, Mansion House, London*, 1873, pp78–9, quoted in Hume, p19
42 Grimes, *The Excavation* etc, p106
43 Library Committee Minutes, 6 July, 5 October 1953
44 Librarian's Annual Reports, 1954, 1955, 1959
45 *Ibid*, 1957–60; Hume, p22
46 *Ibid*, 1950, 1959–66
47 *Daily Mail* and *Daily Sketch*, 7 December 1966. I owe this reference to Mr Peter Marsden
48 Librarian's Annual Report, 1966
49 Librarian's and Director's Annual Reports, 1967–74
50 Librarian's Annual Report, 1966
51 Common Council Minutes, 20 October 1966, p359; Library Committee Minutes, 5 June 1967
52 Merrifield, p22; information privately supplied
53 Peter Marsden, *Roman London*, 1980, pp198–9; I am greatly indebted to Mr Peter Marsden for this and the following paragraphs
54 Marsden, pp200–1; Merrifield, pp22, 196, 273
55 Max Hebditch, 'Towards the Future of London's Past', in *Collectanea Londiniensia, ut supra*, p24

56 See B J Philp, 'The Forum of London: Excavations of 1968–9' in *Britannia*, volume 8, 1977, pp1–64
57 Hebditch, p25; Grimes, *The Excavation* etc, p26; Marsden, pp201–3; Librarian's Annual Reports, 1955–6; Director's Annual Reports, 1966–8; information kindly supplied by Mr Peter Marsden
58 Marsden, p205
59 Director's Annual Report for the Guildhall Museum for 1971
60 Director's Annual Report, 1971
61 *The Times*, 28 December 1971, p6, and 13 January 1972, p4
62 *Ibid*, 4 April 1972, p14, 6 April 1972, p4; Hebditch, pp25–7
63 Hebditch, p26
64 *Ibid*, pp26–7; Library Committee Minutes, 2 October 1972
65 Hebditch, p27; Library Committee Minutes, 3 July 1972, p192
66 Hebditch, p28; Library Committee Minutes, 3 November 1972, pp213–18
67 Library Committee Minutes, 3 July 1972, p192, 3 November 1972, pp213–18; Martin Biddle, Daphne Hudson and Carolyn Heighway, *The Future of London's Past*, 1973, *passim*, but especially pp51–2
68 Hebditch, pp28–9; Library Committee Minutes, 23 July 1973; Biddle, pp51–2
69 *The Times*, 23 July 1973, p13

ABBREVIATIONS

CLRO
Corporation of London Records Office, Guildhall, London

Co Co
Common Council of the Corporation of London

Esher Papers
Esher Papers at the Churchill Archives Centre, Churchill College, Cambridge

GLC
Greater London Council

Harcourt Papers
Harcourt Papers at the Bodleian Library, Oxford

LCC
London County Council

MOL
Museum of London

PRO
Public Record Office

RA
Royal Archives at Windsor Castle

Chapter 7
THE MUSEUM OF LONDON: ITS FORMATIVE YEARS
1965 TO 1987

Pages 159 to 188

1 Harcourt Papers 519, p114; MOL, DC3/6, p224, Laking to Harcourt, 23 May 1913
2 MOL, Exhibit files, A14000–14367, Harcourt to Crawford, 10 April 1916
3 *Royal Commission on National Museums and Galleries, Oral Evidence, Memoranda and Appendices to the Final Report*, 1929, p12
4 MOL, DC4/1934, correspondence between Wheeler and Douthwaite, January 1934
5 CLRO, librarian's report for 1943
6 MOL, DC4/1946, Grimes to Harewood, 16 March, 3 October 1946
7 *The Times*, 30 August 1956, p5
8 MOL, London Museum Director's Report, 7 December 1959
9 *Ibid*, 'Future Premises File', 1958–60
10 *Ibid*, London Museum Director's Report, 1 November 1964
11 *Ibid*, London Museum Trustees' Minutes, 22 April 1964; Director's Report, 22 July 1964
12 *Ibid*, London Museum Trustees' Minutes, 7 February, 23 May 1962; Director's Report, 16 September 1962
13 *Ibid*, 'Future Premises File', Esher to Harden, 6 April 1959
14 *Ibid*, London Museum Trustees' Minutes, 15 November 1961; Director's Report, 7 February 1962
15 *Ibid*, London Museum Trustees' Minutes, 17 July, 13 November 1963; Director's Report, 7 July 1963; Interim Board of Governors' Minutes, 10 July, 6 November 1963; CLRO, Improvements and Town Planning Committee Minutes, 23 July, 24 September 1963
16 CLRO, Co Co Minutes 1966, Library Committee Report, 7 February 1966
17 MOL, London Museum Trustees' Minutes, 22 April 1964; Director's Report, 16 September 1962
18 *Ibid*, Director's Reports, 5 December 1962, 15 April 1963, 24 November 1965; information supplied by Mr Norman Cook
19 MOL, London Museum Trustees' Minutes, 24 February, 24 November 1965; Director's Reports, 24 November 1965, 25 May 1966
20 *Ibid*, London Museum Trustees' Minutes, 25 May, 10 November 1966
21 *Ibid*, 9 February 1967; Director's Report, 9 February 1967; *City Press*, 16 February 1967, p1
22 CLRO, Improvements and Town Planning Committee Minutes, 28 February, 12, 23 May 1967; *The Times*, 25 February 1967, p2
23 MOL, London Museum Trustees' Minutes, 2 November 1967; Director's Report, 22 October 1967; *The Times*, 25 August 1967, p10d
24 MOL, London Museum Director's Report, 22 October 1967; Governors' Minutes, 19 October 1967
25 CLRO, Co Co Minutes, 31 October 1968, Joint Report of Coal, Corn and Rates Finance and Improvements and Town Planning Committees, Appendix A
26 MOL, London Museum Director's Report, 22 October 1967
27 *Ibid*, Director's Report, 25 October 1970
28 CLRO, Co Co Minutes, 25 February 1971, Report of Planning and Communications Committee
29 MOL, London Museum Trustees' Minutes, 11 November 1964, 24 November 1965; Director's Report, 24 November 1965
30 GLC Minutes, 19 October 1965, p588
31 MOL, London Museum Director's Report, 22 October 1967
32 *Ibid*, London Museum Trustees' Minutes, 31 October 1968; Director's Report, 20 October 1968
33 *Ibid*, Director's Report, 16 March 1969
34 *Ibid*, London Museum Trustees' Minutes, 27 March 1969
35 *Ibid*, File in Director's Office, 'Appointment of Trustees etc. 1955 . . .', Harcourt to Prof Douglas, 9 December 1969
36 *Ibid*, London Museum Director's Report, 18 January 1970
37 CLRO, Library Committee Minutes, 1 June 1970
38 MOL, Director's Reports, 25 October 1970, 23 May 1971
39 *Ibid*, Board of Officers' (Finance) Minutes, 12 November 1970; GLC Minutes, 9 March 1971, pp145–6
40 GLC Minutes, 9 March 1971, pp145–6
41 *Ibid*, 26 November 1974, p594; MOL, London Museum Trustees' Minutes, 28 November 1974
42 CLRO, Library Committee Minutes, 1 February 1971
43 Information kindly supplied by Mr G W Rowley
44 MOL, London Museum Director's Report, 23 May 1971

45 Max Hebditch, 'A Museum for London' in *London Topographical Record*, vol XXIV, 1980, pp191–201; CLRO, Co Co Minutes, Report of Planning and Communications Committee, 24 May 1973; *ibid*, Report of same, 25 July 1974; *ibid*, Report of same, 10 June 1976; *ibid*, Report of same, 9 October 1980; *ibid*, Report of same, 21 May 1981. National Theatre and Museum of London Act 1973, c2

46 MOL, *First Report*, 1975–1979, p71

47 CLRO, Co Co Minutes, Report of Planning and Communications Committee, 25 February 1971

48 *Ibid*, Co Co Minutes, Report of same, 25 February 1971, Appendix C; *ibid*, Report of same, 9 October 1980

49 MOL, London Museum Director's Report, 29 October 1972

50 Information kindly supplied by Mr Peter Marsden

51 MOL, London Museum Director's Reports, 23 January 1972, 18 February 1973, 30 June 1974; Hebditch, p198

52 *Ibid*, London Museum Director's Reports, 18 February 1973; CLRO, Co Co Minutes, 4 October 1973, p351

53 CLRO, Co Co Minutes, 16 October 1969, p338

54 MOL, London Museum Director's Reports, 22 January, 28 May, 29 October 1972

55 Except where otherwise stated the rest of this chapter is based on the published annual reports of the Museum of London and on information supplied by members and former members of the staff.

56 Powell and Moya's Preliminary Report to the Interim Board of Governors, 1964, pp24–6 (*copy in MOL Library*)

57 MOL, London Museum Director's Reports, 4 Nov 1973, 30 June 1974

58 These results are summarized in Brian Hobley, *Roman and Saxon London. A Reappraisal* (MOL Annual Archaeology Lecture), 1986, *passim*

59 *Greater London's Rescue Archaeology Service. A Rescue News Special Report*, 1985

60 Chris Ellmers, 'A Museum in Docklands' in *Dockland. An illustrated historical survey of life and work in East London*, 1986, pp81–8

61 Exhibition Catalogue. *The Quiet Conquest. The Huguenots 1685 to 1985*, 1985, pxvi

62 Museum of London Act 1986, c8; CLRO, Co Co Minutes, 24 October 1985, 13 March 1986, Policy and Resources Committee, submitting reports of the Reference Sub-committee

ILLUSTRATION CREDITS

The Museum of London acknowledges with thanks the individuals and organizations who have generously made copyright illustrations available for this publication. The references are to figure numbers.

BOARD OF TRUSTEES OF THE
VICTORIA AND ALBERT MUSEUM
127

B T BATSFORD LIMITED
169

COMMISSIONER OF POLICE FOR
THE CITY OF LONDON
237, 254, 255, 257, 293

CORPORATION OF LONDON:
GUILDHALL ART GALLERY
36, 45

CORPORATION OF LONDON:
GUILDHALL LIBRARY
41, 42, 43, 44, 46, 48, 49, 50, 54, 55, 58, 60, 61, 62, 63, 64, 65, 66, 67, 68, 69, 73, 76, 77, 90, 136, 137, 140, 141, 181, 182, 241, 242, 243, 245, 248, 249, 266, 267, 270, 271, 274, 278, 292, 294

GOVERNOR AND COMPANY OF THE
BANK OF ENGLAND
247

LONDON TRANSPORT
4

NATIONAL MONUMENTS RECORD, RCHM(E)
84, 128, 129, 130

NATIONAL PORTRAIT GALLERY
86, 131

ORDNANCE SURVEY
297, 298

PRIVATE COLLECTIONS
85, 87, 91, 190, 192, 204

SOCIETY OF ANTIQUARIES
47, 51, 175, 351

TIMES NEWSPAPERS LIMITED
228, 268, 276, 277

WORSHIPFUL COMPANY OF IRONMONGERS
71

All other illustrations drawn from the archive and collections of the Museum of London

Every year the Lord Mayor's coach is taken out of the museum to carry the new Lord Mayor in procession from Guildhall to the Royal Courts of Justice in the Strand, where he takes the ancient oath of office. This event takes place in November and the procession is known as the Lord Mayor's Show.

The removal of the coach involves the raising of a specially designed drawbridge and the opening of a steel double door leading on to London Wall, both these features having been included in the architect's original designs for the museum.

353 *Drawbridge being raised*

354 *Screen in the late Stuart gallery being opened*

355 *The coach, having been lowered on to special ramps, is winched towards the exit*

356 *The coach emerging through the ceremonial entrance*

357 *The coach in London Wall*

358 *Two of Whitbread Brewery's shire horses being brought up*

359 *Harnessing the horses to the coach*

360 *The Lord Mayor's coach with all six white horses on 'pre-Show day' training session, outside the museum*